# The Billy Boys

The Orange Arch: Orange ideology, illustrated by symbols

# THE
# BILLY BOYS

A Concise History of
Orangeism in Scotland
WILLIAM S MARSHALL

MERCAT PRESS
EDINBURGH

First published in 1996 by Mercat Press
James Thin, 53 South Bridge, Edinburgh EH1 1YS

© William S Marshall, 1996

ISBN 1873644 523

Set in Ehrhardt at Mercat Press
Printed and bound in Great Britain by
Athenæum Press Ltd, Gateshead, Tyne & Wear

For my late father,
William Hendry Marshall

'I will now take the liberty of assuring his Grace that such a fire has been already kindled in North Britain as must speedily burst into a conflagration not easily to be extinguished'
—*Colonel William B Fairman to the Duke of Gordon at a meeting of the Grand Orange Lodge in London, 1833*

# CONTENTS

# ILLUSTRATIONS

# ACKNOWLEDGEMENTS

This book would not have been possible without the efforts of others with similar or related interests in this particular area of Scottish social history. All references consulted are listed in the Bibliography but I was especially grateful to be able to refer to the works of those authors cited in the Introduction.

Friends encouraged me to pursue this project and offered on occasion quite 'robust' criticism of parts of the manuscript! I thank them for their comments.

I would like to acknowledge the assistance I have received from staff in the reference sections of a number of public libraries in Scotland. In particular, the staff of the Glasgow Room of the Mitchell Library have been most helpful to me over the years.

I am also grateful to the lecturers of the Department of Applied Social Studies at what is now the University of Paisley for their unstinting efforts at educating a classic example of working class underachievement!

My thanks to Seán Costello of Mercat Press for his advice and assistance.

Last, but by no means least, I sincerely thank Morag and my mother for their support and for their patience. I also thank them for putting up with my absences whilst I was writing and preparing the manuscript in what was my spare time.

# BIOGRAPHICAL NOTE

The author is 42 years old and is married. He left school at 15 years of age and commenced work in the textile industry. Following a brief period of working in different parts of Canada, he then graduated from what is now the University of Paisley with a BA (Hons) in Social Science. He currently works in the National Health Service.

# INTRODUCTION

THIS book represents an attempt to outline the social, political and religious history of the Orange Order in Scotland from its origins in the late eighteenth century to the present day. This is no easy task. Orangeism is an unpopular and controversial subject shrouded in misunderstanding, half truths and mythology. However, it remains an important subject which has been seriously neglected by social historians in Scotland for too long, perhaps because it mars the image of the country they are attempting to project.

Such ideological considerations or sensitivities play no part here. The book is not written from any specific theoretical perspective. Rather, it is intended to be a straightforward, matter of fact historical account of the development of the Orange movement in Scotland, interspersed with some comment where this has been deemed to be necessary as an aid to interpretation. Personal views, such as they are, are well signposted.

Indeed, I have striven for that most elusive and probably unattainable of sociological objectives: ethical neutrality. However, since I am not a professional historian or an academic, the book is free of 'jargon'. Nevertheless, I sincerely hope that it will be of interest to academics as well as a wider public including members of the Orange Order themselves.

Of course, all historical writing tends to build on the work of others who have gone before in the field. In this respect, I owe an enormous debt of gratitude to four current authors in particular: Dr Steve Bruce, Dr Graham Walker, Dr Tom Gallagher and the Rev. Gordon McCracken. The work of the last-named on the history of Orangeism in Glasgow has been especially valuable. Without all their respective works this book would have been much more difficult to write.

There is a dearth of primary sources for the serious student of Orange history to research. It is doubtful, given the nature of the movement, whether many lodges in Scotland have a complete set of minute books intact or any other records of historical interest. None at all are lodged with any public library in the country.

Even if original records of this type did exist in any real numbers, it is probable that they would not be made available to outside researchers.

Given this unsatisfactory state of affairs, reliance has to be placed on the few crumbs which are available: my own research and secondary sources—in the main, newspapers. References and allusions to Orangeism are found in some of the material relating to the social history of modern Scotland and if one views these as pieces of a jigsaw then this book represents an attempt at putting together the overall picture. That picture is certainly not yet complete but I believe that a decent start has at least been made to give the broad outline of the subject.

This particular study is timely coming as it does in the wake of the 200th anniversary of the founding of the Orange Order in Ireland. I have not attempted to present a year by year account of its Scottish offshoot but have concentrated instead on some of the key issues and personalities to have shaped the history of the Orange movement in Scotland. However, I have endeavoured to place these issues and personalities against the wider socio-economic background which produced them.

The Orange Order in Scotland has had an interesting if turbulent history. It may come as a surprise to many to learn that the Order is not entirely the homogenous entity it is so often portrayed to be. Indeed, the early history of the movement in Scotland is one of division and schism. It was not until the third quarter of the nineteenth century that the movement finally resolved its internal difficulties by uniting into one body.

Issues around the concept of class stratification pervade Orange history in Scotland. Since its first appearance on Scottish soil, there have been persistent tensions between the leadership of the movement and the rank and file. These tensions have surfaced again and again in a variety of contexts and as responses to specific issues of concern to Orangemen. They have shaped and usually stultified the Order's reponses to the political and religious challenges it has faced and assist in explaining its persistent failure to be a more effective and successful force in Scottish life.

Scottish Orangeism is essentially a by-product of the Industrial Revolution. It was and has remained an overwhelmingly working class organisation. A major theme of this book is an exploration of the relationship between the Orange Order, working class Unionism and the Labour Movement. It will be suggested that these relationships are a good deal more complex than has often been argued by social historians and others in the past.

Orangeism today is regarded as being archaic and reactionary, confined to the margins of society. However, this was not always the case. During the late Victorian and Edwardian era, Orangeism was very much a part of mainstream contemporary attitudes and thinking. Orange ideology provided a viable belief system for those working class Protestants predisposed to notions of Empire and Great Britain's superiority in the world. A major difficulty for the Order now is that whilst the world has moved on, its ideology has remained static and anchored in the Age of Imperialism.

Finally, a few words on the terminology used in the text. When I refer to the Orange Order, I am referring to male, adult Orange Lodges unless otherwise stated. I admit to somewhat neglecting the development of the Ladies' Orange Association of Scotland and the Junior and Juvenile sections of the Order. Strictly speaking, all of these sections, along with the Royal Black Institution, constitute what is the Orange Order.

I have dealt briefly with the Royal Black Institution in Scotland and the Apprentice Boys of Derry Association in Scotland separately.

# Chapter 1
# IRISH SETTLEMENT
# IN SCOTLAND

BY the end of the eighteenth century, the work of the Reformation in Scotland was almost complete. The overwhelming majority of the population, which in 1801 numbered 1.6 million, adhered to one or other of the various denominations of the Reformed faith. Since the time of John Knox, the major religious disputes in the country had been fought within the parameters of Protestantism.

Only pockets of Roman Catholicism remained. These were confined to the Celtic fringe, notably in Gaelic speaking parts of the Western Highlands, some of the Hebridean Islands and Banffshire. The condition of the 'old faith' in the Central Lowlands was so serious that there were only about 6,000 Catholics left in the area by 1780.[1] Only 50 Catholics resided in Glasgow in 1795.[2] Indeed, the entire Roman Catholic population of Scotland barely exceeded 30,000.[3] It was little wonder then that Rome, as early as 1603, had been obliged to relegate the Church in Scotland to missionary status.[4]

However, Roman Catholicism was about to embark upon a quite remarkable revival, ironically enough through the inherently secularising process of economic industrialisation. As the Scottish enonomy boomed, the consequent demand for labour was met, partly, by the arrival of Irish immigrants. Immigration from Ireland was not new, but prior to industrialisation the Irish had come to work mainly as seasonal agricultural labourers. Now their labour was required in the construction of canals and railways; the extraction of coal and ironstone; and the loading and unloading of ships in the docks and wharves.

The Irish were invariably unskilled toilers on the lowest rung of the occupational ladder. They primarily undertook the type of work the native Scots would not or could not perform.

Most of the immigrants who arrived in Scotland originated from the province of Ulster and were Roman Catholics by religion. The principal 'pull' factor in their decision to migrate was the prospect of better wages and upward social

1

mobility. The major 'push' factors were escape from grinding poverty which was exacerbated by religious persecution and denial of political rights.

With legitimate forms of normal social discourse denied to them, Catholics in Ireland were often forced to seek the redress of justified grievances in illegtimate activities. One such episode was the unsuccessful attempted rebellion in 1798 which had been orchestrated by a secret organisation known as the Society of United Irishmen.[5] The repression which followed in the wake of such events often acted as a further stimulus to immigration.

The census of 1841 was the first to give details of the numbers of Irish-born inhabitants in Scotland. As one would expect, the heaviest concentration of settlement was in those parts of the country which were the most industrialised: Ayrshire: 7.3 percent; Dunbartonshire: 11 percent; Lanarkshire: 13.1 per cent; Renfrewshire; 13.2 per cent. The only exception to this trend was in more rural Wigtownshire, where 14.7 per cent of the population was Irish born. Overall, the figures reveal that 4.8 per cent of the population of Scotland was Irish born.[6]

However, these figures actually seriously hide the true picture. If second and third generation 'Irish' are taken into account, then a more accurate figure would be some 10 per cent of the total population.[7]

Of crucial significance was the fact that the Irish were often heavily concentrated in specific localities. Thus, for example, by the 1830s, 75 per cent of the population of Girvan was Irish and immigrants amounted to 80 per cent of the town's handloom weavers.[8] In neighbouring Maybole, a third of the population was Irish.[9] In Crosshill, also in South Ayrshire, 800 of the village's 1,000 inhabitants were either Irish or of Irish descent by the year 1838.[10]

The heaviest period of immigration was the decade between 1840 and 1850 when entire families arrived as a result of the dreadful potato famine which ravaged rural Ireland. By 1851, the Irish constituted 18.2 per cent of the population of Glasgow,[11] and in nearby Coatbridge, the immigrant population rose from 13.3 per cent in 1841 to 49.1 per cent ten years later.[12] This latest wave coincided with the intensive development of the country's coal and iron industry.

The reaction to the arrival of the Irish in Scotland has been summarised thus:

> In general, the attitude of the majority of lowland Scots towards the Irish immigrant was one of settled hostility. This hostility was due to economic, political and religious reasons, one or other of which dominated according to the rank and training of the native but all of which were to some extent present in the minds of those who objected to the settlement of Irish men and women on Scottish soil.[13]

Although generally welcomed as a source of cheap labour by employers, the Irish were detested by native born workers for the same reason. Because they were willing to work longer and often for much less pay, they were accused of stealing jobs from Scottish workers. Competition for unskilled work was intense, especially in the mining and iron industries, a situation which often led to violent confrontation between the Irish and the Scots.

The Irish were occasionally used by employers to break strikes and they were, initially at least, non-unionised. Whether or not they actually did undercut wages is a moot point, but they were perceived as doing so by sections of the native working class and this belief became a festering sore within a number of different occupational groupings.

The other major component of native resentment was the religion of the majority of the immigrants. Roman Catholicism was regarded by many Scots to be superstitious, unscriptural and undemocratic and completely alien to the values of Presbyterian Scotland. The emphasis placed on devotion and ritual by the Catholic Irish was considered to be an example of their lack of intellect and an excuse for moral laxity.

It was unfortunate indeed that the Irish arrived in Scotland in such large numbers at the same time as the appearance of many of the social problems associated with the processes of industrialisation. This situation led some native Scots to the conclusion that the former was the cause of the latter.

So it was that long hours of tedious and often dangerous work, low wages, poor housing conditions, increasing levels of criminal behaviour and greater abuse of alcohol were just some of the problems laid at the door of the immigrant. The Catholic Irish became a convenient scapegoat for all the ills of a society in the midst of profound transformation. As a consequence, they were hated by their fellow workers and treated with barely concealed contempt by the establishment.

This anti-Irish sentiment was in reality a contemporary expression of the latent anti-Catholicism which still lurked beneath the surface of Scottish society. The arrival of the Irish rekindled old flames. Vicious anti-Catholic riots had occurred in Edinburgh as recently as 1779 when individuals and property were attacked:

> ...the building in Chalmers Close, Leith Wynd, used as a catholic chapel was attacked by a mob. After a preliminary onslaught with hatchets and stones, the rabble distributed straw and barrels of tar over the floors and set the house alight. A Popish cat which was making a tardy escape from the building was thrown back by the mob into the flames.[14]

Similar disturbances occurred that same year in towns as far apart as Glasgow, Dundee, Peebles and Perth. It was not until 1793 that a Relief Act was passed in Scotland which effectively abolished the most punitive anti-Catholic laws still on the statute books. However, this was fully 14 years after similar legislation had been passed in England and Ireland.

The delay north of the border reflected establishment fears of reviving Jacobitism in the country. Fear and suspicion of Roman Catholicism continued after the 1793 Relief Act was enacted. As an example, Glasgow had 43 anti-Catholic societies in existence when there were no more than 39 Roman Catholics resident in the city![15]

Although the majority of the Irish in Scotland were Roman Catholics, there were, nevertheless, a significant number of Protestants amongst the immigrant population. Official figures are not available for this period but it has been estimated that about 25 per cent of the migrant Irish were Protestants.[16] As with the immigrant community generally, they too were often concentrated in specific localities.

Economic factors were the principal reasons for Protestant Irish migration. Recession in the domestic linen industry due to restraints on Irish trade and new modes of production forced many handloom weavers into ruin. The only way many of them could continue their trade was by migrating to Scotland where work was plentiful.

Political uncertainties also contributed to their migration across the North Channel. For most of the eighteenth century much of the Ulster countryside had been subjected to intermittent outbreaks of sectarian violence. These disputes often involved secret bodies of armed men conducting military style operations. Attempted rebellions in 1798 and 1803 merely reinforced Protestant expectations of a successful Catholic uprising, emulating that of 1641 when thousands of Protestants were put to the sword.

The weaving communities of South Ayrshire had a strong Ulster Protestant presence as did Calton, the first industrial suburb of Glasgow. This district became a major centre of handloom weaving. In 1831 about 33 per cent of the population was Irish. The immigrant community numbered 6,890 persons and of these 4,202 were Protestants. The total population of Calton was 20,613 persons, thus about 20 per cent of these were Protestant Irish.[17]

The Lanarkshire mining village of Larkhall was another early centre of Ulster Protestant migration. One particular from Belfast could recall that his grandmother recited ballads in Scots Doric even though she had lived in Ireland all her life. He himself had read Robert Burns as a boy.[18]

These examples help to illustrate an absolutely crucial point regarding the question of native reaction to Irish immigration. A distinction was often made: whereas the Catholic Irish were almost universally detested, there was a good deal more tolerance displayed towards the Protestant Irish.

Distinction was indeed the key factor in determining these attitudes. The Catholic Irish brought with them a cultural baggage completely alien to most of contemporary Scottish society. By way of contrast, many Ulster Protestants shared a common heritage with the Lowland Scots, a result of a historical process formed over two centuries.

During the reign of King James VI of Scotland and I of England, the decision was taken to 'plant' thousands of English Anglicans and Scottish Presbyterians in the North of Ireland in order to establish British rule and maintain the Reformed faith on Irish soil. The majority of the Scots settled in the counties of Antrim and Down, although large colonies of them were already well established in these areas prior to the plantation which occurred c.1610-1646. In time, most of the population of Antrim and Down came to be essentially 'Scottish' in speech, custom and outlook.[19]

Not surprisingly, the Ulster Plantation, as it came to be known, was bitterly resented by the native Catholic population and in a very real sense it has never been fully accepted by sections of them to this day.

Of course, the descendents of the 'planters' have viewed the event quite differently:

> Thistle and Rose, they twined them close
> When their fathers crossed the sea
> And they dyed them red, the live and the dead
> Where the blue starred lint grows free
> Where the blue starred lint grows free
> Here in the Northern sun
> Till His way was plain, He led the Twain
> And He forged them into One[20]

Many, if not most, of the Ulster Protestants who migrated to Scotland almost two centuries later, were themselves the descendents of the original Scottish settlers. Indeed some would even have had relatives in Scotland. These familial and cultural bonds made their assimilation into Lowland Scottish society almost a matter of course. They shared a common identity, the same Presbyterian world view and the values and beliefs which stemmed from it.

Significantly, a small minority of the Ulster Protestant migrants[21] had initiated their own unique mechanism for maintaining a separate identity from the Catholic Irish. This was their membership of an Orange Lodge.

# Chapter 2

# THE ORIGINS OF
# SCOTTISH ORANGEISM

THE Orange Order was formed on Monday, 21 September 1795, in the Loughgall district of the County of Armagh as a direct consequence of a violent confrontation in that troubled locality between Protestants resident in the area and a Catholic secret society, known as the Defenders, who had come to attack them.[1] The conflict has come to be known as the 'Battle of the Diamond' and it was a typical example of the sectarian disorder which had ravaged the Armagh countryside for many years. Usually the violence involved rival factions indulging in raids and counter raids for livestock and arms, assaulting individuals and groups at fairs and markets and destroying the property of their opponents.

The Diamond was different. The constant fear of an organised and successful Catholic rebellion led the Protestant victors to form a permanent society for mutual defence:

> Now Armagh County still hold dear
> Grand secrets there were found
> Old Erin's shore we'll still adore
> And that grand spot you know
> Where our true Order first saw light
> One hundred years ago[2]

The new society was named after King William III, the Prince of Orange, who at the Battle of the Boyne in 1690 had secured the future of the Reformed Faith in Ireland. The leading figures in the formation of the Orange Order were James Wilson, Daniel Winter and James Sloan. As it happened, these men were all Freemasons,[3] and they applied Masonic principles of organisation to the fledgling society.

They established a similar hierarchical system of lodges. At the base was the local or private lodge; private lodges were then grouped geographically together to form a District Lodge. District Lodges were then grouped geographically together to form a County Grand Lodge and at the top of this pyramid structure stood the national Grand Lodge of all Ireland.

This structure had an inherently democratic character, at least in theory. Every Orangeman joined his local private lodge in the first instance and elected its officers on an annual basis. These officers were then usually chosen by the membership of the private lodges to represent them at District Lodge level. Officers of District Lodge rank were then eligible for election to County Grand Lodge positions. These officers, in turn, constituted the basis of the national Grand Lodge.

Of equal importance to the future stability of the new society was the creation of a fairly elaborate and secret system of degrees, signs, grips and passwords. These were essentially devised to ensure security within the movement and to inculcate a sense of brotherhood. Some of this ritual may have been based on certain aspects of Freemasonry but it is more probable the bulk of this esoteric content originated from an earlier secret Protestant society, the Orange Boys, which had been founded by the same James Wilson two years previously in 1793.[4]

The Order spread rapidly throughout the North of Ireland. By 1796, at least 315 lodges had been established[5] and moves were begun to give the movement a proper framework. This process was helped along by the establishment of a 'gentleman's' lodge in Dublin in 1797. A Grand Orange Lodge of Ireland was quickly formed in its wake.

The Grand Orange Lodge of Ireland established a uniform system regarding the rules and constitution of the Order; its degrees, signs, grips and passwords became the sole authority for issuing warrants to new lodges.

From 1798 onwards, numbered warrants were issued by the Grand Lodge to Orangemen who wished to set up private lodges in their localities and these documents represented their authority to do so. The warrant was, therefore, equivalent to a certificate of authority and it had to be displayed at all lodge meetings as proof that the lodge was properly constituted. Grand Lodge had sole authority to issue and revoke warrants and maintained a register of all lodges under its control.

The Grand Lodge also issued a declaration outlining the purpose of the Order:

We associate to the utmost of our power to support and defend His Majesty, King George III, the Constitution and laws of this country and the Succession to the Throne in His Majesty's Illustrious House being Protestants; for the defence of our person and properties and to maintain the peace of our country; and for these purposes we will be at all times ready to assist the civil and military powers in the just and lawful discharge of their duty.

We also associate in honour of King William III, Prince of Orange, whose name we bear as supporters of his glorious memory and the true religion by him completely established; and in order to prove our gratitude and affection for his name, we will annually celebrate the victory over James at the Boyne on the 1st of July, old style, in every year, which day shall be our grand area for ever.

We further declare, that we are exclusively a Protestant Association; yet detesting as we do any intolerant spirit, we solemnly pledge ourselves to each other that we will not persecute or upbraid any person on account of his religious opinion but that we will, on the contrary, be aiding and assisting to every loyal subject of every religious description.[6]

The enduring image of Orange iconology: 'King Billy' in heroic pose, crossing the Boyne

Orangemen were given an early opportunity to demonstrate their loyalty to 'King and Country' when rebellion broke out in Ireland in 1798. They enlisted in large numbers in the Yeomanry as well as in special bodies like the Orange Volunteers and, in so doing, played a not insignificant part in crushing the uprising in the North of Ireland. The participation of the rank and file of the movement had been encouraged by their leaders at Grand Lodge and County Grand Lodge level who were often officers in the Yeomanry and Volunteer units.

Orangemen celebrated their part in the victorious campaign in the spirit of the times:

> Poor Croppies, ye knew that your sentence had come
> When you heard the dread sound of the Protestant drum
> In memory of William, we hoisted his flag
> And soon the bright Orange put down the Green rag
> Down, Down Croppies, Lie Down!![7]

The Order had advanced beyond its humble origins amongst the tenant farmers and handloom weavers of Armagh. It was now under the leadership of the nobility with the landed gentry and Members of Parliament counted amongst the membership of the Grand Lodge. In many parts of Ireland the Order had virtually developed into an auxiliary force for the landlords.

A typical lodge at this time would have been composed of the landlord as Master, perhaps the local Church of Ireland vicar or his curate, with the bulk of the membership being the landlord's tenants and servants. The Order remained an essentially rural based movement for some time and the majority of Orangemen were Episcopalians by religious denomination.

The attempted rebellion of 1798 galvanised Protestant opinion to the extent that whatever their economic differences, religious denomination or social status, they all as 'Protestants' had a mutual interest in maintaining the 'Ascendancy'. Fear of militant Roman Catholicism and loss of privilege were the central elements cementing Protestant unity.

The Orange Order, in effect organised militant Protestantism, would become the first line of defence and the natural vehicle of Protestant and Unionist intransigence to any fundamental reform in the structure of Irish society.

The initial channel employed to convey Orange Lodges into Scotland was military. As part of the government effort to suppress the 1798 rebellion, militia regiments were raised in England and Scotland and were posted to Ireland for duty. There can be little doubt that many of those who enlisted in the Scottish regiments would have been Ulster Protestant migrants keen to defend their kith and kin in their time of peril. Some of these immigrant volunteers may even have been Orangemen already, but in any event, Orange Lodges came to be formed in a number of the militia regiments during their service in Ireland.

Some confusion still persists as to which regiment received the first warrant and when. According to one source, the first warrant was issued to a John Gibson of the Argyleshire Fencibles in March, 1798.[8] The warrant number was 421.

However, according to another source, the Argyleshire Fencibles did not receive a warrant until 1799 and the number issued to them was 915 and not 421.[9]

The total number of regiments known to hold warrants issued by the Grand Orange Lodge of Ireland were: LOL 421 Argyleshire Fencibles (1798); LOL ? Dunbartonshire Fencibles (1798); LOL 573 Dumfries Militia (1798); LOL ? Ayrshire Militia (1798); LOL 677 North Lowland Fencibles (1799); LOL 841 Duke of York's Own Highlanders (1799).[10]

When these regiments returned to Scotland, the lodges were probably little more than ex-servicemen's clubs and it is likely most of them did not survive. The one known exception was the regimental lodge established within the Ayrshire Militia under the leadership of Captain John Ramsay. A company of this regiment, the Loyal Carrick Volunteers, had been formed in Maybole in February, 1797.[11] When the regiment returned to Maybole in 1799, the lodge continued to meet and indeed prosper by allowing civilians to join it from the local population. There would have been no shortage of potential recruits given the sizeable Ulster Protestant community in the area and this lodge was, in all probability, the first in Scotland.

However, although it cannot be substantiated, it is possible that entirely civilian lodges were also operating in Scotland at this time which had no connection with the military at all. It is feasible that immigrant Orangemen could have brought over warrants issued by the Grand Orange Lodge of Ireland or perhaps just decided themselves to establish lodges without any formal authority to do so from Dublin.

What is certain is that the Orange movement did not grow at the same pace in Scotland as it did in the north of England, where a separate British Grand Lodge was established at the Star Hotel, Manchester, in May, 1808.[12]

Henceforth, all lodges operating in Great Britain came under, in theory at least, the new Grand Lodge in Manchester. Existing Irish warrants were revoked and replaced by new warrants issued from Manchester. The British Orangemen were led by an ex-soldier and magistrate, Colonel Samuel Taylor of Moston. He had raised and equipped at his own expense a militia regiment, the Manchester and Salford Rifles, which had served in Ireland during the 1798 rebellion.

The Deputy Grand Master was also an ex-soldier and magistrate, Colonel Robert Fletcher of Bolton.[13] He was a man noted for his relentless pursuit of working class radicals in Lancashire and was known to employ a network of spies to assist him in this enterprise.

The new Grand Lodge did not have much to organise north of the border. In 1807, only three lodges were known to be in existence.[14] The first of these was the original lodge in Maybole which was issued with warrant No. 29 by the new authority in 1809.[15]

The second lodge was located in Glasgow and was probably an offshoot of LOL 29. It is known that on 27 June 1813, LOL 106 received its warrant from the British Grand Lodge and that this was issued to John McWilliam, a soldier in the Ayrshire Militia.[16] It is possible that he and other members of the lodge may have moved to Glasgow when demobilised. Since it is also quite possible they were weavers to trade, they may have moved to the city in search of better employment prospects, perhaps in the Calton area.

The third lodge was apparently located in Argyll and would almost certainly have been the regimental lodge of the Argyleshire Fencibles. Nothing further is known about its existence.

The Order's growth and development in Scotland during the period 1800-1830 was somewhat less than spectacular. By 1830, the number of lodges operating under the authority of the British Grand Lodge had risen to about 40.[17] However, there is evidence that there were still a number of lodges operating in the country under the authority of the Grand Orange Lodge of Ireland. This latter body issued seven warrants to lodges in Maybole and Dailly in 1830.[18] The exact number of 'Irish' lodges in Scotland is unknown but it is unlikely to have been as many as those with British warrants. In theory there should have been none at all by this time.

The membership of most of these lodges would not have exceeded thirty in number. Indeed the vast majority would have had considerably fewer than this figure.

Although progress was at a slower pace than in England, a pattern of development was nevertheless already discernible which had important implications for the future prospects of the movement in Scotland. Thus, it was clear by the 1830s that the spread of Orangeism was inextricably linked to parallel developments within the industrial economy of Lowland Scotland.

During these formative years in the Order's development, weaving was of critical importance since it had attracted large numbers of Ulster Protestant migrants into the domestic industry.[19]

The Order had established roots in three main areas of the country. These were all localities where Ulster weavers had settled in permanent residence to work at their trade. In the southern parishes of Ayrshire about ten lodges were in existence. From Maybole, the Order had spread into the neighbouring villages of Crosshill and Dailly. Three lodges were operating in Girvan, two under British and one under Irish authority.[20]

The second area of relative strength was Galloway in the South West of the country. This was the closest part of Scotland to the North of Ireland. In Wigtownshire, lodges were established in Stranraer, Glenluce, Stoneykirk, Newton-Stewart, Creetown, Whithorn and Wigtown. The two lodges in the port of Stranraer were almost certainly founded by the 150 weavers who had arrived from Antrim, Armagh, Londonderry and Down[21] to work in the town. In Kirkcudbrightshire, lodges were founded in the county town itself and Gatehouse of Fleet. It is probable the lodge in Dumfries was a civilian offshoot of the regimental lodge which had been formed in the Dumfries Militia.

Glasgow was the third area where Orangeism had taken root. There were six lodges in existence which were all located in the weaving district of the Calton, an area of concentrated Ulster Protestant settlement. Five of these lodges were operating in 1821, thus there was little growth in the area between then and 1830. Nevertheless, lodges were also formed in neighbouring towns and villages with strong weaving connections: Paisley, Neilston and Pollokshaws.

However, the Order was not merely confined to weaving districts. By the late 1820s, it was already beginning to spread into the rapidly expanding iron and coal mining areas of the country, where demand for labour was prodigious. An increasing number of Ulstermen were finding employment in these industries, a trend which would continue for the rest of the century. Indeed, the coal mining industry, in particular, was to prove the major force in the spread of Orangeism in Scotland.

The earliest lodges in the Scottish coalfield were diffused over a wide area. In Ayrshire, lodges operating under British authority existed in Newton-on-Ayr and Kilmarnock. In Lanarkshire, two lodges were operating in Airdrie with a combined membership of fewer than sixty. A third of these were Scots and most were colliers and ironstone miners.[22]

Further afield, lodges were established in the Midlothian coalfield in East Central Scotland. The first lodge was formed in Dalkeith in 1826[23] and the second in Musselburgh in 1829.[24]

11

The Orangemen of Scotland were, at this time, predominantly Irish in ethnic origin and overwhelmingly working class. It was noted that 'they are perhaps of the best description of the lower orders...they are men humble in life. They are, generally speaking, uninformed; they are disposed to do everything right and proper but they are not educated men.'[25]

They were also, in the fashion of the times, rough and ready. The District Master of the Glasgow lodges, William Motherwell, complained that he had been obliged to suspend most of the city lodges for irregularities and indiscipline. These 'irregularities' included the non-payment of dues: 'The scoundrels in Donaldson's lodge are a set of thievish gamblers who spend all their money on drink and pay very little reverence to their Deputy Grand Secretary.'[26]

Lodges were required to collect monthly dues from members, a part of which constituted a levy to be paid to the Grand Lodge. Many lodges clearly had problems in collecting these monies, which given the social composition of the membership is perhaps not surprising. It cost members five shillings to progress through the two degrees of the Order, a not inconsiderable sum of money to many working men at this time.

The indiscipline of the Glasgow lodges had been noted with concern by the Grand Lodge in London in 1827[27] and again in 1831.[28] In fact, by 1835, the only lodge in the Glasgow area which remained 'regular', i.e., in good standing, was the exclusively bourgeois Royal Gordon Lodge.

Nor was this particular problem confined to Glasgow. In Neilston, the Master of the local lodge, Samuel Thompson, was forced to expel some of his brethren, 'The leaders of a cabal, who by their habits of intemperance had not only brought reproach upon the Institution but had also induced some worthy brothers to withdraw from its ranks...'[29]

In Girvan, the local magistrates had found it necessary to ban local Orangemen from holding their lodge meetings in any of the town's inns and taverns following repeated outbreaks of disorder.[30]

There were some exceptions. The Grand Lodge noted with regret the deaths of Joseph Milligan, the District Master of Maybole, and James Crawford of Paisley, '...who were mainly instrumental in preserving good order and regularity in their respective districts.'[31]

Part of this problem of indiscipline was linked to the excessive consumption of alcohol. In common with other working class clubs and societies, almost all of the country's Orange Lodges met in public houses. Indeed, publicans came to assume a significant role within the Order.[32] There is some evidence, mainly from England, to suggest that the Order was a source of patronage for persons wishing to procure licensed premises, or at least it was perceived to be in the popular imagination.[33]

The Order's declared intention to celebrate publically the Boyne anniversary every year by means of a procession or 'walk' was often the harbinger of serious disorder. Many Irish Catholics were angered and offended by these ritual displays of Protestant tribalism which became, on occasion, the storm centres of Orange and Green antagonism.

By 1821, the Orangemen of Glasgow felt confident enough to hold a public procession through the streets of Scotland's largest city. This was the first recorded 'Twelfth' in the country. It was not a good start:

> Thursday afternoon, the harmony that had marked the Fair was interrupted by a procession of Orangemen. Three lodges met by appointment in the Lyceum Rooms and at half past twelve o'clock, after a variety of reports concerning the route the procession meant to take, they moved off, preceded by a band of music and a number of men with swords and emblems and accompanied by three flags.
>
> While the procession moved along Ingram Street, symptoms of disapprobation were heard. A boxing match took place at the head of Miller Street which divided the attention of the spectators. Turning down Queen Street, the Orangemen proceeded to the Cross; the crowd increased as they went along and epithets of reproach and contempt became louder and more frequent till they entered Prince's Street, when the Orangemen, heartily tired of their procession, seemed to meditate a retreat to some of the numerous taverns in the lane leading from Prince's Street to the Trongate. The crowd observed this and burst upon the parade.
>
> All order was instantly at an end; fragments of Orange belts (sic) were tossed in the air while the luckless owners were stretched on the street or kicked and bandied about among the exulting mob. One of the flags was torn, the Orangemen fled in all directions and in five minutes after the commencement of the scuffle, there was not a vestige of an Orangeman to be seen.
>
> Several of the shops in Nelson Street were shut about twelve o'clock and as a number of Orangemen went into a tavern in King Street, the shops there were shut for several hours. The police repaired to the scene and prevented further tumult.
>
> The procession appeared to excite dissatisfaction in every beholder.[34]

The intended venue of the Orangemen was probably the equestrian statue of King William III which at this time was located in the Trongate. It was indeed unfortunate that the statue was also located in one of the most heavily populated Catholic Irish districts in the city.

Despite this inauspicious start to their public appearances on Scottish soil, the Orangemen decided to hold another procession a year later, the declared aim of which was to collect money towards a subscription fund set up for the relief of distressed Irish immigrants.[35] This procession also did not lack incident:

> The office bearers of seven lodges, one of which was from Paisley and another from Pollokshaws, assembled at nine o'clock this morning opposite the barracks, from whence they marched to the number of 127, in procession to Fraser's Hall in King Street.
>
> In their march they met with little or no interruption, the ceremony not being expected; but in a short time, a number of people collected in front of the hall, among which were a number of zealous Catholics most ready to give battle. About ten o'clock, one of the Orangemen having come out to the street, was immediately jostled and very ill used, upon which, a number of the Orangemen came out in defence of their brother with drawn swords, which, however, they did not use. In the meantime, one of the magistrates, Mr Graham and the Master of Police, came upon the spot and took prisoners of some of the assailants, among them was a true son of the Church, armed in the Irish Fair style with a pitchfork, which he had previously sharpened with much ceremony on the pavement...[36]

In all, about 130 people were arrested and the besieged Orangemen were taken into protective custody.

The city magistrates were determined to prevent any further disturbances of this kind and as a consequence, they banned the Orangemen from holding any future processions in Glasgow.

Orangemen reluctantly obeyed the ban but they continued to celebrate the Twelfth 'privately' in inns and taverns. They were not discreet and often hung their regalia and banners from the windows of these establishments in the full knowledge that such displays were an irritant to the Catholic Irish in their midst. Indeed, only the prompt action of the police and military at one such incident in 1829 prevented another riot from occurring in the city.[37]

Disturbances involving Orangemen erupted in other parts of Scotland as well. In April, 1823, a body of Irish Catholics from the Creetown area decided to set about the Orangemen of neighbouring Newton-Stewart on Fair Day. Scores of armed protagonists fought for hours while the business of the town was suspended and people sought safety in the hills. The Orangemen managed to see off their assailants and held a procession in Newton-Stewart the following day in order to celebrate this 'victory'![38]

In Edinburgh in 1826, a body of about 16 Orangemen was returning from the installation of a new lodge in the mining village of nearby Dalkeith when they were ambushed by a much larger body of Irish Catholics, armed with sticks and bludgeons. Serious injuries were sustained and 12 people were arrested.[39]

Such disturbances did nothing to enhance the reputation of the Order in Scotland. Orangemen were regarded by the authorities as a public menace and part of an Irish 'problem' which had been imported into the country. However, there were elements within the political right who saw opportunities in encouraging the Orange movement. The initiative came from England.

# Chapter 3

# ROYAL PATRONAGE

THE opening decades of the nineteenth century were a period of considerable political and social unrest in the country. The events of the French Revolution had encouraged radical sentiment amongst all classes of society.

The bourgeoisie demanded the reform of the country's political institutions to correspond with their growing status and wealth. The emerging working class were increasingly engaging in collective forms of action, both in the workplace and outside of it. The traditional Tory establishment began to feel threatened by what they perceived to be revolutionary developments.

Since its formation in 1808, the leadership of the Loyal Orange Institution of Great Britain had attempted to court the ultra Tory right by playing on their fears of social upheaval. Although certainly not powerful, the British Orange movement could conceal its limitations and point to the very real services rendered to 'King and Constitution' by Irish Orangemen as proof of their own potential for countering revolutionary activity on the mainland. Orange leaders like Taylor and Fletcher, in their capacity as magistrates, had already demonstrated the possibilities by swearing in a number of Orangemen to act as special constables during the Luddite disturbances in Lancashire.[1]

An increasing number of militant right wing nobles came to see the advantages of supporting and leading a 'loyal' popular movement amongst the working class. For many of these peers within the Protestant aristocracy, the Constitution had to be defended against any encroachment of democracy or populist sentiment. What was at stake was their right to govern the country and they were resolved to resist 'reform' by all available means.

The first peer actively to encourage the Order was Lord Kenyon, who came from a Scottish family. He had joined the Order in 1808[2] and, along with Lord Yarmouth, was instrumental in persuading HRH Frederick, Duke of York, to join also. The Duke, like his father, King George III, was bitterly opposed to the prospect of Roman Catholic Emancipation and he seems to have seen in the

15

Orange movement a useful vehicle to resist it.

There remains some debate as to when the Duke of York actually joined the Order[3] but in 1821 he assumed the office of Grand Master:

> I have to acknowledge the receipt of your letter of the 6th February and to acquaint you that Mr Eustace communicated to me the resolution entered into by members of the Loyal Orange Institution appointing me their Grand Master and with which I felt much gratified and I am sorry that my acquiescence should not have been communicated to you.[4]

The appointment of a member of the Royal Family as Grand Master was a major coup for the Orange movement and the Grand Lodge decided to move its headquarters from Manchester to London, where a lodge for 'gentlemen' had been formed in 1817. This was probably the lodge that the Duke had joined.

However, the tenure in office of the Duke of York as Grand Master was short. He was advised that the oaths undertaken by Orangemen on joining the Order were illegal and he resigned from membership in June 1821. His action was followed by two other Orange peers, Lord Hereford and Lord Lowther.

The legality of their oaths had been a persistent problem for the Order on both sides of the Irish Sea and they had been required to alter them on a number of occasions to remain within the law.

Royal patronage of the Orange Order did not end with the resignation of the Duke of York. In 1827, his brother, Ernest Augustus, Duke of Cumberland, became Grand Master of the British movement and of the Irish movement a year later.[5] Where York had been rather circumspect about his association with the Order, Cumberland was audacious. He was an unashamed militant Protestant, quite uncompromising in his beliefs. When Parliament was debating Roman Catholic Emancipation in 1829, Cumberland strongly advocated its rejection on the grounds that such a measure was unconstitutional and a danger to the liberties of the country.[6]

Despite his and the efforts of the other Orange peers in Parliament, the Roman Catholic Emancipation Act was passed in 1829.[7] Orangemen, of whatever class, regarded the passage of this Act a betrayal of the Protestant character of the Constitution. It was seen as a panic measure undertaken by a government harassed by the reform lobby. Orange leaders became temporarily demoralised in the wake of this defeat but they were determined to prevent any further inroads into the Constitution by the Radicals. The man chosen by the Grand Lodge to spearhead this campaign was the Deputy Grand Secretary, William Blennerhasset Fairman, a retired Colonel of the Indian Army.

Fairman, an individual of abundant energy, flamboyant oratory and fertile imagination, undertook an extensive recruitment tour of Great Britain in an attempt to rally those sections of the nobility who were opposed to further reform to support the Orange cause. He also visited existing lodges and was granted authority by the Grand Lodge to form new ones. In February, 1833, Fairman arrived in Scotland.

Apart from Lord Kenyon, the only Scottish peer who had shown any interest in the Orange Order was George, the 5th Duke of Gordon. He was born in Edinburgh in 1770 and had pursued a military career.

In 1796 he was Colonel of the 92nd (Gordon) Highlanders, serving with them durng the 1798 Irish Rebellion. It was during this campaign that he probably acquired his militant Protestant tendencies. He was promoted to Major General in 1801 and served with the 42nd Highlanders (Black Watch). Gordon was given the command of all forces in Scotland between 1803-1806. He was promoted to General in 1819, serving with the 1st (Royal Scots) Regiment, and later commanded the 3rd Foot Guards.

In between bouts of military service, the Duke was elected MP for Eye in 1806 before being elevated to the House of Lords in 1807. There remains some confusion as to when the Duke of Gordon actually joined the Order. According to one source it was 1813[9] and according to another it was 1831.[10] The latter date is the more likely since as late as 1829, Lord Kenyon was still being referred to as the Deputy Grand Master of Scotland, an honorary title which Gordon later accepted, presumably when he joined the Order.

When Fairman visited Scotland, he stayed for a period with the Duke on his extensive Highland estate in the North East. He gave a valuable insight as to the Duke's actual relationship with his 'brethren' in the proletarian lodges when he noted that although 'He is very zealous in the cause...I do not think he gives himself much trouble'.[11] In other words, Gordon made no effort to communicate with, let alone visit, any of the lodges ostensibly under his charge. He was merely a figurehead to them, preferring the company of the Grand Lodge in London. However, this state of affairs was hardly surprising, given the Duke's social standing and that of most of his brethren.

Fairman kept in regular contact with the Duke regarding his sojourns north of the border and in a characteristic fit of exuberance declared, 'I will now take the liberty of assuring his Grace that such a fire has been already kindled in North Britain as must speedily burst into a conflagration, not easily to be extinguished'.[12]

Despite the rhetoric, Fairman realised the movement in 'North Britain' lacked leadership and, with this in mind, he formed a lodge for 'gentlemen' in Glasgow in 1833.

Fairman was enthusiastically assisted in this enterprise by Laurence Craigie, a journalist who worked for the Tory newspaper, the *Edinburgh Evening Post*. On 6 April 1833, he wrote to Fairman: 'I fervently hope that your progress among the higher classes may be equally successful and that the wealthy of the land may be shamed into something like activity by their inferiors. The Tories have been hitherto most culpably deaf to the calls of their own interest...'[13]

Fairman and Craigie formed the lodge on 19 April 1833[14] with the intention that it should become the nucleus of a Scottish Grand Lodge, as had occurred when similar lodges were formed in Dublin and London. The Duke of Gordon agreed to lend his name to the lodge and become its patron.[15] In June 1833, the lodge recruited its most significant member when the poet and journalist, William

Motherwell, joined. Born the son of a Glasgow ironmonger in 1797, he was educated in Edinburgh and Paisley. He became the Sheriff Clerk Depute for Renfrewshire in 1818 at a time when Paisley was a centre of radical agitation. The radical politics espoused by elements within the local weaving community horrified Motherwell and encouraged his Toryism.

A highly literate man, Motherwell began writing poetry, his first published work appearing in 1827. A year later, he became the editor of the *Paisley Advertiser* before becoming editor of the staunchly Tory *Glasgow Courier* in 1830.[16] He used his position as editor to promote the Orange cause.

Shortly after his initiation into the Royal Gordon Lodge, his newspaper carried the following item:

Appeal to the Conservatives of the West of Scotland: appealing to the patronage of an enlightened and respected member of the British Peerage, rejecting all party distinctions, except those of honesty and truth and recognising those principles only, which secured the Protestant Succession and joined by an indissoluble tie, the welfare of the Church and State, the Gordon Lodge appeals to the support of every well meaning individual and particularly invites into its ranks all who possess the means of swaying the opinions of this great manufacturing and commercial city.[17]

As far as those people who did possess the means of swaying opinions were concerned, the appeal fell on deaf ears. Almost no person of any political influence joined the lodge. Craigie, in a letter to Fairman, approaches an explanation for their reluctance:

It is the wish of many worthy individuals, who have been asked to join our Orange Lodge that a Conservative Club should be organised in connection with it, for the purpose of controlling the local politics of the city and of uniting the Party in a more numerous force than could be mustered under the banner of Orangeism.[18]

Putting it more bluntly, local Tories with political influence and social prestige were not going to risk their reputations by being directly associated with the Order as it existed north of the border.

Unlike the situation in Ireland and, to a lesser extent, England, the Orange movement in Scotland had not rendered any 'services' considered useful by the establishment. Indeed, quite the reverse. The continued existence of what were clearly hooligan elements within the lodges and their propensity to violence had convinced many leading Tories that Orangemen could not be controlled. In addition, the lodges in Scotland were not numerous enough or concentrated enough in any single location for political action to have any prospect of lasting success.

Although it failed in its ultimate mission, the Royal Gordon Lodge did manage to recruit a few Glasgow notables.[19] Its Master was city merchant and brother of the Lord Provost, William Leckie Ewing. The Deputy Master was a solicitor, Robert Adam. Chaplain to the lodge was the Rev. John J Bentley, an Episcopalian. Another notable member was Archibald McLellan, Convenor of the Trades

House and later a city councillor. He was an art collector and he bequeathed to Glasgow its first public art collection and a gallery to store it in. The McLellan Galleries in Sauchiehall Street are still used to this day for a variety of purposes.

When Laurence Craigie died, somewhat prematurely, in 1834, the Royal Gordon Lodge died with him. He had always been its motivating spirit and no one else was prepared to assume his mantle. His death was noted with profound regret by the Grand Lodge in London at its February meeting in 1835. It was decided to erect a tablet to his memory for which Lord Kenyon donated £2 and his close confidant, Colonel Fairman, £1.[20]

# Chapter 4
# OLD BATTLES ON NEW SOIL

THE attempt of the Grand Lodge to mobilise the Orange movement against further Parliamentary Reform met with only limited success. As most Orangemen in Great Britain were urban dwellers, they had no material interest in opposing such measures. Indeed, in parts of England, some Orangemen openly supported reform and one lodge actually turned radical.[1]

The situation in Scotland was slightly different since the movement was not as homogenous in nature. Lodges tended to be located in either small rural communities as in the South West or South Ayrshire or the rapidly expanding industrial towns of the Central Lowlands.[2]

By the 1830s, the southern parishes of Ayrshire had become something of a stronghold of Orangeism. There was also a substantial Catholic Irish population in the county. Not only did South Ayrshire resemble Armagh in its demographic and economic structure but increasingly in its customs and folk traditions as well. It was hardly surprising then that it was in the 'Irish' town of Girvan, with its peculiar local features, that Orange and Green antagonism came to the boil.

Ostensibly, the issue was Reform. Following the successful second reading of the Reform Bill in 1831, local supporters and other radicals in Girvan decided to hold a celebratory procession through the streets of the town. However, they were physically prevented from doing so, on two occasions, by armed Orangemen, incensed by Catholic Irish participation in the proposed event. This intimidation only served to enrage the radicals, who, in turn, threatened to disrupt the Twelfth celebrations of the Orangemen later in the year.

This tit for tat activity, so typical of the Ulster countryside, alarmed the authorities. As the July anniversary approached, local baillies advised the Orangemen against parading through the streets of Girvan. However, the Sheriff informed the magistrates that there was no legal impediment to the Orange procession taking place as planned.

It appears that at least some of the lodges in Girvan took cognisance of the

20

Defenders of the Faith: a Covenanters' Conventicle

warnings and agreed to avoid marching through the centre of the town. However, on the day of the procession, the Girvan lodges were supported by others from Dailly and Maybole and these lodges seem to have entertained other ideas about the route of the parade.

Around 300 Orangemen and their supporters, many of whom were heavily armed, assembled on the outskirts of Girvan. After marching some way, they were met by a body of special constables on a bridge leading into the town. Some discussion followed between the constabulary and the Orangemen on the route the procession was to take and, as agreed, the Girvan lodges began to veer off down a road which avoided taking them into the town centre. This action caused some dissension in the Orange ranks which led to stones and other missiles being thrown at the special constables.

At this point:

A man stepped out from the right of the fifth or sixth file of the Orangemen and deliberately levelled and fired his gun in the direction of the constables and Alexander Ross, one of the constables standing quietly close to the footpath on the left, instantly fell and...immediately expired.

This occurred while the Orangemen and constables were from ten to fifteen yards apart and was followed by several shots in rapid succession from the Orangemen. The attack by the Orangemen now became general in which they employed the firearms, swords, pikes and bayonets wherewith they were armed on the constables and people, men, women and children, indiscriminately cutting and knocking down all who stood before them. The people gave way in all directions and after struggling for a moment and a number of them being severely wounded, the constables gave way likewise...

The Orangemen now rushed in a body into the town, firing their guns and pistols, brandishing their pikes and swords, cutting down those they met, knocking in windows and the like, crying triumphantly, The Town Is Our Own!!![3]

Appalling acts of brutality were committed by Orangemen in Girvan that day for which there could be no excuse. All told, one man was murdered, 12 persons were seriously wounded, including one victim who lost an eye in a vicious assault, and countless others were subjected to a variety of attacks. Several special constables were severely beaten, some into unconsciousness. The only wonder was that there there were not more fatalities, a fortunate occurrence put down afterwards to what had been the drunken state of many of the assailants.

Such 'donnybrooks' were ten a penny in Ulster but Orangemen there often escaped the full force of the law descending upon them since the 'brethern' often occupied the judicial bench. However, in this respect at least, Ayrshire was not Armagh and consequently an Orangeman was convicted for the murder of the unfortunate special constable Ross.[4] This shameful episode was ironic indeed for a society which in England had supplied special constables as its contribution to law and order.

The Glasgow Riots of 1821 and 1822 and the Girvan Riot of 1831 were to a large extent 'Irish' affairs in that the main protagonists were immigrants fighting their old battles on new soil. The riots which occurred in the industrial town of Airdrie in 1835, although beginning in the same manner, escalated beyond a mere Orange and Green confrontation into something much more sinister.

These riots were to demonstrate, amongst other things, Orangeism's ability to harness itself as an ideology to the latent but still potent anti-Catholicism of Presbyterian Lowland Scotland. What occurred in Airdrie were not 'Orange' riots as such but rather anti-Catholic riots within which Orangemen were no more than minor players.

The disturbances began when a party of around a hundred armed Ribbonmen[5] arrived from Glasgow with the declared intention of forcibly preventing the Orangemen of Airdrie from holding their Twelfth celebrations in the town. However, the Ribbonmen failed to make contact with the Orangemen, and perhaps out of frustration at a wasted journey, they decided to assault local inhabitants at will. Several people sustained serious injuries as a result.

Once the Ribbonmen dispersed, the incensed inhabitants of Airdrie indulged in almost a week of violent anti-Catholic rioting in the town. According to the local Roman Catholic Bishop:

Several innocent persons were dragged from their houses or laid hold of on the road as they returned from their work and cruelly maltreated because they were known to be Catholics...On Tuesday, Wednesday and Thursday, meetings of miners were held and a unanimous resolution was passed to expel every Catholic, young and old, from the various works.[6]

The trouble did not end there. A week later a rumour swept the town, started it was alleged, by an Orangeman named Thompson,[7] that a Catholic plot existed to blow the town up with explosives as an act of revenge.

A mob gathered, reported to have been 4,000 strong, which roamed the streets assaulting any unfortunate Catholics who happened to be about. Catholic property was also attacked, including the church which was all but destroyed.

Significantly, the rioters appear to have enjoyed the tacit approval of the local authorities. When the mob attacked the property of a Protestant in error, the head of the Airdrie Police merely pointed out the 'mistake' to them but made no attempt to prevent the destruction of Catholic property. Indeed, one of the Burgh Magistrates was reported to have been 'in the midst of the mob'.[8]

As for direct Orange participation in these events, the Lord Advocate's Deputy, Cosmo Innes, charged with investigating the disturbances, stated: 'I do not think that the leaders or any great part of that mob were Orangemen...'[9]

Given the numerical strength of the Order in the district at this time, this statement is undoubtedly accurate. However, the Order's ideological contribution should not be underestimated. The anti-Catholic sentiment expressed by the inhabitants of Airdrie, not only in religious but in economic terms as well, presented opportunities for expansion to the Orange movement which it was all too willing to exploit.

Orangeism, as an ideology, was well suited to encouraging and nurturing the pre-existing economic, racial and religious prejudices which soured relations between native Scots Protestants and immigrant Irish Catholics for most of the nineteenth century. Anti-Catholicism became the bridge between immigrant Orangemen and some elements of the native Protestant working class.

# Chapter 5

# 'THE ORANGE CONSPIRACY'

FROM its inception in the Armagh countryside in 1795 to its acceptance by certain members of the Royal Family, the Orange Order had lived on the fringes of illegality. The main difficulties revolved around the administering of secret oaths to new members and the existence of military warrants.

The Order had been obliged to alter its oaths on a number of occasions to remain inside the law. It was this very issue which had forced the Duke of York to resign as Grand Master in 1821. However, the real Achilles heel of the Orange movement was the existence of lodges in the Regular Army despite orders from Horse Guards in 1813, 1822, 1828 and 1835 to dissolve them.[1]

The Order had a great many enemies in Parliament, particularly amongst the Radical Whigs, who regarded it as a bastion of reaction. They were always willing to make capital of any opportunity to discredit the Orange movement which came their way. The Radicals managed to persuade the government that the continued existence of Orange Lodges in the Army constituted a threat to national security. In March, 1835, Thomas Finn proposed in the House of Commons that a Select Committee be set up to investigate every aspect of Orangeism in Ireland.

The Select Committee was composed of 27 members, of whom eight were Orangemen, twelve were Radicals and seven were considered neutrals.[2] In April, 1835, the Grand Orange Lodge of Ireland agreed to give the Select Committee its full co-operation in the pursuit of its aims.[3]

In August, 1835, the Duke of Cumberland wrote to the Select Committee that he, as Imperial Grand Master, had not signed any military warrants and had not known of the existence of any lodges in the Regular Army. He did admit to signing a number of 'blank warrants' which, it was further admitted, may subsequently have been used in connection with military lodges but this had been done outside the knowledge of the Duke himself.

Furthermore, Orange MPs were keen to point out the distinction between those military personnel who happened to be Orangemen and actual military lodges, which would perhaps appear more sinister.[4] In the event, the Select Committee accepted Cumberland's explanation of this matter.

Military lodges were, in fact, a legacy of the Irish Rebellion of 1798 which both the Irish and British Grand Lodges had permitted to continue beyond the end of hostilities. Orange leaders were reluctant to discourage enthusiasm for the cause in the ranks, although there is no real evidence that they specifically promoted it either.[5]

The typical Army Lodge consisted of a sergeant and a dozen or so privates. These lodges were organised on a regimental basis. Officers were rarely, if ever, members and many may not even have been aware that such lodges existed in their regiments or units.

The investigation into Irish Orangeism was concluded in early August, 1835. It found that there were about 1,500 lodges in Ireland, each comprising a membership of anything between 30 and 300 men. The total membership figure was given as 200,000. The Grand Lodge had issued 24 military warrants, although most of these were found to be dormant.[6]

The Radicals were not satisfied with the tenor of these conclusions and on 11 August 1835, Joseph Hume, a Scot, proposed that the Select Committee's remit be extended to include the investigation of the Order in Great Britain and the Colonies. This was accepted and another Select Committee was set up for this purpose. Its membership included Lord Kenyon, Colonel William B Fairman and William Motherwell.

The inquiry into British and Colonial Orangeism lasted from 13 August until 31 August, 1835. It concluded that there were 300 lodges in Great Britain with a total membership of 150,000.[7]

The Order came under increasing pressure which was exacerbated when the King, William IV, wrote to the House of Commons in the following terms:

> I have received your dutiful address submitting to me certain resolutions on the subject of Orange lodges in the Army. My attention has been and shall continue to be, directed to practices contrary to the regulations and injurious to the discipline of my troops. I owe it, no less to the dignity of my Crown, to the state of the country and the welfare of my brave and loyal Army, to discourage and prevent any attempt to introduce secret societies into the ranks and you may rely on my determination to adopt the most effective means for that purpose.[8]

Cumberland was still pleading ignorance in this matter, but in response to the Royal Declaration he announced that from 24 August, 1835, all military warrants were 'null and void'.

On 7 September, 1835, the final conclusions of the Select Committee were published. These were: Orangemen controlled the Irish Yeomanry; Orangemen enjoyed a certain measure of immunity from justice in the North of Ireland; Orangemen were frequently engaged in civil disturbances and riots; Orange Lodges existed illegally in the Army and the Order was a source of patronage for persons wishing to procure licences for public houses. In addition, many Orangemen possessed firearms which was a threat to the rule of law.

The Select Committee recommended that all Orangemen should be dismissed from public and military service. It also recommended the complete suppression of the Order.

As far as Scotland was concerned, armed Orangemen had certainly been involved in serious public disorders. Of that there could be little argument. In his evidence before the Select Committee, the Lord Advocate's Deputy in Scotland, Cosmo Innes, traced the increase of sectarianism in the country to the Girvan Riots of 1831. He concluded: 'It will not be possible to restore the West of Scotland to tranquillity and to prevent breaches of the peace occurring occasionally until measures are taken to put down the Orange Lodges and Ribbonmen and every other secret society.'[9]

Despite this barrage of criticism, the Duke of Cumberland had still not made any move either to resign his position as Grand Master or to dissolve the Order. Parliament appears to have stalled on the Select Committee's recommendations in the belief that Cumberland would do the honourable thing. True to form, the Duke maintained a characteristic defiance.

However, whether by chance or design, Joseph Hume produced new 'evidence' against the Order, based on the allegations of one Joseph Haywood, an expelled Orangeman from Sheffield. These allegations amounted to a charge of treason being levelled at the Order.

According to Haywood, Colonel Fairman, during his recruitment tour in 1833, had been sounding out Orangemen as to whether they would have been prepared to support a plot designed to place the Duke of Cumberland on the throne as Regent in place of the Princess Victoria, who was deemed too young at the time to become the monarch. The reigning monarch, King William IV, was to be deposed for sanctioning reform.

It is possible that Fairman may have entertained such bizarre notions if his correspondence is to be taken seriously. In a letter to the Duke of Gordon, written in 1832, he wrote: 'By our next general meeting, we shall be assuming, I think, an attitude of boldness as will strike the foe with awe but we inculcate the doctrine of passive obedience and non-resistance too religiously by far.'[10]

Following Haywood's allegations, Colonel Fairman went into hiding with a letter book the Select Committee were anxious to examine. In the meantime, the unfortunate Haywood died of natural causes and so the Radicals lost their star witness. Nevertheless, the charge of a treasonable conspiracy now hung over the Order on top of all its other difficulties.

The King was not amused and on 25 February, 1836, he informed the House of Commons:

I willingly assent to the prayer of the address of my faithful Commons that I will be pleased to take such measures as may seem to be advisable for the effectual discouragement of Orange lodges and generally of all political societies excluding persons of a different religious faith, using secret signs and symbols and acting by means of associated branches.

It is my firm intention to discourage all such societies in my Dominions and I rely with confidence on the fidelity of my loyal subjects to support me in this determination.[11]

Given the King's 'firm intention', Cumberland was at last compelled to act. The following day, the Duke dissolved the Loyal Orange Institution of Great Britain. After some prevarication, the Loyal Orange Institution of Ireland followed suit in April, 1836.[12]

If the idea of an 'Orange Conspiracy' ever existed, it was almost certainly only in the fertile imagination of Colonel William Blennerhasset Fairman. Whatever else Cumberland, Kenyon, Gordon and other Orange peers like the Bishop of Salisbury and the Marquis of Chandos were, they were not considered to be lunatics. They may have despised Reform and all its implications but they would not have been foolish enough to contemplate a treasonable conspiracy dependent upon such a shaky foundation as the British Orange movement.

The real conspirators were perhaps the Order's many enemies in Parliament whose dogged determination to smash the movement finally paid off. The Select Committee, for reasons of their own, had grossly exaggerated the numerical strength of the Order in Great Britain and hence its potential 'threat'. Rather than the quite absurd figure of 150,000 quoted in the official report, there were, in reality, no more than about 6,000 Orangemen in Great Britain.

In addition, there were only about 500 Orangemen in the Army and they were scattered around the four corners of the Empire. Given these circumstances, the chances of staging a successful military style *coup d'état* were nil.

The Order, of course, had brought much of this hostility on itself. It had failed lamentably to control what was, in many parts of the country and especially in Scotland, an undisciplined and violent rabble. In addition, it had at its head an individual who was universally disliked, and a small part of the Order's difficulties stemmed from the personal malice directed towards the Duke of Cumberland from both Radicals in Parliament and senior establishment figures in society at large.[13]

Finally, Cumberland and Kenyon must shoulder part of the blame for this debacle themselves. They displayed appalling judgement in permitting an adventurer like Fairman to assume the powers he did within the movement. By giving him *carte blanche*, they effectively abdicated their own responsibilities and both themselves and the movement they professed to lead ultimately paid the price in public disgrace and ridicule.

*Chapter 6*

# SCHISM AND DIVISION

WHEN the Imperial Grand Master, the Duke of Cumberland, dissolved the Loyal Orange Institutions of Great Britain and Ireland in 1836, his action did not make the continued existence of individual Orange Lodges illegal. Cumberland had dissolved the movement at the request of the King and also in the realisation that if he had not done so then Parliament would have taken much more draconian measures, probably a total ban backed by the full force of the law. Cumberland's action was really something of a damage limitation exercise since it undoubtedly prevented a worse fate befalling the Orange Order.

In point of fact, a request of the reigning monarch was not the 'law' and so the Orange movement did not disappear, rather it assumed new aliases and went underground, as it were, until the heat died down. As far as the rank and file were concerned, the Grand Lodge could dissolve itself but it had no power to dissolve the movement. Orangemen were incensed that the Order had been officially per-secuted when what they perceived as disloyal and treasonable societies were being openly tolerated.

It was in these circumstances that the majority of Scottish lodges simply realigned themselves with one or other of the two Orange Societies which emerged in the immediate aftermath of the dissolution. These bodies were the Grand Protestant Confederation of Great Britain and the Grand Orange Association of Scotland.

The events surrounding the dissolution had embarrassed most of the British peers who had supported the Order. Most lost all interest in Orangeism, a process which, in truth, had already manifested itself in the aftermath of the Order's failure to prevent Roman Catholic Emancipation in 1829 and Reform in 1832. They realised then that the Order was not going to be an effective auxiliary of Toryism.

Of the Order's leading figures, the Duke of Cumberland, not surprisingly, had maintained a very low profile. In 1837 he left the country to be crowned King

Ernest I of Hanover. Lord Kenyon also bowed quietly out of Orange affairs and died in 1855. The titular head of the movement in Scotland, the Duke of Gordon, died in 1836.

The one Tory Peer who did 'keep the faith' was George William, the 10th Earl of Winchelsea, who had once challenged the Duke of Wellington to a duel over the latter's support for Roman Catholic Emancipation. An enthusiastic Orangeman, Winchelsea was instrumental in keeping the movement intact and alive following the confusion which occurred in the wake of the dissolution. In May, 1836, the Grand Protestant Confederation of Great Britain was formed under his leadership.[1]

In reality, this new organisation was the old Loyal Orange Institution of Great Britain under another name. Winchelsea considered it prudent, both in his interest and the movement's, to make no reference in the title to the word 'Orange' until the dust had settled. This was probably wise given the stigma attached to it at this time.

However, the rank and file were not so circumspect. In 1840, they succeeded in having 'Loyal Orangemen' added to the title. Following more semantic manoeuvring, the title was changed again in 1844, to the Grand Protestant Association of Loyal Orangemen of Great Britain.

By this time the Earl of Enniskillen had become the Grand Master.[2] Thus, those Scottish lodges which were in membership of the GPALOGB, were under the leadership of an Irish peer from an organisation based in England.

According to the new Grand Lodge:

> Its leading and sole principle is a devoted adherence to those Protestant opinions and institutions, for the maintenance of which against the threatened encroachments of Popery, our revered Sovereign, William, Prince of Orange, was called to the throne in these realms.
>
> We bind ourselves in the carrying out of this principle, to undeviating loyalty to the person of the Sovereign being Protestant, to unswerving obedience to the laws and a constant endeavour, individually, collectively and legally to maintain the peace, the good order and the rational liberties of our fellow subjects.
>
> The principle of our Association extends no further.[3]

This declaration was indicative of an organisation on the defensive with its emphasis on obedience to the law and the maintenance of the peace. Well might Orangemen make a point of stating these principles so forcefully given their track record.

It should also be noted that no oaths were administered by or exacted from members but all candidates for admission into a lodge were required to declare their support for Queen Victoria and the Succession to the Throne being Protestant.

As before, only two degrees were recognised, the Orange and the Purple, and a uniform system of signs, grips and passwords was established. The opening and closing prayers for lodge meetings were based on the Liturgy of the Church of England. Needless to say, the GPALOGB remained exclusively Protestant.[4]

Although the GPALOGB had a number of Scottish lodges under its wing, it is interesting to note that, from its inception in 1836, it does not seem to have had a single Grand Lodge Officer who was a Scot. Apart from the Grand Master, the leadership was dominated by members based in England.

Not all Orangemen in Scotland were content to continue having their affairs orchestrated from London. Following the dissolution, a number of them assembled in Edinburgh and formed a rival organisation, the Grand Orange Association of Scotland.[5]

An unknown number of lodges in the country were represented at this meeting and they immediately established a Grand Orange Lodge of Scotland. Of the first ten warrants issued by the new authority, five went to Airdrie District No. 1 and of these, four went to locations where no previous Orange activity was known:[6] LOL 1 Moodiesburn; LOL 2 Chryston; LOL 6 Drumgelloch; LOL 8 Gartsherrie; LOL 9 Shotts. These lodges were all located in coal mining districts and may well have existed before 1836.

For the first time, Orangemen in Scotland had formed their own Society which was quite independent of similar organisations in England or Ireland. Unlike the lodges which transferred to the English-based GPALOGB, these Orangemen were determined to distance themselves from any semblance of aristocratic influence, however nominal this had actually proved to be in practice.

Detail remains obscure regarding the founding members of the new Association but it is likely that the impetus came from three main sources.

The first source was probably the lodges in Glasgow which had been suspended by William Motherwell when he became their District Master in 1833. Apart from their irregularities, which have been noted,[7] the lodges in question had been unhappy at the appointment of Motherwell, since this had been imposed on them by the Grand Lodge in London.

Their preferred choice and the man Motherwell replaced as District Master was a Paisley lawyer, George Donaldson. He had joined the Order as a means of opposing Roman Catholic Emancipation and became the Master of LOL 178 in Paisley. In 1831, he was elected to senior office in the Grand Black Encampment of the Knights of Malta.[8] It is quite likely that given his record in Orange circles, Donaldson would have been a likely candidate as one of the leading figures in the new Association and probably took most of the Glasgow lodges with him into its ranks.

He may well have been assisted in this enterprise by Orangemen still attached to military lodges. The Edinburgh lodges were largely composed of military personnel[9] and there were, perhaps, some others in the country. The warrants of these lodges had been cancelled by the Duke of Cumberland but it is probable they still continued to meet despite this.

Following the dissolution, these lodges would not have been welcome in the GPALOGB since it had been the existence of such lodges which had proved so troublesome to the old LOIGB in the first place. Given these circumstances, those lodges in Scotland still holding military warrants would have been willing to join any newly set up Orange Society.

Indeed, it may not be entirely a coincidence that the founding meeting of the Grand Orange Association of Scotland was held in the military city of Edinburgh. However it may also be the case that by meeting in the national capital the new Association wanted to emphasise its 'Scottish' identity from the start. Perhaps both reasons influenced the choice of Edinburgh for the founding meeting.

The third source of membership for the Association were the previously 'unattached' lodges then in existence. Their actual number is unknown but clearly some of them played a leading part in forming the new body.

If these theories are correct, then it was a somewhat disparate group who came together to form the Association. In such circumstances, it would have been difficult to maintain any semblance of stability without good leadership. The latter quality, so essential to a movement in a period of transition, was not forthcoming, as the events in the following decades were to testify.

# Chapter 7

# THE ORANGE
# AND THE GREEN

THE restructuring of Scottish Orangeism which took place in the wake of the dissolution did not result in either of the two new Orange Societies having any more control over the behaviour of their membership than their predecessors. During the 1840s and 1850s, the Orange movement was again scarred by a series of particularly ugly disturbances and riots, some of which resulted in loss of life.

Most, though by no means all, of these violent outbreaks occurred within the coal mining communities of the country where both the Catholic and Protestant Irish were present in large numbers. The violence tended to be most frequent on those occasions of specific importance to the immigrants such as the 12th of July or the 17th of March (St Patrick's Day). Annual fair holidays were also prone to episodes of sectarian disorder and mayhem.

Glasgow's Orangemen, banned by the city magistrates from holding public processions following the riots of 1821 and 1822, opted for less ostentatious but equally provocative ways of celebrating the Boyne anniversary:

> Tuesday being the 12th of July, two Orange lodges which assembled in Gallowgate Street, exhibited a crown of orange flowers and other insignia from the window of the room in which they meet. This is the first time that any public demonstration of this kind has been attempted in Glasgow for many years and as these party displays are extremely liable to irritate and excite the Roman Catholic part of the population to retaliation, the police interfered and ordered the Orange badges to be removed.[1]

Undaunted as ever by such setbacks, it was noted seven years later: 'Two publicans in the Gallowgate, named respectively, Rennison and Blair, were brought before Baillie Orr on the charge of allowing their houses to be used...as the public reandezvous of Orange lodges.'[2] The publicans were fined a guinea each for hanging flags and bunting from their premises.

A more serious disturbance occurred in Ayrshire in 1847:

In Kilmarnock, on Monday, the Orangemen kept the town in a perfect ferment. They fired pistols from the window of the lodge room between nine and ten o'clock while the streets were crowded with workmen and others going to and from breakfast. This, of course, alarmed some and enraged others and had the effect of immediately causing a crowd to assemble; information was also soon conveyed to the navvies at work on the line of railway between here and Mauchline and these immediately struck work and poured into the town.

About mid day the street opposite the Council Chambers was from the density of the crowd, nearly impassable. The Catholic party, however, still continued peaceable and the Orangemen incensed at this commenced in their lodge room with drum and fife to play 'Croppies Lie Down' and 'Protestant Boys' and other party tunes. This, however, the police immediately put a stop to.

About five in the afternoon, about a dozen of them, armed with drawn swords and pistols, left Mr Morton's and proceeded to the Star Inn in Regent Street. Although they flourished their weapons and seemed anxious for battle, no one molested them. Indeed their appearance was so contemptible that a navvie remarked 'they were not worth the bating'.[3]

That same year, disturbances also occurred at a Twelfth procession in Dundee when local Orangemen were attacked by a hostile mob of Irish Catholics.[4]

Sectarian outrages had become an almost normal feature of life in the Airdrie and Coatbridge area. A massive brawl occurred on St Patrick's Day in 1851 in Airdrie when 300 Orangemen taking part in a funeral procession for a deceased member of the Order were attacked by a mob of Irishmen. Many injuries were sustained by both parties.[5] In an obvious act of revenge two years later, a two-hour long melee occurred in the town between Orangemen and Catholics, this time during a Catholic funeral procession.[6]

Airdrie was also the scene of yet another full scale riot in 1854. During the Airdrie Races, tents selling alcohol were open all night and in one of them, a fiddler hired by a group of Orangemen began playing party tunes. This action provoked many Irish Catholics who were present and a fearful riot ensued in which one man was murdered and several others were very seriously injured.

The deceased was said to have been an innocent bystander simply caught up in the mayhem which occurred. However, as in 1835, there were serious repercussions for the local Roman Catholic community arising from this incident. Anti-Catholic feeling was widespread in the town and was only kept in check by the presence of a troop of the military specially drafted in for the purpose. Several pits in the area struck work in an attempt to expel every Catholic from the workforce.[7]

In Ayrshire, the Dalry area had become another storm centre of sectarian hatred. Serious disturbances had occurred in 1846 and 1847 and by the 1850s, parts of the Garnock Valley seemed to be on a par with the worst excesses found in the Ulster countryside:

On Sunday last a riot of an alarming nature took place at Kilbirnie station. A party of miners from the adjacent village of Borestone visited the former place, ostensibly to enjoy themselves but really with some malicious purpose in view, for the greater number of them were armed with 'jumpers', formidable bars of iron used in their trade. After partaking of stimulants, several houses inhabited by miners, Protestants, were visited but in almost every instance the men were either absent or had concealed themselves. It now became evident that an onslaught by Ribbonmen on Orangemen was contemplated, all the parties sought after being Irish Protestants.

Disappointed and baffled by not seeing the object of their malevolence, the party wreaked their vengeance, first upon the doorposts and windows of the houses of their intended victims and ultimately upon the females and helpless inmates. The poor creature first injured was an elderly woman who was engaged in reading her Bible and the very sight of that hated book aroused to fury the miscreant horde.

They beat the poor creature with their iron weapons until her whole body became a blackened mess. Having some method in their madness, however, they avoided injury to her head and she escaped with her life. She lies dangerously ill however. Several others were seriously bruised but it was astonishing that no mortal injuries were sustained.[8]

The local constable, himself beaten up severely, was powerless on his own to prevent this invasion. It was little wonder that the Sheriff of Ayrshire complained that the Dalry district was '...the very worst in the county, lawless, violent and tumultuous.[9]

The 'Iron Burgh', Coatbridge, had one of the worst records of sectarian strife in Scotland and it was the scene of a particularly vicious riot in 1857 which had serious consequences for the Orange movement:

A riot which assumed a very serious character occurred at Coatbridge on Monday night between eight and nine o'clock, resulting from that deadly animosity existing between the Orange and Catholic factions. It appears that the Orangemen had resolved on celebrating the 12th of July in the usual way by having a procession at Chryston, at which place there was a very large number of Orangemen from all places round about, even to a considerable distance. The Sax Horn and Union Bands left Airdrie at an early hour on Monday morning to play at the procession. So far as we understand, nothing occurred during the day to mar the proceedings.

Unmistakable evidence, however, was apparent at Coatbridge during the day that the Catholics meditated an attack on the Orangemen on their arrival there. At an early hour in the evening many hundreds were congregated about the bridge leading to the railway station, at which place, the Orangemen were to arrive per train. On their arrival and having left the carriages, they proceeded down to the bridge, both bands playing, the Sax Horn in front and the Union in the rear but being informed of their danger, if they walked through Coatbridge, they struck off on a path along the canal bank.

They had not proceeded far until they were overtaken by a dense mob who attacked them in the rear. The bands appeared to be alone the object of their attack and with such violence was the onslaught made, that several of them were severely injured so that medical aid was found necessary, before their arrival home. Their drums and instruments, to a considerable extent, were also destroyed.

The report of firearms was heard from several parties in the crowd during the melee. The windows of several houses were also smashed to pieces. We understand that several of the ringleaders are in custody and that an active investigation is being made by the authorities.[10]

After routing the Orangemen, the mob took control of the town, assaulting anyone and everyone at will. One witness, a collier at Gartsherrie, stated: 'I heard cries in the mob frequently repeated of "Orange buggers, they ought to be ripped up". The mob was running here and there in the streets in parties of twenties and fifties.'[11] Order was not restored in Coatbridge until the military arrived from Glasgow.

From statements made to the police, the occupations of 40 of the Bandsmen and Orangemen can be established. They included eight miners; five colliers; one ironstone drawer; one pitsinker; one pitheadman; one roadsman; one pit brusher; one pit bottomer and seven labourers.[12]

Three of the nine men convicted of mobbing and rioting also had mining industry connections and four were labourers. All but one of these nine men were Irish. They were severely dealt with by the judiciary. Three were each sentenced to four years penal servitude; four to eighteen months imprisonment and the other two to twelve months imprisonment.[13]

The Orange Order did not escape punishment of a fashion either. The authorities, alarmed by both the frequency and the violence of these outrages, at last acted decisively. The Sheriff of Lanarkshire placed a ban on all public Orange processions for the next ten years in the county. His action was followed by his colleagues in the neighbouring counties of Ayrshire, Dunbartonshire, Renfrewshire and Stirlingshire.[14]

In effect, all Orange processions in West Central Scotland were banned forthwith. Orangemen were outraged at what they regarded as a fundamental encroachment on their civil and religious liberty. However, with one exception, the ban was observed by the Order.

The one exception to the ban occurred in the small mining village of Linwood in 1859. Unfortunately, it had fatal consequences:

For some reason or another, which in the meantime is not explained, the authorities in Renfrewshire did not issue proclamations prohibiting Orange demonstrations although this was done both in Lanarkshire and Ayrshire and this circumstance appeared to operate materially in making the Orangemen of this town (Paisley) bold and confident.

As early as six in the morning, the lodge mustered in the High Street to the number of four or five hundred, among whom were a considerable number of women, and, headed by a band of music, they proceeded to parade the town.

Ultimately, they directed their steps to Johnstone and on reaching Millarston...they were attacked by a body of miners. Some of their musical instruments were damaged and severe wounds on the head and parts of the body were given and received by both parties. One of the miners assailing the Orangemen had his head severely cut by a sword. Ultimately, the miners drew off and the Orangemen proceeded to Johnstone.

Here, in the square, they waited some time and had some refreshment and again started on their route, proceeding to Quarrelton and from thence...they turned back and again rested for a time in Johnstone. Shortly after twelve o'clock, they left Johnstone and proceeded to Linwood by the Deaf Hillock Toll, reaching the latter place shortly before one o'clock. Here the Linwood lodge broke off from the procession and the Paisley and Johnstone lodges proceeded on the road to Paisley with the intention of separating at the West Toll. On reaching the bridge over the Black Cart at the south end of the village, they found their further progress opposed by two or three hundred miners, who as soon as they made their appearance, attacked them with stones and bludgeons.

The procession was driven back into the village in disorder but after a short delay they induced four or five of the County Constabulary to accompany them again to the bridge, which they again essayed to cross.

A desperate encounter then ensued in which firearms and knives were freely used, in addition to less dangerous weapons such as bludgeons, paving stones etc. A continued succession of shots were fired but apparently the greater number of them were discharged at too great a distance to do much harm. As the struggle continued, the combatants drew closer to each other and a fearful hand to hand fight followed, the weapons being used, chiefly knives and bludgeons.

Ultimately, after the struggle had lasted about three quarters of an hour, the Catholic party gave way and fled along the road leading to Inkerman. Two or three who dropped behind were very severely handled by the infuriated Orangemen and indeed, in one case in particular, but for the energetic interference of the police, it is questionable if the unfortunate man would not have been murdered. He was pointed out as one who had taken a most prominent part in the melee. After he was in custody, two pistol shots were fired at him.

After the affray was over, the combatants presented a horrid spectacle. On the middle of the road where the fight had been hottest, lay extended the dead body of a strong muscular man, apparently about forty years of age. His skull had been severely fractured and he was stabbed, apparently, with a clasp knife in the left breast. The body was conveyed to the village, whither also, the more seriously wounded were taken. The procession then reformed and accompanied by all who could walk, proceeded to Paisley, which place it reached without further molestation. One extraordinary feature in the day's proceedings was the encouragement given to the Orangemen by the police. In the morning, several of the night force, as soon as they were dismissed, joined the procession in their uniforms.[15]

Another extraordinary feature was the utter determination of the Orangemen to continue with their procession no matter the cost to themselves or whoever stood in their way. They were not only attacked once, on the way out of Paisley, but again on the way back in a savage melee which lasted some three quarters of an hour and resulted in loss of life. Yet, despite these traumas, they were resolved to continue! Fanaticism, fuelled by intoxication, is the only explanation one can offer for their extraordinary conduct that fateful day in Linwood.

The man murdered in the riot was a Roman Catholic, who, it was later alleged, had been an innocent bystander visiting relatives in Linwood. In any event, no one was ever charged with his murder. However, two people were arrested, both Irish Catholics, who were charged with mobbing and rioting. One received six months imprisonment and the other received four months.[16] The fact that no Orangemen were charged with anything would seem to endorse the inference of some police collusion in this disgraceful affair.[17]

Linwood, not surprisingly, remained in a state of excitement for some time after the riot. The authorities stationed 150 troops of the Royal Sussex Militia in Paisley and also swore in a number of special constables in Johnstone in case of further disturbances.[18] It was not long before rumours started circulating in Linwood that the homes of known Orangemen would be attacked in revenge for the riot. In response, about a hundred armed Orangemen marched through the village again in an act of further defiance.[19]

It is clear from the available evidence that many of these sectarian outrages were not simply the result of spontaneous indignation by one party or the other but rather the result of planning. Orangemen often went out of their way deliberately to provoke the opposition but it is equally clear that some attacks on Orange processions, as at Coatbridge in 1857 and Linwood in 1859, were not merely the individual actions of a few hotheads. Something more organised was afoot.

Reference has already been made to the existence of Ribbonism amongst the Catholic Irish community.[20] It is quite likely that the impetus behind some of this agitation came from Ribbon Societies or their equivalents from within the immigrant population. More research has to be undertaken on the extent and nature of Ribbonism in Scotland at this time before definite conclusions on its true impact can be accurately assessed but on available evidence it certainly appears to have played a much more significant role within the Catholic Irish community than has has been realised.

# Chapter 8

# INDUSTRIALISATION: MIDWIFE OF POPULAR ORANGEISM

B Y the 1830s, the industrial landscape of Scotland was undergoing a transformation. The handloom weaving trade was in decline as the textile industry
generally began to recede in importance. Its position as the leading sector of the
economy was supplanted by the growth and development of the coal and iron
industries.

These industries, concentrated in the Central Lowlands, became increasingly interdependent and in addition both were extremely labour intensive. The
new iron companies which emerged not only increased the demand for coal,
they were also involved in the extraction of this precious mineral for their own
consumption.

Lanarkshire was in the forefront of this industrial revolution. The number of
coal mines in the county increased from 139 in 1851 to 187 by 1864. By 1895, the
number had risen to 257.[1] This expansion demanded a large workforce.

In 1841, the number of coal miners in Lanarkshire was 7,226. Ten years later,
the number had doubled to some 15,580. By 1871, the number had risen again to
22,190. Almost half of Scotland's coal miners worked in Lanarkshire pits.[2]

This development was complemented by a corresponding domination in iron
production. In 1854, out of 118 furnaces in blast in Scotland, a total of 68 were
located in the 12 iron works of Lanarkshire.[3] By 1870, the county contained 92
furnaces in blast out of a national total of 158.[4]

Ayrshire experienced similar levels of industrialisation. By 1878, there were
104 coal mines in the county. Of these, 26 were located in the Dalry, Irvine and
Kilwinning area; 32 were located in the Galston and Kilmarnock area; 25 were
located in the Cumnock and Muirkirk area and 21 were located in the Ayr,
Dalmellington and Girvan areas.[5] About 13,000 miners were employed in these pits.[6]

Similar growth occurred in this county's iron industry. In 1854, 30 furnaces
were in blast in the nine iron works spread across Ayrshire. By 1870, this number
had risen to 41 furnaces in blast.[7]

It was the scale of the industrialisation in this part of Scotland during the nineteenth century that ensured the survival and eventual expansion of the Orange Order. This was due to three main factors.

Firstly, the mining of coal and the manufacture of iron were labour intensive industries. The indigenous population could not meet the employers' demand for workers and as a result, immigrants from Ireland and elsewhere were recruited to make up the shortfall. Many of these migrants were Ulstermen, some may even have already been Orangemen; both groups were potential recruits for the Order in Scotland.

Secondly, family and kinship traditions were becoming established. By the middle decades of the nineteenth century, the Scots born sons and grandsons and other relatives of immigrant Orangemen were themselves joining Orange Lodges and in increasing numbers. In so doing, they were gradually transforming the Order from an ethnic mutual aid society for Ulstermen into an institution firmly embedded within 'Scottish' working class life and experience.

Thirdly, these developments coincided with the re-emergence of anti-Catholicism in the wake of continuing immigration from Ireland. The Order was able to exploit the fears and prejudices felt by many native Scottish Protestants towards the Catholic Irish in their midst.[8]

This last factor was of particular importance in the coal and iron industries where the competition for semi-skilled and unskilled employment was most intense between the two social groups. Orangeism, *per se*, was not the root cause of the prevalent sectarianism, but as an ideology it was well disposed strongly to reinforce the pre-existing prejudice held by a not insignificant section of the native proletariat towards the Catholic Irish.

A correlation certainly exists between the development of the coal and iron industries in Lanarkshire and Ayrshire and the growth of the Orange movement in Scotland. In the 1830s, the coal and iron industries were initially concentrated in the Airdrie and Coatbridge areas. It has been noted that when the Grand Orange Association of Scotland organised itself in 1836, there were five lodges in the same area and indeed Airdrie received District Warrant No. 1 of the new Society. When the industries expanded into the Motherwell and Wishaw area during the middle decades of the century, lodges were formed in their wake. Bellshill District No. 8 and Wishaw District No. 16 were established at this time and a separate District Lodge, No. 22, was also set up in Coatbridge in 1863.[9]

This pattern of development continued in the late 1870s, when the Lanarkshire coalfield expanded into the Blantyre and Hamilton areas. It was not long after that Blantyre and Hamilton District No. 33 was established. As the coal and iron industries continued to boom, so too did the membership of the Order. More District Lodges were established at Motherwell, Harthill and Larkhall.

In Ayrshire, by the 1840s, the strength of the Orange movement had shifted from the old handloom weaving communities of the southern parishes of the county into the coal and iron producing districts. Although Maybole District No. 4

Industrialisation: midwife of popular Orangeism. In memory of a coalmining disaster

remained a bastion of Orangeism for some time to come, the real strength was concentrated in the coalfield.

Kilwinning District No. 9; Ayr District No. 11; Patna District No. 12; Dalry District No. 14 and Stevenston District No. 23, formed in 1864,[10] were testimony to a period of sustained growth of the Order in industrial Ayrshire.

The correlation between the expansion of the coal and iron industries and the growth of Orangeism extended beyond the county borders of Ayrshire and Lanarkshire. In Stirlingshire, a good many Orangemen were employed in the coal mines around Slamannan and an Orange Ball was held in the village in 1861 to celebrate the Twelfth. The first Orange procession in the county was held in Slamannan in 1870, which by this time had its own District Lodge, No. 32. Ten years later, the lodges in Slamannan were strong enough to purchase, at a cost of £300, premises for use as an Orange Hall.[11]

A second District Lodge in Stirlingshire, Falkirk District No. 36, was formed in 1876. The impetus for this development had come from lodges organised in the pit villages of Brightons and Maddiston. They were later joined by a lodge organised in Camelon.[12]

It was a similar scenario in West Lothian. By the 1870s a District Lodge, No. 26, was established in the heart of the county coalfield at Armadale and Whitburn.

This was soon followed by the establishment of another District Lodge, No. 48, around the pit village of Broxburn.

The importance of the development of the coal and iron industries to the growth of the Orange Order in Scotland has been emphasised. No less significant in sustaining this growth was the gradual development of the shipbuilding industry on the River Clyde during the middle to late nineteenth century.

Indeed, the steady increase in the number of Orange Lodges amongst the various shipbuilding communities along the banks of the Clyde estuary reflected the expansion of the industry. The catalyst for much of this process was, once again, the importation of Ulster Protestant labour.

In 1853, one Edward Harland opened a shipyard in Belfast[13] but he was soon obliged to import a large number of Clydeside shipbuilding workers in order to train his workforce in the new skills of iron ship construction. Harland's yard was located in the staunchly Protestant east end of Belfast and it seems that a good number of the Clydeside workers brought there forged strong bonds with their Ulster colleagues.

The men shared a skilled occupation, but more than that, they shared a common cultural heritage based on their work ethic and religion. When the Scottish shipyard workers returned home some of them bore a legacy of their Belfast experience: an acceptance of Orangeism. This development was encouraged by the steady importation of Ulstermen into the Clydeside shipyards as the domestic industry entered a period of spectacular growth. It was not long before Orange Lodges began to appear in the Clydeside shipbuilding communities as a result.

The focal point of much of this initial development was Partick. About 1858 or earlier, a District Lodge, No. 15, was formed[14] which by 1864 comprised nine lodges. Ten years later, Partick District No. 15 was the largest Orange jurisdiction in Scotland with a total of 18 lodges operating under its wing.[15] In addition, a further seven lodges were organised in Partick under the authority of a rival Orange Society.[16] Although not all of these lodges actually met in Partick, they were nevertheless located in neighbouring communities with a shipbuilding connection, like Anderston and Whiteinch.

South of the river from Partick, a District Lodge, No. 42, comprising eight lodges, was organised in Govan in 1876.[17] The Order grew rapidly in the burgh and it received a further boost to its membership when Harland and Wolff, the Belfast shipbuilders, opened a yard.

Like a number of other District Lodges in the Glasgow area, Govan had an Ulsterman, one Thomas Hanna, as its first District Master.[18] The extent of Ulster migration into the shipbuilding communities at this time can be seen in the census figures of 1901 which showed the number of Irish born inhabitants of Govan to have been 11.5 per cent of the population and 12 per cent in Partick.[19] A good proportion of these immigrants, perhaps the majority, were Protestants.

Orange expansion north of the river continued unabated. West of Partick, a separate District Lodge was established at Whiteinch in 1889.[20] Prior to this date, the local lodges had been part of Partick District No. 15 but by the late 1880s they were numerous enough to form their own District.

West of Whiteinch, the next District Lodge to be organised was at Clydebank in 1892.[21] It was no coincidence that the local Orange Hall was located outside one of the main gates of the town's biggest and most famous shipbuilding firms, John Brown's. Further down river again, a District Lodge had been organised in Dumbarton as early as 1868 when shipbuilding was an important local industry in that town.[22]

South of the river from Clydebank, a District Lodge had been established in Renfrew in about 1873.[23] However, outside of Paisley, the real strongholds of Orangeism in Renfrewshire were the shipbuilding and port towns of Greenock and Port Glasgow.

Port Glasgow had a long established Orange tradition. One of the oldest lodges in Scotland, 'Nassau' LOL 219 was formed as early as 1829. By 1873, Port Glasgow District Lodge No. 19 comprised some eight lodges which met in an Orange Hall located in the heart of the town's shipyard area.[24] By 1886, it was estimated there were about 300 Orangemen in the 'Port'.[25]

In neighbouring Greenock, District Lodge No. 34 comprised 16 lodges of which 14 met in the town, one met in nearby Gourock and the other lodge met in Rothesay on the Isle of Bute.[26] The number of Orangemen in Greenock at this time was estimated to be about 700.[27]

By 1914, there were 18 lodges operating in the Greenock area. These were organised into two separate District Lodges, No. 34 and No. 35, each of which had its own Orange Hall located in different parts of the town.[28]

The importance of the shipbuilding industry to the growth of Orangeism in Scotland can perhaps best be appreciated when it is noted that the three largest Orange jurisdictions in the country by 1914 were Partick, Greenock and Govan.

What, if any, was the relationship between Orangeism and Capital? Can any meaningful conclusions of a universal nature be drawn? Do the following two case studies tell us anything?

## (i) William Baird & Company

The Scottish coal industry was characterised by a small number of increasingly large iron companies surrounded by a very large number of small colliery owners, some of whom possessed only one mine. Of particular interest was the firm of William Baird & Company of Gartsherrie. Not only because they were the largest ironmasters in Scotland but also because they entertained a somewhat opaque association with Orangeism.

The company was formed by three brothers, Alexander, James and William Baird in 1830. They had already acquired a number of coal mines two years earlier but in 1830 they built an ironworks at Gartsherrie, on the outskirts of Coatbridge. The Bairds were the first ironmasters commercially to exploit the hot blast process of iron smelting which reduced the amount of coal required. This innovative process proved extremely profitable and allowed the company to expand its operations.[29]

In 1844 the Eglinton Iron Works in Kilwinning were acquired, followed by the Blair Iron Works in Dalry in 1852, the Muirkirk and Lugar Iron Works in 1856 and the Portland Iron Works in 1864, all located in Ayrshire. In addition, the company owned 35 collieries, most of which were connected to these various iron works. By the 1860s the Baird workforce was estimated at about 10,000.[30]

The Bairds had a typically paternalistic Victorian attitude towards their workers. At Gartsherrie the company owned 400 dwellings, each with two or three apartments. These were periodically inspected by a committee who awarded prizes to the best kept and imposed fines on those found habitually dirty.[31] Employees were obliged to shop at the company store and send their children to be educated at the company school.[32]

The Baird family were staunch Presbyterians and they took a particularly keen interest in the religious life of their employees. In 1839 they built and largely funded, at a cost of £3,300, Gartsherrie Parish Church.[33] On Sundays the company damped down the furnaces in the iron works between 6.00am and 4.30pm in order to allow as many of their workers as possible to attend church services.[34] In addition, the company employed a full time missionary at Gartsherrie to ensure the spiritual welfare of the workforce was maintained beyond the Sabbath![35]

The most active brother in the management of the business was James Baird. He was the Tory MP for Falkirk Burghs, a constituency which then included Airdrie, between 1851 and 1857, the year he retired from politics. He devoted the rest of his spare time to the Church and in 1873 he donated £500,000 to the Kirk to set up the Baird Trust.[36] James was a strong supporter of the principle of bible instruction in state schools and when he stood for election in 1851, he opposed the restoration of the Roman Catholic hierarchy which had occurred in England, amidst great controversy, the year before.[37]

James Baird's opposition to 'Rome' would have gone down well with what must have been a sizeable Orange element in his workforce at Gartsherrie. An Orange Lodge was operating in Gartsherrie as early as the mid 1830s[38] and the neighbouring district of Sunnyside, where the Bairds owned the local colliery, was regarded as an Orange stronghold.

By 1857 there were about 300 Orangemen in the Coatbridge area[39] and a substantial number of them would have been in the employment of the Bairds, given the extent of their business interests in the town. There is evidence that fewer Roman Catholics were employed at the Gartsherrie Iron Works than in other local iron works.[40] There must also have been a significant number of Orangemen employed at the company's other iron works and collieries in Ayrshire. By 1875, there were six Orange Lodges in the Dalry area, four around Kilmarnock and four around Kilwinning.[41] Indeed, the Eglinton Iron Works actually had an Orange Band which may or may not have had the approval of the company.[42]

The perceived tacit encouragement given to Orangeism by certain employers was noted with exasperation by the forces of law and order. In 1859 the Sheriff of Ayrshire appealed to local coal-mine owners and ironmasters to exert their influence to dissuade their workers from participating in Orange demonstrations:

> If they showed half the alacrity to defend the public against the outrages of their men
> that they exhibit when they demand the civil and military authorities to protect them
> against these men on strike, we should probably never hear more of an Orange
> procession.[43]

The Sheriff was probably overstating his case in suggesting employers could influence their workers in matters of this nature. Whilst the Bairds intruded into almost every facet of their employees' lives, with varying degrees of success it may be added, they were unlikely to have had any sway over their workers in matters 'Orange'. Orangemen being Orangemen would hold processions whether the Bairds or any other employer approved or not. Orangemen regarded such demonstrations as an absolute right,[44] and if necessary, they were often prepared to defy the law to exercise that right.

This raises the question of whether the Bairds utilised Orangeism as a mechanism of control or discipline over their workers. The evidence is circumstantial but it does suggest that, at the very least, they pandered to Orange sentiment where it was in their best interest to do so. However, this may not have been as cynical or pragmatic as it appeared, since the Bairds as a family were staunch Protestants and were, therefore, not necessarily unsympathetic to the established aims and objectives of Orangeism. Indeed, some family members even joined the Order.[45]

If it can be conclusively proved that they did deliberately set out to promote Orangeism, then it should be acknowledged that this was only one of several stratagems open to them as employers for fostering division in their workforce.

## (ii) Orange Patronage in the Shipyards

By 1914 the Orange Order had become firmly entrenched in the shipbuilding communities of Clydeside:

> There was a strong Orange group in the shipyard areas. Many of the skilled boilermak-
> ers of the shipyards had originally come from Belfast in the 1860s; not only the platers
> and riveters were Orangemen but often their labourers and there were 23 shipyards on
> the lower Clyde alone. The Glasgow shipyards had strong links with the Belfast ones;
> in Harland and Wolff in Glasgow, no Catholic was ever employed.[46]

The apparent preponderance of Orangemen within certain shipbuilding trades was not without significance. Being skilled workers or foremen, their craft status gave them some control over the labourers they were required to hire. Although much of the 'evidence' is anecdotal in nature,[47] Orangemen have been accused of practicing religious discrimination against Roman Catholics in two ways: firstly, by denying them entry as apprentices into the trades concerned and secondly, by refusing to hire them, even as labourers.

An interesting perspective on this question as it relates to the Belfast shipyards has been advanced.[48] It can be equally applied to the Glasgow shipyards. The argument is that the skilled workers in the shipyards, as well as in other related industries like engineering, formed an artisan élite which was virtually coterminous with established trade unionism. Crucially, it was also a predominantly 'Protestant' elite.

This is an important point, since it should be remembered that craft trade unionism already had pre-existing rules of entry and apprenticeship, specifically designed to exclude the unskilled. Thus:

> Although the presence of Orangemen amongst the artisan élite ensured that where possible they would discriminate, they were able to do this not because of Orangeism but because of the structure of craft unionism. Orangeism was not a product of craft exclusiveness. Rather, Orange ideology determined that those in a position to exercise craft control, did so in a particular way.[49]

Orangemen were able to discriminate in the selection of hired labour because of the existence of a predominantly 'Protestant' workforce with the necessary skills required for building ships and their own dominant position within certain craft unions. This ensured that they were able to utilise the existing mechanisms of craft control as a source of patronage, not only for their 'brethren' but more generally for their co-religionists as well.

This fact may have made the Order more attractive to Protestant workers who had no bargaining power in the labour market. Thus, the Order was more useful to the unskilled worker than to those who were already part of the artisan élite.

The discrimination which confronted Roman Catholics in the shipyards, although real enough, arose from their lack of opportunities within society generally which they had inherited from birth, rather than simply the existence of a significant number of Orange artisans and foremen. It would be more realistic to assert that Roman Catholics were denied entry to apprenticeships because they were, as a social entity, generally unskilled and the craft unions had restrictive rules of entry precisely to debar the unskilled.

This highlights an obvious point in relation to the questions posed at the beginning of this section. In a very real sense, employers did not necessarily have to utilise Orangeism as a stratagem to control their workers, since they were not faced with an organised or homogenous entity. The working class were sadly divided and not just by religion but perhaps more crucially by craft and social status.

Of course, Orangeism by its very nature was sectarian and divisive and as such, useful to employers as a barrier to notions of class consciousness. However, the Order did not lend itself to 'control' by them since, as a proletarian movement, it was largely beyond their ken.

Of more relevance was the impact of Orangeism on the growing labour movement. The existence of Orangeism amongst Protestant workers in Scotland was a problem which was to haunt socialists in the years to come.

*Chapter 9*

# REORGANISATION OF THE ORANGE MOVEMENT IN SCOTLAND

AMIDST the turbulent decades of the 1840s and 1850s, the Orange movement itself had been undergoing yet more reorganisation. By 1855 the English based Grand Protestant Association of Loyal Orangemen of Great Britain (GPALOPG) was claiming a total number of 2,000 primary lodges in membership, organised within almost 100 District Lodges.[1] In addition, the GPALOGB had established a system for affording pecuniary relief to members in need.

This latter point was important because any lingering legal anxieties the GPALOGB harboured were removed in 1855 with the passage of the Friendly Societies Act. This Act gave legal protection to societies with benefit functions and recognised their right to organise branches on a national basis. Although aimed primarily at working mens' insurance societies, the Act was vague enough in definition to allow the GPALOGB to shelter under its terms as a benefit society.

A number of Scottish lodges were attached to the GPALOGB[2] but in time they came to desire more autonomy in running their own affairs. The Friendly Societies Act may have afforded these lodges the opportunity to reorganise the Orange movement north of the border, for that same year a separate Grand Orange Lodge of Scotland was established.

This display of independence proved attractive to the rival Grand Orange Association of Scotland with the result that the two societies amalgamated to become the Grand Protestant Association of Loyal Orangemen of Scotland.[3] For the first time since the introduction of Orangeism into Scotland, the country at last had a unified system of organisation to which all Orangemen belonged.

The headquarters of the new Grand Lodge continued to be the King William Tavern, Gallowgate, Glasgow. This establishment had previously served as the headquarters of the Scottish lodges belonging to the old Confederation. However, in 1858 the Association acquired their own premises at 33 Candleriggs, Glasgow, which served the purposes of both the Grand Lodge and a number of local primary lodges in the area.[4]

The Grand Lodge immediately undertook the sensitive task of completely re-issuing new warrant numbers to lodges, although cognisance was taken of the desire of some lodges to retain their existing warrant numbers. Amongst the latter were three of Scotland's oldest lodges still in existence, with warrants dating from the earliest period of Orange history: 'King William' LOL 102 Paisley; 'Brunswick' LOL 106 Glasgow; and 'Nassau' LOL 219 Port Glasgow.

The first Grand Master of the Association was Dr Robert Clements, a licentiate of the Royal College of Physicians and Surgeons.[5] He lived and practised medicine in the Gallowgate. It was Dr Clements who led the procession at Chryston in 1857 from which Coatbridge's returning Orangemen were attacked.

Dr Clements died, somewhat prematurely, at the age of 46 years in 1861. He was succeeded as Grand Master by another Glasgow physician, Dr John Leech.[6] The son of a minister, Leech qualified as a doctor in 1828. He was a founder member and the first Secretary of the Glasgow Southern Medical Society in 1844. It is not known when he actually joined the Order but he was probably a member of the Glasgow lodge LOL 1688, which provided a lot of officers to the Grand Lodge at this time.

Leech presided over a rapid expansion in the membership of the Association in Scotland, especially in Ayrshire and Lanarkshire.[7] A similar rate of progress was also being made in the Glasgow area. When the Association was formed in 1855, only one District Lodge, No. 3, was known to have been in existence and Leech was its first District Master. However, by 1864, the number of District Lodges in Glasgow had risen to four.

In 1862, Glasgow District No. 17 was formed. A year later, Parkhead District No. 21 was formed when a warrant was issued to one James Clyde, a weaver who had come to Calton from Maybole. An Orange pedigree if there ever was one! In 1864, Glasgow District No. 24 was formed.[8] The total number of primary lodges in Glasgow at this time was 29.

In the neighbouring burgh of Partick, nine primary lodges were in existence and another three lodges were operating in the burgh of Rutherglen, to the east of the city near Parkhead.[9] To the south of the city, a District Lodge was established at Thornliebank and Pollokshaws in 1868.[10]

By 1870, there were 71 primary lodges operating in and around Glasgow, established under the authority of the Association. This figure was almost double the number of lodges there had been in the city in the early 1860s.[11]

Although by this time firmly established as a creature of industrialisation, the Order also continued to make progress in its original heartlands of the rural South West. Maybole District No. 4 continued to be strong numerically and before long a separate District Lodge was established for Galloway. The District Master was Gilbert R Murray, a landowner who had an estate at Chapelrossan, which he periodically loaned to the Association for Twelfth demonstrations in the area.

Galloway District Lodge consisted of primary lodges located in Stranraer, Glenluce, Leswalt, Port Logan, Portpatrick, Drumore, Sandhead, Wigtown, Stoneykirk, Newton Stewart, Gatehouse of Fleet and Dumfries. At a Twelfth rally held in the grounds of Murray's estate at Chapelrossan in 1876, the parish minister of Stoneykirk, the Rev. McDougall commented: 'he did not know any Association which had prospered so much in their district as the Orange Society. He was within the mark when he said their number had increased tenfold.'[12]

The growth of the Association had, indeed, been remarkable. The number of District Lodges established under its authority had more than doubled in the space of 15 years. In 1862, there were 15 District Lodges in existence, rising to 21 by 1864.[13] By 1876, the number of District Lodges established in Scotland was 32 and rising.

The number of primary lodges operating under the authority of the Association in Scotland at this time was approximately 200.[14] Just how many actual Orangemen there were is more difficult to determine. In the absence of primary sources, this figure can only be estimated. Taking the number of primary lodges, both Association and Institution (see below) to be about 270, then membership would have been in the region of 13,500 in 1876.[15]

The unity of the Orange movement, so recently achieved in 1855, was short-lived. In 1859, a number of primary lodges, mainly in Glasgow, Partick, Greenock, Edinburgh and parts of Ayrshire, withdrew from the Association and joined the Liverpool based Loyal Orange Institution of Great Britain.[16] The reasons for this development remain obscure but it may have been due to the disillusionment some Orangemen must have felt in the aftermath of the Coatbridge and Linwood riots.

At precisely the time when the Order was growing, both in numbers and in confidence, it must have been a severe blow to the self esteem of many Orangemen and the morale of the movement generally to be associated with the public disgrace emanating from these disturbances. Some blame must have been directed to the leadership of the Association for their failure to control and discipline elements of the membership, especially after the Linwood disaster.

This shameful episode had been particularly damaging to the Orange movement at a time when it was attempting to recover some measure of respectability within society at large. The lodges which left the Association in disgust joined the English based Institution and as a result, relations between the two sets of 'brethren' north of the border remained somewhat strained for some time to come. In reality, the two societies went their separate ways whilst pursuing common aims and objectives.

The dissident lodges were welcomed by the Institution and were permitted to establish a Provincial Grand Orange Lodge of Scotland under its authority. Ironically enough, the headquarters of this new body were set up in the same Glasgow street as the Association, at 20 Candleriggs.

In 1875, the Provincial Grand Master was Robert Andrew of Edinburgh and the Provincial Deputy Grand Master was Robert Adam of Glasgow.[17] The Scottish branch of the Institution was to produce a number of individuals who would later play an important part in the development of Orangeism in Scotland, including two future Grand Masters, William Young and William McCormick and the militant evangelical, Harry Alfred Long.

By 1875, the Provincial Grand Lodge had 69 primary lodges in membership, organised within seven District Lodges.[18] It is interesting to note that the Institution's areas of strength in Scotland were the shipyard communities of Clydeside. This suggests that the Institution lodges probably had a higher proportion of Ulstermen in membership than the more established Association and perhaps, more significantly, a higher proportion of skilled workers and artisans as well. This latter point, if correct, may also help to explain the split of 1859, since as members of higher social status, they may have been keen to distance themselves from less respectable elements within the Orange movement as a whole.

# Chapter 10

# EVOLUTION OF A POPULAR MASS MOVEMENT

WITH the exception of Linwood in 1859, the Orangemen of Scotland reluctantly accepted the ten year ban on Twelfth processions which had been imposed on them. In most cases they had no alternative. The authorities had tired of the scenes of disorder which often accompanied these occasions. Thus, in Lanarkshire:

> Every precaution was taken in the county to prevent the occurrence of the disgraceful scenes which generally follow from the processions of Orangemen. Sir Archibald Allison issued a proclamation prohibiting these processions and Captain MacKay of the County Police followed this up by taking energetic precautionary measures. He had a hundred of his men, along with four mounted assistant superintendents, stationed in the districts of Coatbridge, Moodiesburn and Airdrie and they kept up communications with each other as far as Glasgow. The men, half of whom were armed with cutlasses, would have been prepared to repress any attempt at procession or disturbance had the Orangemen been bold enough to defy the proclamation...[1]

Local Orangemen obviously noted these 'energetic precautionary measures' and no attempt was made at a demonstration.

In the light of such restrictions, Orangemen were obliged to find less ostentatious ways of celebrating the Boyne anniversary. These tended to take the form of localised private functions. Thus, in Airdrie in 1860, they held a ball in the Trades Hall[2] and in Langloan in 1861 the local lodge held a supper in the Eagle Inn.[3] Any more public manifestation of Twelfth activity was stamped on, as the lodge in Langloan discovered in 1864, when they erected an 'Orange Arch' in the village. No sooner was it erected than the police dismantled it.[4]

The authorities in Ayrshire were no less vigilant in their policing of Orange activity: 'Great preparations were made by the Sheriff for suppressing any demonstrations by the Orangemen throughout the county. A large number of the Ayrshire Yeomanry, the Royal Sussex Militia and the Royal Engineers were sent to the various mining districts but...nothing took place to call for their interference.'[5]

The Orangemen of Glasgow, banned since 1822 from holding Twelfth processions in the city, were equally frustrated. When the Glasgow Police discovered that a railway booking for 700 'excursionists' to visit the statue of the poet, Robert Burns, in Ayr, was in fact a clandestine gathering of city Orangemen, the excursionists were prevented from boarding their train.[6] Similarly, an Orange excursion to Garelochhead by steamer was cancelled when the steamer company realised who their passengers were.[7]

However, as time went by these restrictions were gradually relaxed and by the late 1860s, Orangemen were again being permitted to hold public processions. These initially took the form of church parades in which no banners were displayed by the lodges and no party tunes were played by their bands.

A number of church parades were held in 1868 including one in Glasgow, when 600 Orangemen marched in procession to Kingston Free Church for a service conducted by the Ulster-born Rev. Robert Gault, a Grand Lodge Chaplain.[8] Even the Orangemen of Paisley were allowed back on the streets and this time they were the souls of discretion: 'They walked two abreast and each wore an Orange necktie (sic) and carried a Bible in his hand.'[9] About 200 took part in this procession to the Episcopal Church and there was no trouble.

The propaganda value of such occasions to the Order should not be underestimated since they demonstrated to the authorities and the public at large that Orange processions need not necessarily lead to scenes of disorder and mayhem.

The acid test of a Twelfth procession was yet to be attempted. The Order moved gingerly at first by staging a series of small local parades to mark the Boyne anniversary. In 1870, the Orangemen of Paisley held a procession in the town before setting off on an excursion to the resort town of Millport on the Isle of Cumbrae.[10] A year later, a procession of about 150 marched through the streets of Busby on the outskirts of Glasgow without incident.[11]

The final act of encouragement for the Order was the repeal of the Party Processions Act in 1872.[12] Although this Act had originally been directed against Orangemen in Ireland, its repeal ended any remaining doubts Orangemen in Scotland may have had regarding the legality of their own processions.

That same year, Glasgow witnessed its first Twelfth procession for 50 years. It was organised by the Institution although an invitation was extended to Association lodges to participate. The authorities, still circumspect, allowed the procession on the condition that the parade route remain private to the Orangemen themselves and that no party tunes be played by bands within the city limits.

The Orangemen readily accepted these conditions. A total of 11 Institution lodges and 20 Association lodges, accompanied by eight bands, mustered on Glasgow Green. They were led by Provincial Grand Lodge Officers of the Institution, including the Rev. R H Dignum of Partick, the Rev. R A Gowans and Harry Long in an open horse drawn carriage and marched in procession by Cathcart Road to Busby where a rally was held upon their arrival. About 1,500 took part in the procession which passed off without incident.[13]

So was set a pattern which, aside from the interruptions of two world wars, has remained an annual ritual in the social calender of Lowland Scotland to this day. The 'Orange Walk' was about to embed itself as a custom eagerly anticipated by sections of the Protestant working class and just as eagerly detested by other sections of society.

In 1873 the Association organised the largest Orange demonstration ever held in Scotland up till that time. Almost 200 lodges, both Association and Institution, took part. In total, about 10,000 Orangemen participated in the procession which started in Glasgow and ended in Cardonald, a suburb to the west of the city:

Shortly before ten o'clock in the forenoon, the various lodges in connection with the Orange organisations in the city, each adorned with numerous banners all bearing the well known figure of the Prince of Orange and each accompanied by an instrumental band, were observed entering the Green, one after the other and marching in the direction of the Flesher's Haugh, where they were formed into the order of procession...they left the Green by the west gate about eleven o'clock, proceeded by upwards of a dozen carriages, most of which were drawn by a pair of horses and occupied by a number of ladies and gentlemen connected with the Orange organisations.

Proceeding over the Albert Bridge, accompanied by an immense crowd, the line of march was along Clyde Terrace, up Portland Street, through Oxford Street and King Street, into Paisley Road and thence on to Cardonald Hill...

There were about 90 banners and flags, all waving in the sunshine, while the sashes and other Orange emblems worn by the brethren of the Order went to form a picture which we heard a Scotch 'wifie' not inappropriately characterise as 'a braw sight'. As the procession entered the field, the different bands, 38 in number, 5 of which were accompanied by pipers, played a number of party tunes, conspicuous among which was 'Boyne Water'.[14]

At the rally which followed this procession, speeches were delivered by Orange leaders from Canada, England, Ireland and the United States of America. They were in Glasgow for a meeting of the Imperial Grand Orange Council of the World. This international body of Orangemen was formed in Belfast in 1866 and continues to meet at regular intervals. It provides a forum where the various Grand Lodges throughout the world can discuss matters of mutual interest and concern. The fact that Glasgow was chosen as the venue for the 1873 sessions attests to the growing significance of Scottish Orangeism at this time.

Twelfth processions in Lanarkshire were also resumed in 1873. The venue was the Orange stronghold of Airdrie but the authorities were leaving nothing to chance:

Chief Constable MacKay, with a force of about 100 constables, was present from an early hour; the Burgh authorities had the full force mustered and 70 men of the lst Royal Dragoons, presently stationed at Hamilton, rode over early in the morning and were kept stationed in a secluded spot about a mile from the town in readiness to gallop in case of a disturbance. There were also 50 Dragoons in readiness in Edinburgh to come off, per special train, if telegraphed for.[15]

As in Glasgow, this procession also passed off without incident.

Twelfth processions were also resumed in Ayrshire that same year. About 3,000 Orangemen paraded through the streets of Ayr and were led by the Grand Secretary of the Association, Professor Thomas Macklin, the Rev. John Thomson of Kilmarnock and Harry Long. Again, no disturbances were reported.[16]

In 1873 the leadership of the Association had again changed hands. Dr John Leech had died in 1869 and was succeeded as Grand Master by George McLeod, who had been Deputy Grand Master. A Glasgow businessman, but native of Halkirk in Caithness, McLeod was a manufacturer of tartan and plaid and often appeared at Orange functions in full Highland dress. He led the Association very capably until 1873 when he retired from office.[17]

The new Grand Master was a man of financial means and some social standing, Chalmers Izett Paton, who owned an estate at Belstane near Edinburgh. He owed his position to the fine arts firm established by his father in Edinburgh, Hugh Paton, a Carver and Guilder by Royal Warrant. The family were of Covenanter descent which may help to explain Paton's strong religious convictions. In 1879, he wrote a popular text entitled 'Catechism of the Principles of the Reformation'.[18]

Paton was an energetic Grand Master who liked to appear at Twelfth processions riding on horseback. He was determined, as a matter of priority, to seek a rapprochement with the Institution lodges in Scotland. There had been a certain amount of ill feeling between the Association and the Institution in the wake of the schism of 1859 but this mutual antagonism began to dissipate through time. The staging of joint processions in the early 1870s underlined the growing spirit of co-operation between the two bodies.

Tentative negotiations about amalgamation were begun at this time, a process Paton strongly encouraged. However it was not until 1876 that real progress towards unity was achieved when representatives of the Association and the Institution met on neutral ground in a London hotel. Chalmers Paton and the Grand Secretary, Thomas Macklin, represented the Association and amongst those representing the Institution were the following District Masters: William McCormick of Ayrshire, David Lang of Glasgow, Thomas Anderson of Partick and Hugh Magill of Greenock.[19]

The conference was held under the chairmanship of the Imperial Grand Master, the Earl of Enniskillen, and lasted two days. It ended in success when it was decided to amalgamate the two bodies. The new organisation was to be known as the Loyal Orange Institution of Scotland and Chalmers Paton was elected its first Grand Master.[20] In effect, the lodges belonging to the old Institution were transferred to the Association and re-issued with new warrant numbers, where duplications occurred.

Paton's role in unifying the Orange movement was officially recognised by the new Grand Lodge at its first meeting: 'The most important item of home news is the happy union of all Scotland and under the superintendence of one Grand Lodge and all agree in ascribing the honour and advantage of this happy union to the untiring exertions of the Most Worshipful Grand Master.'[21]

The union brought additional strength, vitality, confidence and unity of purpose to the Order which after almost 80 years of friction and schism was at last truly united as one body.[22] Membership had grown steadily in the previous two decades and was beginning to embrace a wider social base. Although still overwhelmingly a movement of the industrial working class, the Order had succeeded in attracting a small petit bourgeois element as well as a sprinkling of professionals. This element helped to imbue the Order with a much more respectable image and responsible demeanour than had been the case in the past.

At least four new District Lodges were created in the immediate aftermath of the union: Calton, Cowcaddens, Govan and Falkirk.[23] This growth was sustained through the remainder of the century. District Lodges were established at Motherwell in 1878; Anderston in 1881; Kirkintilloch in 1882; Gorbals in 1883; Whiteinch in 1889; Clydebank in 1892 and Maryhill in 1899.[24] During the same period other District Lodges were also set up at Harthill; Larkhall; Blantyre and Hamilton; Irvine and Broxburn.[25]

The creation of many of these new District Lodges reflected the expansion of the shipbuilding industry on the River Clyde and the continuing development of the Scottish coalfield during the closing decades of the century. In particular, the spread of Orangeism into the Lothians and Fife was related almost entirely to the social mobility of the mining labour force. As migrant miners and colliers moved from exhausted pits in Ayrshire and Lanarkshire to find work in the new pits of East Central Scotland, so the Orangemen amongst them established Orange Lodges in their new localities.

The oldest existing lodge in Fife is 'True Blues' LOL 198, which was formed in Kelty in 1903.[26] This was followed by 'Fifeshire Purple Heroes' LOL 207 in Cowdenbeath, formed in 1909, and 'Chosen Few' LOL 220 in Lochore, formed in 1910, when a warrant was issued to a number of miners who had come from the west to find employment in the area.[27] In 1911, these three lodges formed Fifeshire District No. 45, the same year as a fourth lodge was formed in the county. This was 'Havlin's Royal Brigade' LOL 265, which was located in Valleyfield and recruited most of its membership from the local pits.[28]

The year 1911 also saw the formation of East Lothian District No. 44.[29] The oldest existing lodge is 'Eastern Star' LOL 184, formed in Prestonpans in 1907.[30] It was originally known as 'Inniskilling Purple Guards' in recognition of the fact that its founding members were a company of the Irish Fusiliers who were stationed at Cockenzie. The other founding members of District No. 44 were 'True Blues' LOL 228, which was formed in the pit village of Tranent in 1910 and 'Conservative' LOL 252 in Musselburgh and Fisherrow.[31]

By 1914 the Orange Order in Scotland had evolved into a popular mass movement, spanning the industrial heartland of the country. Its membership embraced both sexes and all ages.[32] These members were predominantly Scottish born, although many, if not most, probably had an Ulster Protestant family background.

Although they were almost all working class, Orangemen were not so easily categorised in terms of social status as some sociologists and social historians have suggested. If occupation is taken as one indicator, then it is clear from the available evidence that Orangemen were just as likely to be unskilled or semi-skilled workers as 'labour aristocrats'.

What was equally clear was the membership boom the Order was enjoying. At a Twelfth procession held in Edinburgh in 1902 the then Grand Master, William Young, announced that the attendance of 25,000 was the largest turnout the Order had achieved up till that date.[33]

At Greenock, the following year, Young noted with satisfaction that 1,500 new members had been initiated into the Order between 1901 and 1903.[34] Many of these new recruits were young. One newspaper, commenting on a Twelfth procession at Rutherglen in 1906, pointed out: '...the extraordinary number of youthful demonstrators who infused the greatest enthusiasm into the proceedings.'[35] The following year, a Twelfth procession was held in Motherwell: '...which was over three miles in length and took nearly two hours to pass a given point. There were 114 bands and over 1,000 banners and 34 flags.'[36]

According to one source, there were about 400 Orange Lodges in Scotland by 1914. Of these, 107 were located in and around Glasgow.[37]

If these figures are correct, and there is no reason to suspect them, then the total number of Orangemen in Scotland would have been about 20,000. In fact, this may well be a slightly conservative estimate, given that it is based on an earlier calculation of a primary lodge's average strength.[38] In addition, female adult, junior and juvenile lodges were all starting to make headway at this time and if they are added, membership may well have been closer to 25,000 and growing as wives, sweethearts and children of Orangemen joined the ranks in increasing numbers.

Another sign of the Order's growing prosperity was the erection of impressive new headquarters for the Grand Lodge in 1914. The old headquarters in Candleriggs had long outlived their usefulness and for some years the Grand Lodge had been obliged to hold its meetings in a variety of hired halls throughout Glasgow.

A major fund-raising effort was launched to find the £5,000 required to finance the venture. Contributions were raised from primary lodges and countless efforts were made on the part of the membership as private individuals to raise the money. A number of special events were organised, including a football match between Glasgow Rangers and Partick Thistle, the proceeds going into the fund.[39] Donations were also forthcoming from prominent persons sympathetic to the Order. These included the then leader of the Conservative and Unionist Party, Andrew Bonar Law, and leading Glasgow businessman, Sir Charles Cleland.[40]

Although born in the Province of New Brunswick, Canada, Bonar Law had strong Ulster Protestant connections. His father was an Ulster Presbyterian minister and he had a brother still living in Coleraine.[41] Bonar Law had spent a good deal of his life as an iron merchant in Glasgow and was a local MP. He was to become a fearless champion of the Unionist cause during the Ulster Crisis of 1912-1914.

Cleland had made his money in a successful stationery business.[42] A local councillor in Glasgow, he became a magistrate in 1901. Cleland was chairman of the Glasgow Conservative and Unionist Association in 1914 and was an Orangeman, being Honorary Deputy Grand Master of Scotland.[43] Like Bonar Law, he too had family ties in Ulster, as one of his daughters had married Sir Richard Dawson Bates, who would become the first Home Secretary in the Northern Ireland government in 1921.

Enough money was eventually raised for the new headquarters and the work was completed in 1914:

> The new headquarters of the Lodge are situated at the corner of Cathedral Street and North Frederick Street. The building, which was erected at a total cost of £5,000 has its main frontage facing Cathedral Street. It is built of smooth sandstone and is five stories in height. There is a balcony on the Cathedral Street side of the building and immediately above it, is a sculptured representation of King William. On the ground floor of the building are situated a large lodge room, committee and retiring rooms and a public office for the Grand Orange Lodge of Scotland. A large hall, capable of seating 600 people, is situated on the first floor, together with committee and retiring rooms. On the second floor and in the upper stories are a number of committee and lodge rooms of various sizes...[44]

The Grand Lodge had, indeed, come a long way from its original meeting place in the back room of the King William Tavern in the Gallowgate and its new headquarters symbolised the steady progress the Order had made in the latter half of the nineteenth century.

# Chapter 11
# ORANGEISM AND SOCIETY IN VICTORIAN SCOTLAND

ORANGEISM in Scotland was and continues to be an essentially working class affair. By the closing decades of the nineteenth century, what came to be regarded as the 'traditional' working class had found its niche in society. Working people had discernibly improved their material position in that they tended to be better fed, clothed and housed than their forefathers. Employment was more readily available and their children were better educated following the advent of a national state funded education system in the 1870s.

Entire communities had evolved based on an ethic of communal solidarity and mutual aid. Most adult males were literate and many of them were enfranchised. Membership of a trade union was now legal. Leisure time too gradually became more available to the masses with visits to the music halls and attendance at football matches becoming very popular forms of entertainment.

An entirely new and distinct culture had developed during this period, as the working class or, perhaps more precisely, the urban industrial proletariat as a 'class' assumed its place in Victorian society.

Orangemen were not immune from these wider societal developments and Orangeism, viewed as a cultural and social phenomenon offering its own unique world view within this more universal milieu, came to represent a somewhat perverse manifestation of working class society's central tenets: mutual aid and solidarity.

If the Order had simply remained a 'Kick The Pope' organisation only, it would not have survived long enough to become the institution it now is in working class life. Rather, it developed and grew in tandem with the class it was an integral part of, precisely because the Order mirrored working class values and to some extent, working class aspirations, no matter how negative and reactionary its ideology was.[1]

The importance of the Order in Scotland as a focus of Irish Protestant identity within the immigrant community generally has been noted.[2] This situation persisted for some time as immigrants from Ulster continued to be a significant source of recruitment until at least the outbreak of the Great War in 1914. In the years between 1876 and 1881, 83 per cent of Irish immigrants into Scotland came from the province of Ulster and of these, 58 per cent came from the four counties with clear Protestant majorities: Antrim, Armagh, Down and Londonderry.[3] Although simplistic correlations should be avoided, the membership boom the Order enjoyed at this time suggests the two events were not entirely unconnected.

The identification with the 'old country' made by many of the lodges during this period is not in doubt. Amongst the examples: 'Antrim True Blues' LOL 78 Glasgow; 'Armagh True Blues' LOL 98 Glasgow; 'Enniskillen True Blues' LOL 155, Paisley; 'Lily of Loughgilly' LOL 280 Shettleston; and 'Sons of Ulster' LOL 348 Port Glasgow.[4]

Upon their arrival in Scotland, Orangemen from the Killyman district of Tyrone formed 'Killyman True Blues' LOL 148 in Whiteinch and 'Killyman True Blues' LOL 712 in Motherwell.[5] Another Motherwell lodge, LOL 670, was formed in the mid 1870s by an Ulsterman named Nelson. He and his five sons were its founding members and when the father died, the lodge was named 'Nelson's Purple Heroes' in his honour.[6] 'Falkirk Blues' LOL 120 was another lodge formed by Ulstermen in 1876.[7]

How many other lodges in Scotland were formed in similar circumstances is unknown but there must have been a significant number. However, in the absence of primary sources, it remains impossible to determine what percentage of the Order's membership was Irish born or Scottish born at this time.

Certainly, by 1914, membership of an Orange Lodge had become in many working class families a tradition, a family affair. The familial custom whereby a son on reaching adulthood joined his father's lodge was well established. Indeed, it was and still is not uncommon for three generations of the same family, grandfather, father and son, to be members of the same lodge together.[8]

Not for nothing is the Orangeman's favourite and best known song entitled, 'The Sash My Father Wore':

> It's old but it is beautiful
> And its colours they are fine
> It was worn at Derry, Aughrim
> Enniskillen and the Boyne
> My father wore it as a youth
> In bygone days of yore
> So on the Twelfth, I proudly wear
> The Sash my father wore[9]

The rituals of family life increased these bonds. It was not uncommon for distinctly Orange families to intermarry and they would often hold their wedding reception in the local Orange Hall. Similarly, there were Orange funerals with members in full regalia acting as pallbearers and marching in procession behind the coffin of the deceased. Orange ritual would often be read at the graveside.

Marriage and funeral services were sometimes conducted by Orange clergymen.

So it was, then, that important family occasions were also Orange occasions, reinforcing the strong family and kinship traditions which membership of the Order entailed.

It was not until 1909 that the principle of adult female Orange Lodges was accepted in Scotland. Up to this point, membership of the Orange Order was restricted to males. The breakthrough came when one Harriet Wilson formed a ladies' lodge in 1909, but it was denied recognition by the Grand Lodge. Undaunted, in true Orange spirit it may be added, the lodge applied to the Loyal Orange Institution of England for membership and was accepted by them. This encouraged other women in Scotland to form ladies' lodges and before much longer, the Grand Orange Lodge of Scotland was obliged to recognise their existence and take them under its jurisdiction.[10]

Ladies' lodges proved popular and a Ladies' Orange Association of Scotland was formed which has greatly added to the strength and vitality of the Order. Juvenile and Junior lodges were also established in the early years of the new century, the first juvenile lodge being formed at Paisley.

Membership of an Orange Lodge offered a wide range of social activities beyond the monthly meeting, esoteric ceremonies and the annual processions. From the 1850s onwards, most District Lodges hosted an annual Orange and Protestant Soiree to which members, along with their wives, sweethearts and friends, were invited. These gatherings were very popular and consisted of an evening of music, dancing and loyal and patriotic speeches from senior officials of the Order and invited guests sympathetic to the movement. Tea and a light supper were usually provided as well.

Another well attended occasion on the Orange calendar was the annual Burns Supper.[11] Excursions and trips 'doon the watter' by steamer to seaside resorts like Rothesay and Millport were also eagerly anticipated by members. In addition, lodges frequently held dinners and dances, often as a means of raising additional revenue, in order to purchase new regalia or furnishings for the lodge room. Who knows how many romances developed in Orange Halls the length and breadth of the country as a result of these gatherings?

A growing number of Orangemen were also forming their own distinct flute and drum bands. Lodges hired bands to play for them at the annual processions, but at this time, most bands had no real connection with the Order as such. They tended to be town bands or pipe bands.

This situation gradually changed during the late nineteenth century, as Orangemen began forming 'Orange' bands, dedicated to playing Orange tunes and they were permitted to practice in Orange Halls. The average band would consist of 12-16 flutes, four to eight side drums and a bass drum, or on occasion, a Lambeg drum. These bands also charged lodges for their hire, the fees received going towards the cost of instruments and uniforms.[12]

Membership of an Orange Lodge could also offer some measure of financial security, a not unimportant matter in an age of no state funded national assistance.

In theory, from 1855 onwards, lodges were able to afford their members pecuniary relief in times of distress like sickness or bereavement. In practice, very few lodges had an organised system for collecting premiums or paying benefits. However, the Order had registered itself under the terms of the Friendly Societies Act of 1855 and it regarded its benefit function to be an integral part of its philosophy.

By the turn of the century, the movement in Scotland was sufficiently large and well organised for this long-standing ideal at last to become a reality.

The Grand Lodge organised the Orange and Protestant Friendly Society from its headquarters in Candleriggs, Glasgow. Membership was extended to all Protestants, male and female, over the age of 16 years, subject to a medical examination. Contributions were paid according to age and benefits were awarded according to an accepted scale, agreed upon joining the Society.[13]

The Orange and Protestant Friendly Society could not have hoped to compete with the larger and more established Friendly Societies. Although open to anyone of the Protestant faith, its clientele was almost wholly composed of Orangemen and their families.

Branches of the Society were organised around the structure of the Order's District Lodges. There were 26 such branches in the Glasgow area by 1912.[14] That same year, the Society had 10,000 members in Scotland,[15] which represented about one third of the total membership of the Loyal Orange Institution of Scotland, at this time.

These activities gave to Orangeism an important social dimension which should not be underestimated. They contributed to what can be described as an 'Orange Culture', which exists to this day.

# Chapter 12

# ORANGEISM & IDEOLOGY IN VICTORIAN SCOTLAND

ORANGEMEN continue to adhere to an established set of politico-religious beliefs and ideas which can be collectively termed 'Orangeism'. This ideology furnishes Orangemen with a distinct world view which has been articulated and constructed around a number of inter-related theories. The relationship between these various theories is illustrated in Table 1, p. 62.

The actual historical roots of Orangeism are traceable to the events which surrounded the life and times of King William III, the Prince of Orange, who accepted the offer of the thrones of England, Scotland and Ireland in 1688. It was the subsequent victory of the Williamite forces over those of the Roman Catholic, King James II at the Battle of the Boyne in July 1690 which secured the future of Protestantism in Ireland.

However, Orangemen make even grander claims for this victory, that it was nothing less than the establishment of democracy in the English speaking world: 'The principles of representative government, of religious liberty, of popular control and of the right of every man to be responsible for his religion to his own conscience alone has spread throughout all civilisation in the wake of the Banners of William, who was the father of all constitutional progress.'[1]

Orangemen believe that what 'King Billy' delivered the nation from was papal tyranny when the last vestiges of the autocratic rule of the Stuart dynasty were finally removed. In their place came the concept of civil and religious liberty with the establishment of freedom of assembly, freedom of speech and freedom of worship. Orangemen have therefore concluded from these historical processes that democratic institutions are an adjunct of Protestantism whereas the absence of such institutions in society is a consequence of Roman Catholicism.

Protestantism is equated with democracy and by implication, progress. On the other hand, it is argued that Roman Catholicism is innately undemocratic and by implication, backward.

Orangemen regard the Constitution of the United Kingdom, based as it is on

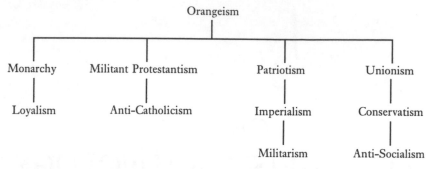

Table 1

the concept of civil and religious liberty, to be an essentially 'Protestant' set of institutions and traditions. However, the Order emphasised that the nation had to be eternally vigilant in defence of these principles. In 1879, Chalmers Paton, Grand Master of Scotland, warned: 'There is, in fact, but one deadly enemy of the British Constitution and that enemy is Popery.'[2]

Orangemen saw the hand of 'Rome' in almost every reform or threat to the government and institutions of the country and they were resolved to oppose every manifestation of what they regarded as 'papist aggression' within society at large.

Orangemen were and have remained amongst the most enthusiastic supporters of the monarchy, an integral part of the Constitution. Of course, the Throne and more importantly, the succession to it, is an exclusively Protestant institution. Amongst the resolutions passed at the annual Orange rallies, there was and is always one affirming support to the sovereign and the National Anthem is sung at the close of every lodge meeting.

The Crown is an important point of reference for Orangemen since it enables them to demonstrate their 'loyalty', not necessarily to the government of the day but to the Head of State. It therefore provides a non-party political focus for the Order's brand of Loyalism.

When Queen Victoria celebrated her Golden Jubilee in 1897, the Imperial Grand Orange Council of the World were meeting in Glasgow. The President of the Council and Grand Master of British North America (Canada), Nathanial Clarke Wallace mused: 'We way ask, to what chief causes under providence have the glories of Victoria's reign been due? If I sought an answer to the question, I should find it in these; the Protestant Faith, an Open Bible and popular government.'[3]

Again, the simple equation is made: Protestantism equals Democracy. Put in the British context, civil and religious liberty and representative government are guaranteed by a constitutional monarchy remaining Protestant. The latter point should be understood. Orange support for the monarchy is conditional; the condition being that the monarchy remains a Protestant institution.

Queen Victoria reigned over a vast empire and the Order believed this had

Imperialism: bringing white Anglo-Saxon Protestant civilisation to the grateful heathen

been achieved as the direct result of the practical application of civil and religious liberty. Orangemen fully supported the concept of 'Empire', seeing in that enterprise a noble crusade to civilise the world in white, Anglo-Saxon, Protestant attitudes and values.

It was no coincidence that at this time an increasing number of lodges began to exhibit Imperialist sentiments on their banners. Amongst the most common themes depicted were portraits of Britannia, whilst the Bible and Crown was another much displayed design . However, the most popular banners were those which depicted Queen Victoria handing a Bible to a kneeling African prince or potentate, with an accompanying inscription which read 'The Secret of Britain's Greatness'.[4]

The Order's commitment to the British Empire went far beyond mere symbolism. To begin with, a number of Scots-born Orangemen had played a significant part in Empire building.

The first Prime Minister of the Dominion of Canada in 1867 was the Glasgow-born Sir John A MacDonald. A member of LOL 834 in Kingston, Ontario, MacDonald is said to have got the idea for the political confederation of Canada from the organisational structure of the Loyal Orange Association of British North America.[5]

The Lesmahagow born Alexander Muir was a member of LOL 142 in Toronto.[6] It was Muir who composed the National Song of Canada, 'The Maple Leaf Forever', the words of which would stir the heart of any Orangeman:

> In days of yore, from Britain's shore
> Wolfe, the dauntless hero came
> And planted firm Britannia's flag
> On Canada's fair domain
> Here may it wave, our boast and pride
> And join in love together
> The Thistle, Shamrock, Rose entwine
> The Maple Leaf Forever[7]

The first Governor General of Australia, appointed in 1901, was John Louis, the 7th Earl of Hopetoun. Hopetoun was a Deputy Grand Master of Scotland at the time.[8]

Imperialism became an important component part of the political philosophy of Orangeism during the late Victorian and Edwardian era. Within Scottish society generally, there existed a strong imperialist popular culture. Expressions of this sentiment included pride in Scottish regiments serving overseas in the Regular Army and in the work of Scottish missionaries like David Livingstone and Mary Slessor. It is not altogether surprising that the Boys' Brigade, an organisation at least initially imbued with a strong Presbyterian 'Bible and Crown' ethos, should have been formed in Glasgow in 1883.[9]

Allegiance to the Empire was also based on the economic benefits it brought to Scottish workers and capitalists alike. Not for nothing was Glasgow known as the 'Second City of the Empire'.

Scottish commerce and industry was largely dependent on imperial markets, giving workers a considerable stake in the continuance of Empire trade. Orangemen were well represented in a number of industries, with the largest share in this trade including shipbuilding, engineering and steel making. It is little wonder then that they so readily identified with Imperialism.

This identification with Empire and its economic benefits encouraged Orange leaders to present a pluralist conception of industrial relations to Orange workers. Orangemen were asked to believe that their best interests lay with the personal prosperity of major employers and industrialists.

When such men stood for Parliament, Orangemen were expected to support them. Electoral support for the Bairds' political aspirations has already been noted.[10] Another case in point occurred when the Govan shipbuilder, Pearce, stood for Parliament in 1880. At one of his election rallies, Thomas Wetherall, Deputy Grand Master of Scotland, explained to the audience: 'Mr Pearce is the very gentleman to represent us...I am addressing working men, a great body of working men and allow me to tell you that Mr Pearce has increased the great credit that has always accrued to Clyde built ships...and for that he deserves your good support.'[11]

In 1908, William McCormick, Grand Master of Scotland, addressed an Orange rally in Clydebank, appropriately enough, in the following terms, when he urged: 'the return of a strong Unionist and Imperialist government to power, thus securing industrial prosperity and contentment throughout the Empire.'[12]

These sentiments were not the exclusive property of Orangemen. They were shared by people of all classes. Amongst skilled workers, in particular, they held a powerful sway, and it should be remembered that almost all skilled workers in Scotland at this time were Protestants.

These workers readily identified with Empire and all that suggested about Protestant 'superiority'. It attested to their own predilection towards the values of hard work, thrift and honesty. The 'respectable' working class had found their place in the sun and the sun would never set on the British Empire.

Such attitudes tended to reinforce anti-Catholic sentiment at home and, in so doing, played into the hands of organisations like the Orange Order. Of course, the Order regarded itself as the last true remaining repository of Reformation truths and values; on the other hand, it is worth examining the nature of the Order's 'Protestantism'.

It will be suggested here that the notion of 'Protestantism' embraced by the Order was, and in fact remains, more of a cultural phenomenon than a religious one.

The Order is a 'Protestant' association in the sense that membership is restricted to Protestants only. Candidates for admission into an Orange Lodge are required to make a declaration on an open Bible and the Bible remains open for the duration of every lodge meeting. The Bible, along with the Crown, are symbolically carried at the head of all Orange processions.

Lodge meetings are opened by prayer and closed by prayer. Each lodge appoints a chaplain, although very few lodges in Scotland had an actual clergyman for this post. As members of an avowedly Christian organisation, Orangemen are expected to fulfil certain obligations, including the active participation in the life and work of the Church. However, the religious element which exists within the Order is not to be regarded by Orangemen as a substitute for the Faith but rather as a complement to it.

In reality, the Order has always had a less than happy relationship with the established churches in Scotland. This partly stems from the dilemmas inherent within Protestantism itself. The Order dares not embrace any specific theological doctrines for fear of alienating potential recruits from one particular denomination or the other. Thus, for example, expressing support for the doctrine of predestination may deter from membership all but the most zealous of Presbyterians and so on.

This, dare one say, almost catholic tolerance towards Protestants of whatever denomination is a consequence of the Order's desire to appeal to as wide a potential membership as possible. In this sense, if in no other, the Order can be said to be ecumenical. However, this pluralist approach has also led to an inevitable dilution of genuine religious content in the movement as a whole.

Of course, in practice, the only persons likely to be concerned with precise theological statements are an interested laity and a professional clergy. More often than not both these groups of people have tended to keep their distance from the Order. Although clerical support for the Order from within the established churches was at its peak in the late Victorian and Edwardian eras, there has never been more than a very small minority of clergymen willing to associate themselves with the Order.

Another reason for the Order's failure to attract more of the clergy was that the established churches, and in particular the Church of Scotland, were themselves undergoing social change. By the turn of the century, the Kirk was increasingly becoming a middle class institution. It embraced middle class attitudes with a predominantly comfortably-off laity and a professionally trained ministry. The Kirk seemed more interested in spreading the Gospel in the Dark Continent than the dark tenement hovels of industrial Scotland.

This apparent lack of concern for the spiritual welfare of the industrial proletariat left the Protestant working class largely unchurched. In addition to what was a general neglect of Protestant workers at this time, the Kirk, as the most quintessential of Scottish institutions, would not have wished to encourage what it no doubt still perceived to be an essentially 'Irish' organisation whose unruly reputation offended middle class sensitivities. Even if the majority of Orangemen had been regular church-goers, it is open to doubt whether they would have been welcome in many Kirks.

The Order tended to attract a higher proportion of clerical support from the smaller independent evangelical churches and missions scattered around the industrial belt. The 'No Popery' stance of the Order which so many Kirk ministers found distasteful, at least in public, held no such fears for many of the evangelical preachers of the day. Harry Alfred Long is a prime example here but other Orange clergymen falling into the same category included the Ulster born Rev. Robert Gault of the Free Church Anti-Popish Mission in Partick[13] and the Rev. James Brisby of the Christian Union Church in Calton.[14]

Although these clergymen and others like them had enthusiastic congregations and were always given rousing ovations at Orange rallies, they only succeeded in getting a small minority of Orangemen to pay anything other than lip service to the obligations of their Faith.

Orangemen enjoy the religious trappings which surround the Order but they are less interested in the responsibilities which flow from them. It could be said of most Orangemen, then and now, that they were Bible loving if not Bible reading! It is instructive that, in comparison with Ireland, the Order in Scotland had only brief flirtations with both temperance[15] and Sabbatarianism,[16] finding no real or lasting support amongst the membership for either.

However, lodges in Scotland have always been keen to invoke a sense of identity with the nation's religious past. Many lodges are named after famous Reformers like John Knox and George Wishart whilst others carry portraits of the Reformers on their banners. Similarly, famous Covenanters like Alexander Peden and Richard Cameron have lodges named after them and banners depicting their portraits.

These contrast with the many lodges in Scotland who chose instead to identify with their Ulster origins. However, Orangemen will argue that the men who defended Derry's Walls so heroically in 1688-89 were of the same stock as the men who defended the Faith in the hills and byways of West Central Scotland during the 'Killing Times' of the Covenanting period. They fought and died for the same cause.

This is what 'Protestantism' is to Orangemen: it is the blood of the martyrs and defence of the Faith. It represents a badge of cultural identity in a world inhabited by Papists and Atheists.

Although Orangeism was never intended to be a substitute for the Faith, in reality, this is what it became for many Orangemen. There is, in fact, a good deal of religious symbolism in the Order's secret ceremonies, passwords, rituals and signs.

There are two degrees associated with membership of the Loyal Orange Institution of Scotland. The first degree is known as the 'Orange' and is conferred upon a candidate on his admission into membership of a lodge. After what may be termed a probationary period, usually about six months, a member is 'raised' to the second degree, known as the 'Royal Arch Purple'. Only upon receipt of this degree is a member regarded as a true Orangeman or, to be more accurate, a true Orange and Purple Man.

The esoteric nature and content of these degree ceremonies have an important psychological function, apart from any intrinsic worth they might bestow on the recipients. They are intended to inculcate a strong sense of brotherhood and unity of purpose to the membership.

The ceremonies themselves are based on episodes from Old Testament history and a clear identification is evoked with the various trials and tribulations of the Ancient Israelites. Like the Hebrews of old, Orangemen also believe they too are a 'Chosen Few'. They too are crying in the wilderness, they too have the one true faith.

This religious symbolism, evoked in secret, esoteric ceremonies, is a very neglected aspect of Orangeism but it should not be underestimated. It provides an important insight into the Orange 'psyche'.

# Chapter 13

# 'NO POPERY!'

THE Orange Order in Scotland approached the last quarter of the nineteenth century with a great deal of confidence and optimism for the future. Membership was on the increase both in numbers and across social class and the movement resolved to enter fully the political process.

The passage of the Reform Acts of 1867 and 1884 had enfranchised the urban-dwelling male proletariat. This included most artisans and other skilled workers, the so-called 'respectable' working class. Orangemen were well represented within these occupational groupings and they were disposed as a body to exercise their newly acquired political muscle in defence of 'Protestantism'.

The enemy, as always, was 'Popery', and the Order was determined to oppose the Roman Catholic Church achieving any measure of influence or power within the institutions or structure of Scottish society. 'Rome' and its representatives were not to be trusted. As proof of this assertion, Orangemen pointed to history, asserting that whenever Rome was in power, persecution of non-Catholics followed in its wake. Examples of this persecution offered by the Order included the terrors of the Spanish Inquisition or the massacre of the Huguenots in France.

The Order was convinced that the Roman Catholic Church, through their political allies or 'dupes', were involved in a treasonable conspiracy to destroy Protestantism in Great Britain and Ireland by undermining the essential features of the Constitution. Orangemen never viewed the Roman Catholic Church as anything other than a completely homogenous entity whose principal aim was to reverse the work of the Reformation in the British Isles and throughout the Empire.

When the government decided to restore diplomatic relations with the Vatican in 1887, the Order was outraged:

That the overthrow of Protestantism, within the three kingdoms being the avowed object of the Papacy; the proposed establishment of diplomatic relations with the Pope seems only part of the conspiracy for the said overthrow of the Protestant religion; and the attempt to govern the Irish Jesuits by their masters, the Jesuits of Rome, is not statesmanship but insanity![1]

In fact, the Order regarded the Jesuits as particularly worthy of suspicion. They were viewed by Orangemen as the 'shock troops' of the counter-Reformation. At an Orange rally in Dumbarton in 1875, Thomas Macklin, Grand Secretary of the Association, described the Society of Jesus as: '...those incessant and insidious plotters and disturbers of the peace.'[2]

Although the Order was not the sole conduit of anti-Catholicism in Scotland at this time, it was certainly to remain the most enduring and unremitting receptacle of 'No Popery' in the country.

Orangemen retained an essentially Reformation view of Roman Catholicism. The Reformation had been a democratising process, both at the level of the individual and at the level of society. Protestantism was a Bible-based religion and most Protestants accepted the Bible as the Written Word of God. The Bible became accessible to every believer and was translated into every known European language. It was no longer the sole property of the Church of Rome as it had been in the past to interpret for the faithful as it saw fit. The role of the priesthood, as the mediators between God and man, was diminished. In its place, the Reformation had established a priesthood of all believers.

This represented a crucial distinction in the practice of Christian faith and led Orangemen to argue that Roman Catholicism remained pagan because it was unscriptural in its essence: '...instead the tradition of the Church is granted equal authority with the Holy Scriptures in all that relates to faith and religious practice.'[3]

The Order concluded that this 'tradition' represented a fundamental error; it was a tradition immersed in idolatry and superstition. Such a view of Roman Catholicism was also held by a number of Protestant denominations and sects as well as the evangelical wings of most of the mainstream churches.

The Order, in its literature and in its public pronouncements, regularly trotted out a whole catalogue of what it considered to be theological errors inherent within Roman Catholicism. On questions of doctrine, the main criticisms focused on the celebration of the mass (transubstantiation), confession and purgatory.

The veneration of the Virgin Mary (Mariolatry) was considered to be another of Rome's major errors. Many Protestants were offended at descriptions of her as the 'Queen of Heaven' and the prayers of intercession which were offered to her in churches. The erection of statues in her supposed image was regarded as blasphemous and a direct contradiction of the Second Commandment.

Particular wrath was directed at the Pope. The Order maintained that the doctrine of Papal infallibility and various other claims made by the Bishop of Rome were not only false but blasphemous. Indeed, far from regarding the Pope as the successor of St Peter and the Vicar of Christ on Earth, he is seen as the anti-Christ, as foretold in the Book of Revelation. Orange clergymen did not hesitate in identifying Rome with 'Mystery, Babylon the Great, the Mother of Harlots' and the Pope as the 'Son of Perdition'.[4]

Putting these long standing historical arguments aside, Rome was also attacked at the more basic level of Scottish society. Charges of immorality were often levelled against priests and nuns. Priests were accused of sexual perversion because of their celibacy, which was considered unnatural, and the nature of the confessional.

The convent life of nuns was another Orange hobby-horse. Calls for the government inspection of convents and monasteries were regularly made at Orange meetings and rallies. The suggestion was that many of the women in these premises were being kept there against their will. It was also implied that many nuns were leading immoral lives and that the remains of murdered children and aborted babies would be found in convent and monastery grounds, if inspected.

Whatever its credibility or legitimacy, the critique of Roman Catholicism offered by the Order was a strong one which was not entirely out of step with prevailing attitudes in Victorian society. The fact was there was deep suspicion of the Roman Catholic Church in the country at this time and anti-Catholicism manifested itself in all classes of society.

That particular problems should exist in Scotland was not surprising. For almost three centuries, Presbyterianism had been the predominant form of religion in Scotland. Its style of worship and practice was simple, even austere. It was characterised by the preaching of the Word with a strong emphasis placed on good moral behaviour.

The contrast with Roman Catholicism could not have been more striking, with its emphasis on devotion and ritual. These traits were particularly prevalent in the Irish Church, whose clergy insisted on reinforcing these traditions of worship within the immigrant community in Scotland.

The authority these priests enjoyed amongst their parishioners was also an alien concept to Presbyterian Scots. The Reformation had partly been a rejection of hierarchical authority in matters of religious faith, and Scottish Presbyterians in particular had endured a long and bitter but ultimately successful struggle against the imposition of ecclesiastical authority during the Covenanting era.

Within the Kirk, parishioners had long enjoyed the right to select their ministers and there had evolved a democratic structure of church government. This was essentially a pyramidal framework with Kirk sessions at the base, leading up to local Presbyteries and Synods, which in turn led to the national Annual General Assembly.

These varying structures of church government allowed Orangemen to argue that Presbyterianism and the other Non-Conformist denominations accepted the concept of rule from the bottom upwards whereas Roman Catholicism was inherently undemocratic because of its hierarchical structure which insisted on rule from the top downwards.

Irish immigration revived Roman Catholicism in Scotland from the somewhat moribund state it had fallen into by the end of the eighteenth century.[5] It coincided with the industrialisation of the Scottish economy and all that meant in terms of social upheaval. This encouraged a measure of anti-Catholic sentiment, although it is important to remember that anti-Catholicism only came to preoccupy a small minority of the host population.

It was perhaps fortunate that the one institution which should have been most concerned with the resultant growth of Roman Catholicism at this time, the Kirk, was itself too preoccupied with its own problems. The Kirk was in a crisis at exactly the same time as the heaviest period of Irish immigration into the country.

In 1843 the 'Great Disruption' occurred when the Church of Scotland split into two main factions over the question of patronage.[6] About 37 per cent of its ministers and between 40 and 50 per cent of its parishioners left the Kirk to form the rival Free Church of Scotland.[7] However, far from being a sign of weakness in the established faith, the split resulted in the expansion of both churches. This was indicative of the strength of feeling Scots had for their Presbyterian tradition.

The two great Presbyterian churches battled it out for the soul of the nation. They were too concerned with their own and each other's internal affairs to be worried about the growing encroachment of 'Rome'. Thus, 'No Popery' became marginalised to the fringes of both Kirks.

The Free Church had probably attracted a much higher proportion of evangelical ministers than remained in the Church of Scotland but out-and-out anti-Catholic ministers were a small minority in both. However, an important exception in the Free Church and one of the best known clerics of his times was Dr James Begg.[8]

Begg was a prolific anti-Catholic propagandist. When the Scottish Reformation Society was established in 1850 from within the body of the Free Church, Begg became the editor of its monthly magazine, the *Bulwark*. This publication was entirely devoted to pointing out and criticising what it perceived to be religious error in the Roman Catholic Church.

Begg was also instrumental in setting up the Protestant Institute of Scotland as an educational centre to combat Popery. He embarked on extensive lecture tours where he denounced the 'evils' of Roman Catholicism and wrote a best selling book entitled *Handbook of Popery*.

These activities brought Begg to national prominence. Although he was not a member of the Orange Order, he certainly articulated an essentially Orange view of Roman Catholicism:

> that considered theologically, it was the anti-Christ of scripture, the deadly enemy of the Gospel of Christ; that considered politically, it was a great gigantic system of despotism and the right arm of all the despotisms of Europe; that considered socially, it was the most complicated curse to any country or neighbourhood in which it prevailed and that considered historically, it presented a series of the most fearful degradations of man and insults to God which history has ever exhibited...
>
> It was more to the purpose at present to reflect on the fact that Popery was not only aggressive but that it was assuming that attitude avowedly with the determination not to cease until Protestantism in every form was extinguished...[9]

Begg's strident criticism of Roman Catholicism was perhaps of more significance to Orange clergymen than it was to ordinary rank and file members of the Order. This is not to deny their importance as a key ingredient of Orange ideology, but disputes over theology were primarily the domain of clerics and an educated and interested laity. However, criticism of Rome's perceived theological errors provided a focus for the Order's often-made assertion that it was essentially a religious society. Indeed, the Order regarded itself as a part of the historical process of Protestant Witness which began in the Reformation, continuing through the Covenanting period and up to the Victorian era of biblical criticism and scientific discovery.

This constant and unremitting criticism of the Roman Catholic faith often degenerated into contempt and ridicule. This resulted in the most negative impact imaginable for community relations. Although the Order was quick to claim that its criticism was directed at Roman Catholicism as an institution and not at Roman Catholics as individuals, the distinction was very often blurred.

In theory, the claim may have been true but the actual practice suggested otherwise. There is no doubt the anti-Catholicism preached by the Order's senior officials and clerics encouraged many, if not most, Orangemen to be personally antagonistic to, and intolerant of, individual Roman Catholics. This has contributed, in no small measure, to the cancer of sectarianism which continues to permeate community relations in Lowland Scottish society.

The negative attitudes towards Roman Catholics held by most Orangemen were reinforced by what they saw as the sociological implications for society arising from Rome's theological errors. When the Catholic Irish arrived in Scotland in such large numbers they were often blamed for the marked increase in social problems like alcoholism, vice and petty crime.[10]

Of course these social problems tend to be symptomatic of any society involved in the process of industrialisation but, rather than accept this view, the Order blamed the Roman Catholic Church: 'We attribute the vast number of Roman Catholic criminals and the degradation and immorality prevailing among Roman Catholics generally, to the anti-Christian doctrines and pernicious code of morals enjoined by the Roman priesthood...'[11]

In summary, the Order was utterly convinced that the Roman Catholic Church was involved in a conspiracy to destroy Protestantism in the British Isles and the Empire. It would achieve this aim by undermining the essential features of the Constitution. This was the Papacy's hidden agenda. It was the Order's mission to expose this hidden agenda and to resist it. The Order would do this by fully entering the political process.

# Chapter 14

# 'PROTESTANTISM BEFORE POLITICS'

DURING 1872 the Education (Scotland) Act was passed. Prior to this development, education had largely been the domain of the established church, the Church of Scotland. However, for a variety of reasons, not the least of which was the 'Great Disruption', this situation was no longer tenable. In effect, the Kirk handed over the responsibility for education in its schools to the state. The Act allowed for the establishment of popularly elected school boards with full management powers over such matters as staffing and the content of the curriculum.

Although education had now become a government responsibility, the Kirk and the other churches were nevertheless determined that religious instruction would remain an integral part of the school curriculum. In particular, it mounted an energetic campaign to ensure that Bible instruction and study would continue in the new school system, despite calls for the complete secularisation of education from certain sections within society.

The principle of Bible instruction in state schools or 'Use and Wont', as it was known in Scotland, became a rallying cry for concerned Presbyterians and other Protestants. The cudgels were also taken up by the Orange Order.

Defence of 'Use and Wont' presented the Order with a unique opportunity to enter the political process in a meaningful way and on an issue it could support quite unequivocally. Orangemen accepted the challenge with enthusiasm and in so doing attempted to ingratiate themselves with the established churches and their political allies, the Conservative Party.

An alliance with the Order was a not wholly unattractive proposition for the demoralised Tories at this time. Many leading Grand Lodge officials were themselves Conservatives, including the Grand Master of the Association, George McLeod, who in 1871 was praised by the Glasgow Conservative Association for his 'vigorous and manly stand' in defence of 'Use and Wont'.[1]

The first school board elections were held in 1873 and Orangemen stood as candidates all across Lowland Scotland. In Paisley, for example, of the fifteen candidates who stood for election, two were Orangemen and both were sucessful: the Rev. James Dodds and the Rev. William Fraser.[2]

Fraser was the minister of the Free Middle Church in the town and was a great admirer of his fellow Free Churchman, Dr James Begg. A Highlander by birth, Fraser had spent part of his childhood in Belfast. He was a strong Conservative and served on the Paisley School Board until his death in 1879. His funeral oration was delivered by Begg and his widow was later presented with an engraved address by Paisley District No. 6 in recognition of his services to the Orange and Protestant cause.[3]

The largest school board in Scotland was Glasgow, and Orangemen were to become almost permanent fixtures on it for the next 50 years. Indeed, the Order enjoyed a notable success at the first election in 1873 when one of its candidates, Harry Alfred Long, topped the poll with a quite remarkable 108,264 votes.[4]

However, it should be remembered that whilst Orange sucesses like Fraser in Paisley and Long in Glasgow were noteworthy, they were tempered by the knowledge that 'Rome' had its successes as well. The Roman Catholic Church also contested these elections and was usually successful in getting out the vote for its candidates: for example, at the Glasgow election of 1873 Roman Catholics won second, third and fourth places on the school board.

The first chairman of the Glasgow School Board was Alexander Whitelaw, who although not himself an Orangeman, was a relative and partner in the staunchly Protestant family firm of William Baird & Company of Gartsherrie. He was a trustee of the Baird Trust and was the author of a number of religious pamphlets.[5] He was elected as a Conservative MP for Glasgow in 1874, becoming the first Tory to represent a Glasgow seat for over 40 years, a fact welcomed by George McLeod at the annual Twelfth rally of the same year.[6]

Orange chairmanship of the Glasgow School Board was only delayed until Sir John N Cuthbertson assumed the office. He had unsuccessfully fought two previous contests before being elected in 1879. Cuthbertson served on the school board for almost 25 years and was chairman for 18 of those. He became strongly identified with Christian and philanthropic work.[7] He was a director and later Honorary President of the Working Mens' Evangelistic Association.[8] Cuthbertson stood unsuccessfully for Parliament as a Conservative on two occasions: at Kilmarnock Burghs in 1880 and St Rollox in 1885.

The stance the Order had taken in defending Bible instruction in state schools through its active participation in the school board elections was proving beneficial to its future progress. At least one Kirk minister, the Rev. John Wilson of Renfrew, had joined the Order because he had been impressed by its support for 'Use and Wont'.[9] He could not have been the only cleric who saw the Order in a new light at this time and it is interesting to speculate on just how many other recruits were similarly attracted into the Society.

The school board elections were of crucial importance to the development of the Orange Order in Scotland. They afforded the Order a point of entry into the normal mainstream channels of political discourse for the very first time. They

'If God be for us, who can be against us?': David and Goliath

allowed the Order to broaden its horizons within society at large and to start exercising the political muscle its numerical strength offered. Orangemen were being elected into responsible positions in society as a result of openly and demo-cratically engaging in the political process.

This development represented a quantum leap forward for an organisation which only a mere 14 years earlier, following the riots at Coatbridge and Linwood, had been stigmatised in the public imagination as a drunken, violent, Irish rabble. The Order was becoming aware of its potential at the same time as other forces in society were becoming equally aware of that same potential.

The involvement in the school board elections of Tory grandees like John N Cuthbertson and Alexander Whitelaw in Glasgow or Colonel Archibald C Campbell in Renfrew opened the door further to the Order's growing political ambitions towards cultivating its links with the Conservative Party. This was a strategy the Order regarded as vital to its declared aim of defending and promoting Protestant interests.

The school board elections also brought to prominence two of the most colourful Orangemen and characters in Glasgow life during the last decades of the nineteenth century: Harry Alfred Long and the Rev. Robert Thomson.

Harry Long was not a native of Glasgow. He was born in Cambridge in 1826 and had been given a strict religious upbringing which included a period of education at the Free Church Normal School in Glasgow. He spent some time teaching in England before returning again to Glasgow in 1847 at the invitation of St Jude's Episcopal Church. A committed evangelical, Long moved from St Jude's and opened an evangelical mission in the Saltmarket district of Glasgow's east end.[10]

From these premises, Long combined a programme of social work amongst the destitute and the poor with a systematic campaign of Bible-based evangelism. To assist him in the latter enterprise, Long formed, in 1869, the Glasgow Working Mens' Evangelistic Association,[11] dedicated to the following aims: 'The objects of the Society are to preach the Gospel; give Biblical instruction; hold educational classes...public lectures...sermons on the Lord's Day...and the usual open air meetings during the Summer on Glasgow Green.'[12]

Long became a controversial, if popular, speaker on Glasgow Green, drawing large crowds to his meetings in this public park in Glasgow's east end. He liked nothing better than to enter into raucous debate with Roman Catholic and atheist opponents. He was dubbed by his growing army of followers the 'Glasgow Green Faith Defender' in recognition of his strident and uncompromising views on 'religious error'.[13]

About 1873 Long expanded the work of the Working Mens' Evangelistic Association by adopting a more overtly anti-Catholic stance. Its stated aims now embraced a commitment: '...to stem the tide of Popery in Glasgow and to offer effective opposition to the infidel propaganda coming to Glasgow at selected intervals from London.'[14]

Appealing to 'pious operatives', the Association is alleged to have distributed over two million religious tracts, many of which were edited by Long himself.[15] Its leadership also seems to have been dominated by Orangemen, although the Association was not, *per se*, a specifically 'Orange' organisation. Apart from Long, who was the Association's Secretary, its first President was Thomas Wetherall, a Deputy Grand Master of Scotland. In 1882 Sir John N Cuthbertson became Honorary President of the Association.[16]

Long immersed himself in his charity work. He is said to have assisted over 2,000 people in finding employment, and fed in his mission a total of 4,000 people over the years.[17] He also obtained medical help for the destitute and poor when this was required.

His undoubted popularity with many of Glasgow's citizens was reflected in his quite extraordinary success in the city's school board elections. He easily topped the poll in 1873 but he also repeated this feat in 1885, 1891 and 1894. Long was assisted in his election campaigns by an organisation he formed known as the 'Knoxites'. In reality, this was a well motivated group of his brother Orangemen.

Long's fame spread far and wide. In the late 1890s, he was called to Brisbane in Australia to lead a 'Bible in the schools' campaign there as well. He returned to Glasgow in 1900 in time to contest the school board election of that year. He again topped the poll.[18]

Long's ability to mobilise the Protestant vote was not lost on the Conservative Party. A Tory all his life, Long was appointed a Vice-President of the Glasgow Conservative Association in 1887 in recognition of his services to the cause.[19] He became a pivotal figure in the growing relationship between the Tories and the Order at this time.

At an Orange gathering in 1874 Long had acknowledged that he and they had worked 'hard and valiantly' for the return of a Conservative government and he reiterated the view expressed by his fellow Grand Lodge Officer, George McLeod, that: 'Every true and sound Orangeman was a Conservative in politics.'[20]

It is of interest to contrast the career of the Orange evangelical and 'missionary', Harry Long, with that of the Orange cleric, the Rev. Robert Thomson. Whilst both men were equally strident in their anti-Catholic views, Long tempered his with a degree of realism which Thomson seemed unable to grasp. Thomson was a prime example of a cleric for whom anti-Catholicism became something of a cottage industry. Although such people were, and still are, often regarded as eccentrics at best and fanatics at worst, the fact remained there was always a market for their services and an audience who lapped up everything they had to say.

Thomson first came to national attention when he stood unsuccessfully as an Independent candidate in Kilmarnock Burghs during the general election of 1868. At this time, he was an assistant to his brother, the Rev. John Thomson, an Orangeman and minister of St Marnock's Parish Church in the Ayrshire town.[21] Robert Thomson had stood for Parliament on a populist platform which included the disestablishment of the Church of Ireland, the reclamation of land used by the aristocracy for hunting, shooting and fishing to be re-cultivated to feed the poor, triennial Parliaments, and voting by secret ballot.[22]

Thomson then appears to have had a political conversion on a Pauline scale, for he turned completely to the right. He moved to Glasgow, joined the Orange Order and became minister of Ladywell Parish Church. It was in Glasgow that his career as an anti-Catholic demagogue really took off.

In typical style, he once told an Orange gathering that: 'he was the only Protestant that ever preached a sermon in St Peter's Square, Rome. He preached on the occasion of his visit when a number of Protestants present were about to follow the example of the Romanists in kissing the Pope's toe.'[23]

Thomson became a favourite figure of ridicule for the Glasgow Tory satirical magazine, the *Baillie*, which took great delight in calling him 'Rubbart'.[24] In time, he also became an embarrassment to the Order itself, starting with his conduct over the restoration of the Roman Catholic hierarchy in Scotland in 1878.

The restoration of the Roman Catholic hierarchy in Scotland was a consequence of the enormous growth in the Roman Catholic population during the nineteenth century. Immigration from Ireland had been the main cause of this increase. In 1780 the Roman Catholic population had stood at 30,000 but, by 1878, this figure had risen to some 300,000. Of more significance was the fact that of this total some 220,000 were concentrated in the conurbation around Glasgow.[25]

Militant Protestants were alarmed at this development but the vast majority remained quite indifferent to the growth of Roman Catholicism in their midst. Presbyterians were too preoccupied with their own internal disputes and rival church building programmes to be unduly concerned with 'Rome'. Therefore, there was no hysteria in Scotland to match the furore which had occurred in England when the Roman Catholic hierarchy was restored there in 1850.

What hostility there was came from predictable quarters. The Order was outraged and in 1877 the Grand Lodge of Scotland sent an urgent telegram to the Prime Minister, Benjamin Disraeli, explaining its opposition:

> that according to the law of this country, a profession of Protestantism is essential to the occupancy of the throne, and the title of the House of Hanover to the throne depends upon the Protestantism of the Constitution. That there is now a very public report circulated in all the newspapers and contradicted in none, that the Pope is about to establish, by his own authority, a Popish hierarchy in Scotland. That the establishment of a Popish hierarchy would be in direct violation of the Constitution and laws of this Protestant kingdom, in which ever since the Reformation, the authority of the Pope has been both abjured and proscribed by pointed, positive, solemn and Parliamentary enactments.
>
> That the adherents of the Pope in Scotland have hitherto had ample freedom of worship and the fullest toleration so that, if they demand more, it cannot be for merely religious purposes but as tending to their final ascendancy as a political party with a supreme head, foreign and hostile to the religion and liberties of this Protestant kingdom. May it therefore please your lordship to take into your serious consideration the statements of this memorial and to preserve intact the existing laws of the United Kingdom; the conditions of the Union between England and Scotland and the fundamental principles of the Constitution, as established in 1688-89.[26]

The Order was somewhat obsessed with the idea of Popish plots and conspiracies against the British state, and this notion surfaces again in this communication to Disraeli, where reference is made to the fact that the restoration '...cannot be for merely religious purposes...' For the Order, the restoration represented a direct threat to the Protestant nature of the Constitution and the Protestant character of Scotland.

Not to be outdone by the Grand Lodge, Thomson went one better. He actually sent a telegram of protest directly to the Pope! It read: 'If your threatened hierarchy is promulgated in Scotland, proceedings will be taken against you in the Court of Session.'[27]

The news of Thomson's telegram was apparently greeted with loud laughter at the General Assembly of the Church of Scotland.[28] This reaction alone demonstrates the extent to which Thomson and his ilk had been marginalised to the fringes of the Kirk.

Thomson was also in danger of becoming marginalised to the fringes of the Order as well. At the annual Twelfth rally that same year he became embroiled in a quite extraordinary platform dispute with two other Orange clergymen present, the Rev. Peter McLachlan of Gallowgate and the Rev. James MacKay of St Clement's, Glasgow.

Thomson publicly accused McLachlan of failing to protest against the restoration of the Roman Catholic hierarchy at a meeting of the Glasgow Presbytery. McLachlan, somewhat taken aback at this unexpected outburst, called Thomson to order. MacKay, a well respected figure within the Order, reprimanded Thomson and pointed out to him that the place for such comment was the relative privacy of the Presbytery and not a public Orange gathering.[29]

Undeterred by such setbacks, Thomson stood for election to the Glasgow School Board in 1879. He was unsuccessful and finished bottom of the poll. He stood again in 1882 and was elected[30] and served on the school board until his retirement in 1889.

Thomson and Long represented two sides of the same coin. Both were fervent in their anti-Catholic, militant Protestant views, although they went about their work in different ways. The 'No Popery' politics of Orange leaders like Thomson and Long represented the Order's perceptions in late Victorian Scotland. As the Order moved closer to the Conservative Party, it never lost sight of its determination to put 'Protestantism' before politics.

*Chapter 15*

# THE ORANGE AND UNIONIST ALLIANCE

POLITICS in Scotland had been dominated by the Liberal Party by the mid-Victorian period. However, the extension of the franchise, initially to the better off sections of the working class, offered new political opportunities to the Conservatives to break the Liberal hegemony.

The possibility of a national Tory revival had manifested itself during the various school board elections of the 1870s when local Conservatives enjoyed a measure of success over the defence of 'Use and Wont'. The opportunity of exploiting religious issues for national political gain became apparent. This could be a dangerous strategy to adopt but its chances of success were certainly enhanced by the policies being enacted by the Liberal Party.

In 1869 the Liberal government had disestablished the Anglican Church of Ireland, much to the chagrin of Irish Protestants. There were elements in the Liberal Party who wanted to pursue a similar course of action in relation to the Church of Scotland. In addition, it was the Liberal government which had introduced the Education (Scotland) Act in 1872 which many Scots regarded as the undermining of the traditional religious upbringing of the nation's children.

These policies alarmed and dismayed many of the Liberal Party's traditional Presbyterian and other non-Conformist supporters. Some started to look towards the Conservatives in order to preserve the Protestant character of the nation. This allowed the Tories to assume the mantle of being the party of Queen and Constitution, Church and Nation.

Such an appeal had an attraction for middle class Presbyterians who cared enough about the future of their church in an increasingly secular age, but something more basic was required if the Conservative Party was going to attract the votes it needed from working class Protestants. Tory strategists, no doubt impressed by the Order's apparant ability to mobilise the vote in school board elections, hoped it would harness the same effort to the Conservative cause in local and national elections.

The Conservatives decided to embark upon a strategy of playing the 'sectarian card' in those constituencies, of which there were many across West Central Scotland, essentially working class in social composition and bitterly divided on religious and ethnic grounds. A distinctly populist brand of Conservatism was adopted, characterised by what may be termed Protestant Unionism.

This strategy was not merely the result of cynicism or opportunism. There were a number of leading Conservatives sympathetic to militant Protestant aspirations and concerns and all Tories were, of course, Unionists.[1] The important point is that this particular political philosophy was reserved for those seats where sectarian feeling could be utilised to electoral advantage.

Protestant Unionism embraced a series of policies and slogans designed to appeal to working class Protestants in general and to Orangemen in particular. Something of a 'True Blue' frame of reference developed between party and voter. The twin pillars of this framework were patriotism and royalism. This ideological superstructure was underpinned by an economic policy committed to the maintenance of Empire trade, from which, it was argued, Scottish workers had especially benefited.

These political views were synonymous with Orangeism and they were intended to be. The Tories hoped the Order could provide a grassroots campaign machine for the party in those working class seats where it had a chance of winning. Thus, the Order was expected to 'deliver' the vote to Conservative candidates when required to do so.

For their part, Orange leaders were ready and willing to enter into a political alliance with the Conservatives. Unlike the previous attempt at a collaboration made earlier in the century, the circumstances were now favourable to the success of such an enterprise. Orangemen realised that passing resolutions at Twelfth rallies or holding mass demonstrations were all very well but if the Order was going to achieve its own aims and objectives then it had to enter fully into the political process.

Thomas Wetherall, Deputy Grand Master of Scotland, urged all Orangemen: 'to endeavour to consolidate the parties belonging to the Conservative interest and to bring them together in a firm and compact body in spite of all opposition.'[2]

In fact, by the end of the 1870s, firm links were being established between Orangemen and Conservatives at the local grassroots level in many West Central Scotland constituencies. There is evidence which suggests that there was in fact a good deal of Orange involvement in the formation of a number of Conservative Associations at this time.

Thus, for example, at the inaugural meeting of the Paisley Conservative Association in 1878, a large number of the founding members were Orangemen. These included Alexander Pollock, who moved that the Association be set up, and Peter Burt, who seconded the motion. Another Orangeman, A N Gardner, submitted the rules of management whilst four others were elected to the management committee.[3]

Pollock, who owned a dry-salting business in Paisley, was elected a Vice-President of the Association, and Gardner, a printer, was elected treasurer. Of even more significance was the programme adopted by the Paisley Conservatives:

> to maintain and defend the fundamental principles of the Constitution which secure the perogatives of the Crown; the Protestant Succession; the privileges of Parliament and the prevention of all undue pressure of class on class; to resist all attempts to subvert our Protestant faith while granting full religious liberty to all sects and while opposing all unnecessary and unwarrantable changes in existing institutions, to support every well considered measure tending to promote the material, social, and moral well being of the people and to improve the financial, administrative and judicial systems of the country.[4]

It should be noted that the assumption is made that members of the Paisley Conservative Association will be Protestants and that all attempts 'to subvert our Protestant faith' will be resisted. Such a manifesto clearly reflects Orange concerns and Orange principles. It is interesting to speculate on how typical the Constitution of the Paisley Association was in comparison to the Constitutions of other Conservative Associations in West Central Scotland. If it is indicative of the norm then it testifies to the influence the Order was exercising on the Tories at this time.

These grassroots links were being reinforced in other ways. It was becoming fairly common practice in certain areas of the country for Orange Lodges to meet in official Conservative Party premises. Thus, for example, a number of lodges in Govan met in the local Conservative Rooms,[5] and in Greenock, both 'Albion' LOL 270 and 'St John's Defenders' LOL 505 chose to meet in the local Conservative Club rather than the Orange Hall in the town.[6]

It was also around this time that some lodges began the practice of naming themselves after prominent Conservative politicians. These included; 'George McLeod's True Blues' LOL 71 Townhead; 'Lord Blythswood' LOL 97 Greenock; and 'John N Cuthbertson' LOL 204 Cowcaddens.[7] Such identification of the lodges with leading Conservatives like Cuthbertson and Campbell (Lord Blythswood) was also indicative of changing political circumstances. Whilst leading Orangemen like Chalmers Paton, Thomas Wetherall and Harry Long were active Conservatives, the luminaries of the party had kept their distance from the Order. Lending one's name to a lodge was one thing; actually joining a lodge was quite another. However, by the 1880s, the Grand Lodge hoped this situation might change, given the new spirit of co-operation existing between the two bodies.

As an inducement towards this aim, the Grand Lodge established a lodge for gentlemen, known as 'Beaconsfield's Purple Guards' LOL 690, in Glasgow, during October, 1880.[8] Its status was intended to be similar to that of the Royal Gordon Lodge formed some 50 years earlier. Unfortunately for the Order, like its famous predecessor, LOL 690 also met with only very limited success.

Its first public meeting was held in June, 1881 at McGregor's Hotel, Glasgow and was mainly notable for the number of gentlemen invited who subsequently sent their apologies for non-attendance.[9] For the small number who did attend,

Queen and Constitution: Queen Victoria. 'God Bless Her!'

Chalmers Paton, elucidated: 'Why am I an Orangeman?...I am a Protestant and a Briton, a loyal subject of her most gracious majesty, Queen Victoria and loyal to the British Constitution, defined and established by the Revolution of 1688, of which Constitution, Protestantism is not merely an integral and essential part, but the very basis.'[10]

This declaration must have impressed at least one of the gentlemen present, one Allan Gilmour of Eaglesham, for at the lodge's first annual soiree later in the year, he announced: 'Whether we call ourselves Tories or Conservatives; Orangemen or loyalists; let us be found side by side and fighting against one common foe ...and under one common banner; the banner of loyalty and in defence of our common cause; the Crown which we adore; the Church which we venerate and the Constitution which we are determined to defend.'[11]

That same year, the lodge held an extraordinary and special meeting, the purpose of which was to initiate 'two prominent gentlemen'. At this meeting, the lodge's chaplain, Robert Stewart, pointed out:

The time has been, brethren, when to be an Orangeman was to be everything that was low and disgraceful. He was looked down upon by all political parties, by all associations. But we have now entered on a better and on a brighter era. And how has this been achieved? Simply because we are getting men into our ranks who are able to lead us; men of education; of principle; of ability. And so it will be. The more our principles are known, the more we will be respected.[12]

Stewart was only partially correct in his analysis of the movement's standing at this time. The image of the Order had indeed improved but his somewhat optimistic view of its appeal to the upper classes would not be borne out in reality. The Order would always be able to attract some men of social standing and political influence but not nearly enough of them to make any real impact on the levers of power in Scotland.

The Order would remain an essentially proletarian movement, led by Grand Lodge officers drawn primarily from the lower echelons of the middle class, with a sprinkling of minor aristocrats. The proletarian nature of the Order was both its great strength and its great weakness.

Unfortunately, the identities of the 'two prominent gentlemen' admitted into membership of LOL 690 has remained a secret. Thus, some educated guesswork is required. Among the possibilities were Allan Gilmour, if he had not been admitted into formal membership of the lodge at the earlier meetings he attended, John N Cuthbertson, James Bain and Colonel Archibald C Campbell. The latter two gentlemen seem the most likely, given their backgrounds and views.

James Bain was born in Glasgow in 1819 and spent his early working life in the employment of Baird's of Gartsherrie. He then entered municipal politics, becoming a councillor in 1863, a baillie in 1867 and finally, Lord Provost of Glasgow in 1874.[13]

As Deputy Chairman of the Clyde Trust, Bain anticipated the need for greater dock and wharf accommodation. He later became President of the Chamber of Commerce and was appointed a Lord Lieutenant of Lanarkshire. Bain was an enthusiastic freemason but his association with Orangeism was more difficult to quantify.

Following his knighthood, Bain chaired the Glasgow Orange and Protestant Soiree in 1879 and reminded his audience that:

This is not the first Orange meeting I have been at. I was at an Orange supper thirty years ago. But how different a supper is our gathering tonight. Then, the drink was hot punch, now it is the cup that cheers but does not inebriate, now wives and sweethearts are present and children too...[14]

The fact that Bain chaired the Glasgow soiree suggests that he may already have been a member of the Order but if he was not then he would almost certainly have been interested in joining LOL 690 when it was formed in 1880. The establishment of what was intended to be an informal bridge between the Order and the Conservative Party would have attracted Bain, who by this time, had national political ambitions.

Bain stood for Parliament as a Conservative in one of the Glasgow seats in 1880. His platform included his strong opposition to the mooted disestablishment of the Church of Scotland. Although finishing bottom of the poll in a five man contest, Bain's candidature was indicative of the Order's growing significance to the Conservative Party.

Bain left Glasgow to live and work in Cumberland. The Bairds had extensive business interests in this part of England, where interestingly enough, Orangeism was also rife amongst many of the workers in the local iron works and coal mines. Bain eventually achieved his political ambition when he was elected the Conservative MP for Whitehaven.[15]

The other most likely recruit for LOL 690 was Colonel Archibald C Campbell, the 1st Lord Blythswood. The discreet Colonel was to become perhaps the key figure in cementing the relationship between the Order and the Conservative Party in Scotland.

Archibald Campbell was born in 1835, the oldest brother in a family of nine children. At the age of 19 years, he joined the Scots Guards and was severely wounded at Sevastapol in the Crimean War. He also saw military service in Canada where he may have first come into contact with the Orange Order.

Following the death of his father, Campbell retired from full military service. However, old soldiers never die. He maintained an interest in the military, serving as a Lieutenant Colonel in the 4th Battalian of the Argyll and Sutherland Highlanders (Renfrewshire Militia), and for a time, commanded the 3rd Battalion of the Highland Light Infantry (Volunteers), based in Glasgow.[16]

Campbell devoted the rest of his life on the family estate to his main interests, religion, politics and science. He was a devout Presbyterian, who, at his own expense, renewed the ancient churchyard at Inchinnan, near Renfrew, where the family estate was located. The current parish church of Inchinnan displays the Campbell family tree on a mural in the vestibule. Campbell was also a generous subscriber to the restoration fund of Paisley Abbey and was a strong defender of Bible instruction in state schools.

It was probably his strong religious convictions which led Campbell into politics. He fought his first national election in 1868 as the Conservative candidate for Paisley but finished second in a poll of three. His platform included support for Reform, votes by ballot, Bible instruction in state schools and opposition to the disestablishment of the Church of Ireland.[17]

Although not a member of the Orange Order at this time, Campbell began to court Orange support seriously. He stood again for Parliament in 1873 in the semi-rural seat of Renfrewshire and was elected this time. The constituency contained a number of localities where the Order was numerically strong, including Johnstone, Pollockshaws and Renfrew. At an election rally in Renfrew, the chairman of the meeting, the Rev. Gillan stated: '...that Colonel Campbell is an uncompromising enemy of Popery. He opposes every practice that has either emanated from or that leads to the Church of Rome.'[18]

Campbell became a regular attender at the annual Orange and Protestant Soirees, especially in Paisley. Later that same year, he told an audience of about 1,000 Orangemen and friends: '...it gives me great pleasure and I feel it indeed to be a very great honour, to be allowed to be associated with those whom I feel to be so thoroughly in unison with the principles I have been taught and the principles which I trust I may have life and health to uphold in the country.'[19] Campbell was congratulated during this meeting both on his election to Parliament and his election to the Renfrew School Board.

Campbell lost his Parliamentary seat the following year and fought it again, unsuccessfully, in 1880. He then threw all of his considerable energies into completely re-organising the Conservative Party in Glasgow. He wanted to embrace the various working men's associations under the umbrella of the Glasgow Conservative Association. The idea was to place them *en rapport* in order to co-ordinate the activities of the various associations with Conservative sympathies in the city.[20]

A special meeting was called in November 1880 and the Glasgow Conservative Association was reconstituted along the lines of Campbell's proposals. A number of leading Orangemen were also present at this meeting, including Thomas Wetherall and Thomas Stewart,[21] and others like George McLeod, Harry Long and William Young were also members of the Glasgow Conservative Association.

These personal contacts ensured that Glasgow's Orange Lodges established links with the Glasgow Conservative Association as envisaged by Colonel Campbell. The significance of the new relationship between the two bodies was amply demonstrated in 1884 when the Conservative Party leader and future Prime Minister, Lord Salisbury, visited Glasgow. After being introduced to the leading members of the Glasgow Conservative Association, he was then introduced to a delegation from the Grand Orange Lodge of Scotland. The various other Party groups and dignitaries were obliged to take their turn in the queue.[22]

Relations between the Order and the Party were finally institutionalised in 1893 when the Conservatives set up their Western Divisional Council. The Order was allocated an official place on this policy-making body of the Conservative Party.[23] William Young, Deputy Grand Master of Scotland, was the Order's first representative on the Council.

Campbell had been instrumental in effecting these important initiatives which he considered were essential if the Party and the Order were to realise their full potential and progress in the future.

By this time Campbell had almost certainly joined the Order, probably LOL 690.[24] He stood again for Parliament in 1885 for the constituency of Renfrewshire West and was elected. In so doing, he became the first Orangeman to represent a Scottish seat in Parliament and he would not be the last. Campbell held the seat until his retirement from public life in 1892 when he was elevated to the peerage as the 1st Lord Blythswood.

Lord Blythswood became an Aide-de-Camp to Queen Victoria, a position he retained under her son, King Edward VII. Both men were enthusiastic freemasons.[25] It was perhaps regrettable for both the prestige and future development of the Orange Order that Lord Blythswood could not have been persuaded to adopt a more high profile or public rôle within the movement. A man of his integrity, social standing and personal connections would have encouraged others from the same background to come forward and bite the bullet.

There is little doubt that he could have had the position of Grand Master if he had wanted it when Chalmers Paton died in 1889. Certainly, his life was already very full as an MP and he was also at this time the Grand Master Mason of the Masonic Order in Scotland. He may have considered the equivalent role in the Orange Order to be rather too onerous on top of his other commitments and responsibilities. It would certainly have been more 'political'.

In matters Orange, Lord Blythswood preferred a more discreet background rôle. Like most Tory grandees, he recoiled from public demonstrations but felt more comfortable with the relative privacy of the annual Orange and Protestant Soirees. However, that background rôle was, nevertheless, quite considerable. He, more than perhaps any other single individual, cemented the relationship between the Orange Order and the Conservative Party, often in the face of a marked reluctance from sections of opinion in both bodies. It was little wonder then that his death in 1908 was described by the Grand Master, William McCormick, as: 'a great loss to the Orange and Unionist cause'.[26]

When the Conservative Party and the Orange Order entered into their political alliance, there were great expectations on both sides. The Tories expected the Order to deliver the vote and whilst it was true that the Order did 'deliver' working class votes for Conservative candidates, that is about all that can be stated with any degree of certainty. What the significance of the 'Orange Vote' actually was in any given constituency at any given time remains a matter of pure speculation.

The 'Orange vote' only existed in the sense that there were a number of constituencies in West Central Scotland which contained a sizable Orange presence but this fact on its own could not guarantee the election of a Conservative candidate. Unlike Belfast or Liverpool, which were much more ethnically segregated,[27] there was not one single Parliamentary constituency in Scotland where Orangemen were concentrated enough to ensure the electoral success of their chosen candidate. Therefore, great care must be taken when discussing the Orange vote; it was always episodic or particular in character and never a universal phenomenon.

If there was one Parliamentary constituency at this time where the Orange vote may have had more significance than usual, then it was the seat of Renfrewshire West. Lord Blythswood won the seat in 1885 and held it until his retirement in 1892. His successor as Tory candidate was one Charles Bine Renshaw, a director of the carpet manufacturers, A F Stoddart of Elderslie, who were and still are major employers in the Johnstone area. Although not an Orangeman himself, Renshaw was one of the very few Tory grandees who was not afraid to associate himself publicly with the Order.

Renshaw seriously courted the considerable Orange support his predecessor had cultivated in the constituency and was ably assisted in this enterprise by his election agent, one Alexander MacFarlane. A native of Paisley, MacFarlane was the Secretary of the West of Scotland National Union of Conservative Associations. Perhaps of more significance to Renshaw's future prospects was the fact that MacFarlane was an Orangeman and an office bearer in the Grand Lodge.[28] He was, therefore, ideally placed to mobilise the Orange Vote on Renshaw's behalf by ensuring voter registration.

Renshaw retained Renfrewshire West for the Conservatives in 1892. He sent a letter of gratitude to the local Orange Lodges for their support.[29] He won the seat again following the General Election of 1895. A year later, he addressed a Twelfth rally in Renfrew:

> he was there that day to recognise the help they had received from the Orange body in all parts of Scotland in returning the Unionists to power. It was greatly...to the fact that such a number of those who were connected with Orange organisations had co-operated with Liberal Unionist and Conservative organisations, that their success was due.[30]

Renshaw exaggerated the importance of Orange support for Conservative candidates in other parts of the country but there is little doubt that it constituted a significant element in his own electoral success in 1895 and thereafter.

However, it would be wrong to extrapolate the importance of the Orange Vote in one single constituency to other constituencies with similar characteristics across the country. Rather, what is required is for each constituency to be analysed in its own right in order to avoid simplistic generalisations being made about this complex phenomenon.

A cautionary reminder in respect of this point was provided in that very same electoral year of 1892 in Perth where William Whitelaw was elected as Conservative MP for the Tayside city. In so doing, he became the second Orangeman to enter Parliament representing a Scottish seat. However, what is ironic here is that the Orangeman Whitelaw should win in a constituency with almost no Orange Vote, whilst Renshaw, who was not a member of the Order, won his seat thanks partly to the sizable Orange vote which existed in his.

William Whitelaw was born in 1868, the third son of Alexander Whitelaw the MP for Glasgow from 1874 until 1879. He was a part of the Baird family dynasty. A lieutenant in the Airdrie Troop of the Lanarkshire Yeomanry Cavalry, Whitelaw was also a director and eventual Chairman of the Highland Railway Company.[31]

Unlike his father, William Whitelaw actually took the step of joining the Orange Order. He told an electoral meeting that: 'he had the honour to belong to the body of Scottish Orangemen and there was no better organisation on the Unionist side.'[32]

A few days later Whitelaw attended a Twelfth demonstration in Govan where the Deputy Grand Master, William Young, congratulated him on what was a remarkable victory in Perth. Whitelaw was later accorded the title of Honorary Deputy Grand Master of Scotland by the Grand Lodge.[33] In point of fact, Whitelaw only won the Perth seat because of a split in the Liberal vote. He only held the seat until the next General Election in 1895 when the Liberals won it back.

Whitelaw stood again in 1900 without success and he next stood for election in Banff and Stirling Burghs in 1907 and again was unsuccessful in both constituencies.

Having given up politics, Whitelaw devoted the rest of his life to his extensive business interests. He died in 1946.

# Chapter 16

# 'HOME RULE MEANS ROME RULE'

T HE one political issue which cemented and indeed came to dominate the relationship between the Orange Order and the Conservative Party was the strident opposition of both to the concept of Irish Home Rule. In 1886 the Liberal Prime Minister, William Ewart Gladstone, formed a government which was dependent for its survival on the goodwill and support of the Irish National Party and he immediately set about framing a Bill which would restore a parliament to Ireland.

Although party politics at Westminster partly dictated this course of action, Gladstone genuinely believed in devolving power back to the Irish. He hoped the somewhat limited form of self government he was proposing would lay the basis for a lasting settlement of the 'Irish Question'.

The proposed legislation, which followed the Liberal government's disestablishment of the Church of Ireland and various land reforms, dismayed the Protestant population and had the effect of galvanising them into a united effort to oppose the Bill. All shades of Protestant opinion, working class and middle class, Anglican and Presbyterian, urban and rural, came together as one and were resolved to oppose Home Rule, which they perceived as a threat to civil and religious liberty in Ireland. The Union had to be maintained at all costs since, for Protestants, 'Home Rule was Rome Rule'.

Of course, Gladstone anticipated strong opposition to his proposals from the Protestant minority in Ireland but he probably underestimated the intensity of that opposition. He also underestimated the damage his Irish policy would have on the Liberal Party. In effect, the Liberals split over Home Rule with almost all of the party aristocracy and many other Liberals who were certainly not aristocrats departing to form the Liberal Unionist Party.[1] An electoral pact was then struck between the Liberal Unionists and the Conservatives which ensured they were not in opposition at future elections and thus the anti-Home Rule vote was not divided.

The issue of Irish Home Rule came to dominate British politics for the next 40 years. In Scotland, it reinforced the bond between the Orange Order and the Conservative Party, as no other issue did. It gave their relationship the kiss of life. However, it could be argued that each group had its own perceptions as to what the issue at stake actually was.

The Order was in no doubt: the issue was religion. Orangemen viewed Irish Home Rule as yet another concession to Roman Catholicism. It followed a long line of such 'concessions' including Emancipation in 1829, Disestablishment in 1869, and various land reforms.[2] Home Rule was the last straw. The Grand Master, Chalmers Paton, expressed Orange frustration:

> ...each concession made in the hope that it would satisfy the Papists and make Ireland peaceful. And what had been the result: murder! Peacefulness, loyalty, contentment? No but louder and still louder the cry...Give, Give. The truth must be spoken, the British government and legislature had not been faithful to the Protestant Constitution of Britain.
>
> It behoved all true Protestants to set themselves with all their might to the resistance of further Popish aggressions.[3]

For the many expatriate Orangemen in Scotland, the campaign and impending struggle against Irish Home Rule was profoundly personal. They had often left family and friends behind in Ireland and were naturally anxious for their safety should actual hostilities commence. The issue presented them with an immediacy and sense of urgency which their more mundane anti-Catholic preoccupations did not.

At their annual Twelfth rally, held that year in Springburn, the Orangemen of Scotland passed the following resolution: 'that this meeting protests in toto against the principle of Gladstone's Home Rule Bill as leading inevitably to the separation of Ireland from Great Britain and further declares that the present union of Liberals and Conservatives must in the interests of the Empire be continued.'[4]

For their part, the Conservatives perceived the 'Irish Question' primarily along class lines. The defence of the 'Protestant Ascendancy' in Ireland was the defence of the principle of private property rights. If such rights could be eroded in Ireland, how long would it be before they could be eroded in Great Britain and other parts of the Empire? The rot had to be stopped and it would have to be stopped first in Ireland. This realisation is not to deny the obvious commitment of many Tories to Protestantism and the Union, but the economic perceptions of the Party underpinned its ideological alignments.

The issue of Irish Home Rule marked something of a turning point in the electoral fortunes of the Conservative Party in Scotland. When Gladstone's Bill was defeated in the House of Commons[5] another General Election was called which resulted in the return of a Conservative government under the leadership of Lord Salisbury. The Conservatives and Liberal Unionists won 19 seats between them in Scotland, a result which went some way to eroding the Liberal hegemony which had previously prevailed in the country. Indeed, the Liberals lost about two thirds of their seats in West Central Scotland where the Tory appeal to 'Protestant Unionism' was at its most potent.

The defeat of the Irish Home Rule Bill in 1886 was met with great rejoicing by Orangemen and Unionists on both sides of the North Channel. Bonfires of celebration were lit around the hills of Belfast. Of more lasting significance was the establishment of improved political relations between Irish Unionists and British Unionists, firstly in the Ulster Loyalist and Patriotic Union and later, the Unionist Clubs. Orangemen in Scotland played their part in fostering these political ties in 1889 when they elected Colonel Edward J Saunderson, leader of the Ulster Unionist MPs at Westminster, to be their new Grand Master.

As expected, the Province of Ulster was the main centre of opposition to Home Rule in Ireland. At a huge gathering held in the Ulster Hall, Belfast, Lord Randolph Churchill roused his audience with a rallying cry which Unionists would repeat over and over again in the years to come: 'Ulster Will Fight and Ulster Will Be Right'.

Churchill added a few lines of poetry which summed up the mood in Ulster:

> Sail On, O Ship Of State
> Sail On, O Union Great
> Shall Ulster From Britain Sever?
> By The God Who Made Us: Never!!![6]

However, the Union came under threat again in 1892 when the Liberals were returned to power following the General Election of that year. This latest Irish Home Rule campaign, leading up to the election, was marked in Scotland by the appearance for the first time of Conservative candidates and election agents appealing directly for support at public Orange rallies and private meetings. This development was indicative of the strong alliance the two groups were enjoying at this time of great peril to the Union.

The first occasion on which this happened seems to have been in 1890 when the election agents for the constituencies of North Ayrshire and South Ayrshire both attended the County Grand Orange Lodge of Ayrshire's rally at Kilbirnie.[7] The following year, election agents addressed the County Grand Orange Lodge of Lanarkshire and the Lothians rally at Coatbridge.[8] In 1893, Alexander Whitelaw, the Conservative candidate for North East Lanarkshire, attended the County Grand Orange Lodge of Lanarkshire and the Lothians rally at the mining village of Benhar, outside Harthill.[9]

In Glasgow in 1892 the Conservative candidate for the College division of the city, John Stirling Maxwell, went one better and actually addressed a private meeting of Cowcaddens District No. 10 which was located in his constituency:

The Chairman (District Master) had said it was not usual for a candidate to address an Orange Lodge...Why not? It had certainly never occurred to me to refuse the invitation. There might have been in the past some neglect of the Orangemen by the Conservatives but I think that probably arose from the fact that the Conservatives were sure of the Orange Vote.[10]

On taking office, Gladstone again set about introducing a second Irish Home Rule Bill. In June, 1892, a great Unionist convention was held in Belfast with the utmost solemnity and attended by 21,000 people. Although the convention was opened by prayers from both the Church of Ireland Primate and the Irish Presbyterian Moderator, the mood of many present was extremely militant.[11] Various Unionist groupings were already importing arms, and rifle clubs were being set up all over Ulster to resist Home Rule—by force, if necessary.

The mood was apparently no less strident in Scotland. At the annual Twelfth rally held at Petershill in 1893, the Grand Secretary of Scotland, Thomas Macklin, himself an Ulsterman, declared: 'Should traitors impose on the North the dire necessity of civil war, Ulster would marshal her sons and the Orangemen of Scotland would join them and the watchword from rank to rank, from man to man, would be No Surrender!!'[12]

This was extraordinary language from a senior and respected Grand Lodge Officer but it underlined the very real anxieties which many expatriate Orangemen felt at the time for their kith and kin in Ireland.

The 'traitors' referred to by Macklin were, of course, Her Majesty's democratically elected government. In the event, physical resistance to Home Rule was not necessary since Gladstone's Bill was again defeated, this time in the Tory dominated House of Lords.

Another Home Rule crisis had come and gone. Two years later, in 1895, the Conservatives were returned to office.

As early as 1876, Harry Long had warned his political allies: 'The Orangemen of Scotland had often been viewed as the mere tools of the Conservative Party, following wherever the Premier led; but they were not the children of any Conservative Party but of King William.'[13]

The point was clear. Orange support for Conservatism was not to be taken for granted. Indeed, Orange support for Conservatism was conditional, the condition being that the Conservative Party defend and promote Protestant interests when required to do so. Staunch Tory though he was, Long put it quite simply: 'Protestantism before Politics'.[14]

In actual fact, the Orangemen and the Conservatives were not 'natural' allies, despite statements from Grand Lodge Officers which suggested otherwise.[15] There were obvious class differences between them which led many Tories to shy away from Orange support or involvement at any level. Some Conservatives found Orange rhetoric and traditions both repellent and vulgar.

For these Conservatives, the Order was too preoccupied with the single issue of anti-Catholicism to be really useful as a long term political ally. Pragmatists realised that serious political parties who crave power have to concern themselves with more than one issue. They have to be prepared to make compromises and ditch unpopular or outmoded policies when necessary. They have to swim with the tide when required or sink without trace.

This was a stark reality which lay at the heart of the tensions experienced in Orange and Conservative relations. The Conservatives often had to put expediency before principle in order to survive. The Order, on the other hand, had no such qualms. Compromise was not a word in the Orange vocabulary. The Order represented a distinct world view which remained fixed and unassailable despite the passage of time or fashion of the day.

In practical terms, the alliance between the Orange Order and the Conservative Party in Scotland was a marriage of convenience, and like all such marriages, there was no real love between the contracted parties. Rather, the agreement reached by the two parties constituted a commitment to pursue together specific aims and objectives of mutual interest and advantage. These were, essentially, religious issues such as the defence of 'Use and Wont' in state schools or opposition to the disestablishment of the Church of Scotland.

This is not to deny the early and significant Orange involvement in the formation of some Conservative Associations in West Central Scotland or the official presence of the Order in the inner councils of the Party, but these developments did not make the Conservative Party in Scotland a de facto 'Protestant' party. It might reflect Protestant interests and values in certain circumstances but it never became the bastion of Protestantism which, by comparison, the Ulster Unionist Party became.

In fact, by the late nineteenth century the Conservative Party was already expanding its social base in order to appeal to the increasing numbers of professional people living in the suburbs. The affluent middle class were about to become the backbone of Conservatism in the future. Such people tended to regard Orangeism with disdain.

The biblical fundamentalism of Orange clergymen like Gault or Thomson was completely at odds with the more liberal interpretation of scriptural truth they were accustomed to hearing in their pews on Sunday mornings. Bourgeois sensibilities and respect for law and order were offended by the sporadic outbreaks of violence which still attended Orange processions on occasion.

The changing face of Scottish Conservatism simply reflected social realities. By the 1890s, specifically religious issues were becoming less and less important to society at large. People were now living in a material world and Scotland, or at least industrial Scotland, was becoming much more secular in its general outlook. What 'Protestants' there were in the Conservative Party and in the Kirk for that matter tended to be middle class and whilst many working class Protestants continued to support, in principle, both institutions, they tended to be active members of neither.

Of course, Conservative candidates continued to promote 'True Blue Protestantism' and play the sectarian card in a number of working class constituencies in West Central Scotland for some years to come. The issue of Irish Home Rule was of great benefit to them here but Orangemen were becoming increasingly exasperated at what they perceived to be differences between Conservative practice and theory on those issues dear to their hearts. Echoing the sentiments expressed by Harry Long over 20 years earlier, the Grand Master, William Young, warned the Tories in 1897 that: 'Orangemen would only support a Conservative candidate

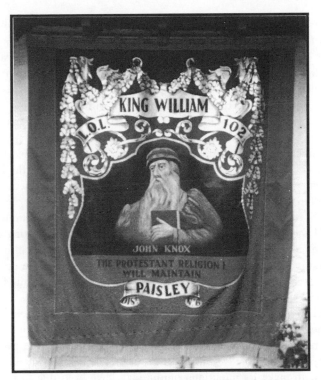

Leader of the Scottish Reformation: Maister John Knox

where they supported Orange principles. In the last election, Orangemen were the means in the West of Scotland of returning a great number of Unionist candidates and expected great things of a Unionist government.'[16]

The Grand Master may have expected 'great things' from his government but he did not get them. Indeed, Orange disillusionment with the Conservatives continued unabated. Government proposals to endow a Roman Catholic University in Ireland and its weak response to the issue of Ritualism in the Church of England[17] infuriated Orangemen. They regarded such developments as yet further concessions to Popery and a betrayal of their support.

A year later, a quite blistering attack on the Conservatives was made by the Rev A G Townsend, a Grand Chaplain of Scotland, at the annual Twelfth rally, held that year at Bellshill:

> The Glasgow MPs could come to their Orange soirees and talk a lot of amiable non-sense and take their votes at election times but when Protestantism was at stake, they sat like a lot of dumb dogs. Mr Balfour and other Unionists were smiling now on rebels and traitors...while they insulted the Orangemen and those who placed them in power. Let them as Orangemen be neither Conservatives or Liberals in the future but Protestants first and foremost.[18]

Orange criticism of the Conservative government stopped briefly following the outbreak of the Boer War in 1899. The Order supported the government's handling of the South African crisis which it apparently regarded as a struggle for civil and religious liberty.[19] Orangemen were encouraged to rally round the flag for the defence of the Empire.

However, criticism was resumed following the end of hostilities in 1902. The decision of the government that same year to ban an Orange procession at Rostrevor in Ireland was bitterly resented, particularly when the government appeared to be adopting a much softer line with Nationalist organisations like the United Irish League. For Orangemen, it seemed history was repeating itself. In the 1830s, they had also been penalised for their 'loyalty' whilst treasonable societies had been allowed to flourish.

Orange disgust with the government was now complete. At the annual Twelfth rally in 1904, held at Dumbarton, a resolution was passed supporting the Grand Lodge of Scotland's efforts: '...vis à vis the forming and working of an independent political organisation within the Association; a political organisation unfettered by any party ties and free to act either with or against any party in the interests of Protestantism.'[20]

This call of the Grand Lodge for independent political action was an extremely radical step which, if enacted, would have had serious implications for the Scottish Conservatives at this time. However, there appears little evidence that any such organisation actually got off the ground. The fact that the Grand Lodge was prepared to make its intentions public may have been due to rank and file pressure on it to take some sort of independent stand from the Conservatives who were now perceived as being soft on 'Romanism'. What the Grand Lodge was probably doing was firing a shot across the bows of the Conservative Party's complacency whilst hoping to appease its own critics within the rank and file of the movement at the same time.

This attempted show of political independence by the Grand Lodge was somewhat shortlived. The political storm clouds were again gathering as the country went to the polls in the General Election of 1905. The prospect of a Liberal victory raised the spectre once again of Irish Home Rule.

Perhaps sensing the disaster which was about to befall the government, the Grand Master, William Young, urged all Orangemen to: '...see that their names were on the voters lists in the coming September (date of election) and let them try to lead others to do their duty and support the Unionist Party at the next election.'[21]

Whatever reservations the Grand Master or any other Orangeman had regarding the commitment of the Conservatives to Protestant principles, the alternative was worse. The result, a landslide election of a Liberal government, ensured that Irish Home Rule would be back at the forefront of British politics. It gave the kiss of life to Orange and Conservative relations.

# Chapter 17
# 'MEN OF THE RIGHT STUFF'

ORANGEMEN in Scotland braced themselves for the struggle which lay ahead. It was inevitable that at some point in the future the Liberal government would introduce its third attempt at delivering Irish Home Rule. It occurred in 1910. Following a second General Election that year, the Liberals were again dependent on the Irish National Party to remain in office. The price of Irish support was Home Rule.

Well might Orangemen on both sides of the North Channel look to scripture for solace and support: 'Entreat me not to leave thee or to return from following after thee; for whither thou goest, I will go; and where thou lodgest, I will lodge; thy people shall be my people and thy God my God.'[1]

The Liberal government introduced a Government of Ireland Bill which provided for the establishment of a bicameral Irish Parliament. As with previous proposed legislation on this issue, the Bill actually represented a limited form of Home Rule but nevertheless it was still resisted with vigour by Unionists on both sides of the Irish Sea. However, this time, the government's majority in the House of Commons ensured its successful passage in 1912.

This action precipitated perhaps the gravest constitutional crisis of the modern era. The Protestant population in Ireland, particularly in Ulster where they formed the majority, were determined to maintain the British connection and have nothing whatsoever to do with Home Rule. Ulster Unionists were prepared to defy the government and by physical force, if necessary. The Orange Order was to play a full and leading part in the drama that was about to unfold.

Political opposition to Home Rule was channelled through the Ulster Unionist Council, under the strong leadership of Dublin QC, Edward Carson, and Belfast millionaire businessman, Captain James Craig. They were a formidable duo and they led a formidable movement.

The campaign got under way when a special day was set aside for the signing of a document[2] which committed those who signed it to opposing Home Rule by 'using all means which may be found necessary'. This document was known as the Ulster Covenant and it was based on the old Scottish Solemn League and Covenant of 1580 which established the principles of Presbyterianism in Scotland. This identification with the historical Scottish Covenant was not merely symbolic but representative of the close links existing between many people in both countries since the time of the Plantation of Ulster by Scottish settlers.

The Ulster Covenant was signed by a total of 471,414 men and women in Ireland and Great Britain. It had been made available for signature in Scotland in the various Unionist Rooms and Orange Halls across the country.[3] In Edinburgh some signed it on the 'Covenanters Stone' in the old Greyfriars churchyard.[4] Carson embarked upon a series of meetings and rallies in Great Britain in support of the Ulster Covenant.

In June 1913, Carson visited Glasgow and Edinburgh. Although his visit was staged under the auspices of the Scottish Unionist Party, there was a strong Orange presence at all of the functions he attended. Carson was met at the Central Railway Station in Glasgow by a huge cheering crowd and a number of leading Unionist and Orange officials including the Grand Master, the Rev. David Ness, and two Honorary Deputy Grand Masters, the Glasgow businessman, Charles Cleland, and Glasgow solicitor, Digby S Brown.

The main rally in Glasgow was held in the St Andrew's Hall and was attended by a full house of 5,000 people. So great was the demand to see and hear Carson that an overflow meeting of 1,000 people had to be arranged at the last minute outside the hall. The rally was also attended by four Scottish Unionist MPs,[5] most of the Irish Unionist MPs and leading officials of the Grand Orange Lodge of Scotland. Most of Carson's speech was devoted to emphasising the close socio-religious links between Ulster and Scotland.

After the rally he was escorted through the streets of Glasgow by a procession of about 5,000 Orangemen and a number of bands. Carson, who was not an emotional man, was visibly moved by the enthusiasm and support he had received from the Loyalist community in the Second City of the Empire. He told them: '...with you behind us, we care not a straw for the government and its allies.'[6]

Later that same year the Grand Orange Lodge of Scotland reiterated its position on Irish Home Rule when the following resolution was passed at the annual Twelfth rally, held in Paisley:

> We, the Orangemen of Scotland are satisfied that the proposals of the Home Rule Bill are a peril to the Empire; endanger the peace, progress and prosperity of Ireland and gravely menace the liberties of our fellow subjects in that country. We therefore pledge ourselves to aid them to the uttermost in their resistance to these proposals and in their determination to remain within the Union, as the sole guarantee for fair and equal treatment of all Irishmen of every creed and race.[7]

This was not to be mere rhetoric. The situation in Ulster was developing into a crisis. In January, 1913, the Ulster Unionist Council had united the various groups of 'volunteers' which had been emerging into a single body to be known as the Ulster Volunteer Force. This body was, in effect, a private army, which would be mobilised forcibly to prevent Home Rule being introduced in the North of Ireland. It quickly recruited 100,000 men between the ages of 17 years and 65 years, all of whom had signed the Ulster Covenant.

It was initially under the command of a leading Irish Orangeman, Colonel R H Wallace, and the Orange Order was its main recruiting ground. The various Orange Lodges in Ireland provided companies for the UVF, and Orange Halls were used for drilling and training the volunteers. A massive and largely clandestine arms smuggling operation was put into place and eventually the UVF was fully armed and equipped. It also had a new Commander, a retired ex-Indian Army Officer, Sir George Richardson.

A significant number of Orangemen in Scotland also joined the Ulster Volunteer Force. In Glasgow, seven companies of the UVF were formed, which were attached to the following District Orange Lodges: Calton, Cowcaddens, Clydebank, Kinning Park, Partick, and Rutherglen. These companies were euphemistically described as 'athletic clubs', probably for legal and security reasons.[8]

The strength of the Glasgow contingent was put at 1,000 fully trained men and about as many again partially trained. They were under the command of one Captain Webb, assisted by Lieutenants H Gordon and John Forbes and Sergeant Major John Vance.[9]

The Glasgow companies of the UVF held a parade in the city in March 1914 at which they were presented with their colours in the City Hall by the Rev. Professor Dr Cooper. About 500 men took part in the parade, and it was reported: 'A number of the officers and men wore war medals. The marshalling of the procession in George Square was witnessed by a large crowd. Perfect order prevailed and the men, who appeared to be well trained, marched with military precision. A special guard of about 30 men, armed with rifles, protected the colours.'[10]

A meeting was held after the parade which was presided over by Digby S Brown, Honorary Deputy Grand Master of Scotland, and a number of Grand Chaplains, including the Rev. James Brisby, the Rev. A J Campbell and the Rev. A MacLaren. Interestingly enough, none of the more senior Grand Lodge Officers were in attendance.

The guest speaker was the Marquis of Graham. He stated the Unionist position with great clarity:

There were in the North of Ireland, thousands of men born under the same flag and bred under the same system of government as the Scottish people. They were men who were contented with that system of government, though they were not contented with the present government. It was proposed now to drive these men out from under that flag and from under that system of government to another system. The proposal to put these men out of the Union was part of a political bargain...

Had not the Ulstermen a perfect right to protest being made the pawns in this political game? When they in Scotland remembered what their own country had passed through for the sake of religious freedom, their hearts warmed to these Ulstermen.

What were these volunteers for? They were out to back up the Ulstermen in their fight. They were men of the right stuff!!! Ulster would fight and Ulster would be right!!![11]

The leading figure behind the formation of the UVF in Glasgow seems to have been the Rev. James Brisby. An Ulsterman by birth, Brisby was an independent evangelical preacher who had established a church in the Calton district of the city. He was very much in the same mould as one of his predecessors and fellow countryman, the Rev. Robert Gault.

Brisby had been elected to the Glasgow School Board in 1909 as an Independent Protestant candidate and had already made a name for himself in Glasgow as a militant Protestant. At the annual Twelfth rally, held in Blantyre in 1914, he declared that in Ulster: 'Every man had his rifle with one to spare for those who came from Scotland to assist.'[12]

Whether Brisby had the official 'sanction', as it were, of the Grand Orange Lodge of Scotland for raising companies of the UVF, or whether he acted solely on his own initiative is not certain. The Irish Grand Lodge had backed the formation of the Ulster Volunteer Force to the hilt but the circumstances in Scotland were very different. On the one hand the Scottish Grand Lodge would want to be seen as reacting in a responsible manner to what was an extremely grave situation, but on the other hand it was equally obliged to be responsive to the pressure from its own rank and file, many of whom, of course, were Ulstermen by birth.

It was likely that, given this difficult dilemma, the Grand Lodge simply turned a blind eye to all paramilitary activity at this time. In any event, whether the Grand Lodge approved or not, it was clear that a number of Orangemen in Scotland were quite prepared to take up arms in defence of Ulster.

Whilst Loyalists on both sides of the Irish Sea were making their various preparations, the actual Home Rule Bill itself was proceeding somewhat tortuously through Westminster. It had been defeated twice by the House of Lords in 1913 but the government was utterly determined to see it become law. This was finally achieved on 18 September 1914, by which time the country was at war with Germany.

With the Empire now at war, the Home Rule legislation was put on ice. However, the sense of 'betrayal' was keenly felt in Ulster:

> She had pleaded and prayed to be counted still
> As one of our household through good and ill
> And with scorn they replied
> Jeered on her loyalty, trod on her pride
> Spurned her, refused her
> Great hearted Ulster
> Flung her aside[13]

It has been suggested that the response of the Loyalist and Orange community in Scotland to the Ulster Crisis of 1912-1914 was not as enthusiastic or as significant as in other parts of the country, notably Liverpool.[14] However, the evidence suggests the contrary. Whilst it is true that a crowd reported to be in the region of 100,000 people greeted Carson on his arrival at Liverpool, the Liverpool contingent of the UVF only mustered about 1,500 men in total.[15] This figure compares unfavourably with Glasgow. In addition, units of the UVF would almost certainly have been formed in other parts of Scotland, most probably Ayrshire and Lanarkshire. Furthermore, Loyalists in Scotland were actively involved in the elaborate gun-running operation organised by the Ulster Volunteer Force. Arms were stored for onward shipment to Ulster in towns across Scotland, including Leith, Clydebank and Renfrew.[16]

Apart from political, religious and physical support, financial assistance was also given to the Ulster Unionists in their struggle. Orangemen in Scotland donated at least £612, a not insignificant sum from a largely proletarian membership.[17] This contribution compares quite favourably with the £660 donated to the cause by the Scottish Conservative Association.[18]

Orangemen and others in Scotland played their full part in Ulster's struggle against Home Rule and many were prepared to fight and die, if necessary, but when their sacrifice did come, it was not in the North of Ireland but in the bloody battlefields of Belgium and France.

# Chapter 18

# THE EMPIRE AT WAR: THE ORANGE RESPONSE

TWO of the most important elements in the political philosophy of Orangeism—patriotism and loyalty—were put severely to the test with the outbreak of the First World War in 1914. However, it should be acknowledged from the outset that Orangemen in Scotland, as elsewhere in the British Empire, did not fail that test. The Orange Order is justifiably proud of the courage and commitment displayed by its membership during that terrible conflict.

The Order had always exuded a somewhat military character and many of its senior officials and leading figures in Scotland had come from a military background, including the Duke of Gordon, Lord Blythswood and Colonel Edward J Saunderson. Many military men tended to see war as a purifying experience which tested manhood. It was an experience which recalled nations to their sense of purpose and individuals to their sense of duty. Some even believed that war fulfilled destinies granted by God.

The Empire was at war and Orangemen viewed the Empire as the cause of freedom. The Order, worldwide, fully supported the war effort. Sir James H Stronge, Grand Master of Ireland, spelled out what was expected of Orangemen everywhere:

> It is not for Orangemen to limit their patriotism to service on our shores or to wait until the law compels them to take up arms. It is for us to do our duty betimes and with a good will as citizens of a great united Empire, trusting that God will deliver us from the dangers both foreign and domestic, by which we are now encompassed.[1]

There can be little doubt that Orangemen in Scotland did do their duty. According to one source, 85 per cent of the male membership of eligible age enlisted before conscription.[2] This is an impressive figure which compares favourably with Orange recruitment in other countries. It should also be borne in mind that this percentage might have been even higher but for the probability that a

Patriotism: the 36th (Ulster) Division at the Somme

significant number of Orange workers on Clydeside would have been exempted from military service owing to their preponderance in certain industries, such as shipbuilding and engineering, which the government considered crucial to the war effort.

Although actual source material detailing the activities of Orangemen from Scotland in military service is scarce, there is no such dearth of information regarding other countries. It is worth looking at some of this material since it indicates likely levels of comparison. It should also be remembered that many of the Orangemen who enlisted in the Australian, Canadian and New Zealand armed forces would have been Scots-born immigrants.

In Ireland the Ulster Volunteer Force, composed primarily of Orangemen, enlisted almost 'en masse' in the British Army to become the 36th (Ulster) Division. Whilst training in England, the Division was issued with at least 20 military warrants by the Grand Orange Lodge of England[3] to set up Orange Lodges in the ranks. On arrival at the Western Front, the lodges in the Division continued to hold meetings, initiate new members and even held processions when possible.[4]

The 36th (Ulster) Division suffered horrific casualties at the Battle of the Somme in July, 1916, losing 5,500 officers and other ranks, killed, wounded or missing in action, in just two days' fighting.[5] Many soldiers wore their Orange regalia going over the top and charged into the enemy shouting 'No Surrender' and 'Remember the Boyne'.[6] The courage displayed by the 36th (Ulster) Division won it four Victoria Crosses. As a consequence of this heroism, the Somme has become almost as revered as the Boyne in Orange tradition.[7]

In Canada the war effort was directed by an Orangeman, Sir Samuel Hughes, the Minister of Militia. It has been estimated that about 60,000 Orangemen in Canada enlisted in the Canadian armed forces.[8] Orange Halls and Orange Lodges were recruiting centres in 1914.[9]

The County Grand Orange Lodge of Toronto had 6,742 men in uniform by July, 1916.[10] Over 50 per cent of the Royal Grenadiers, a Toronto regiment, were Orangemen.[11] In 1918, the Provincial Grand Orange Lodge of Ontario West reported that some 600 of its members had been killed in action or had died from their wounds.[12]

It has been noted: 'The Loyal Orange Lodge had virtually transferred itself bodily to Flanders fields and in 1917, the Grand Lodge did not meet because of the desperate situation. Scarcely a regiment sailed overseas without a number of Orangemen among the officers and in the ranks.'[13]

Orange Lodges were organised in a number of Canadian regiments.[14] The total number of Canadian Orange casualties in the war has been estimated at about 8,000.[15]

The response from Australia was no less enthusiastic. In November 1916 the Grand Orange Lodge of Victoria pointed out: 'The Orangemen of Australia have, with their brothers in other parts of the Empire, responded nobly to the call for men. Many of our lodges have been depleted of their most active working members, so much so, that in many districts, lodges find it difficult to hold regular meetings.'[16]

Members from no fewer than 101 Orange Lodges in the State of Victoria alone enlisted in the Australian armed forces. Indeed, the first Australian to lose his life in the war was a member of a lodge in Melbourne.[17]

The Victoria Cross was won by three Orangemen during the war:[18] Robert Quigg, 12th Battalion, 36th (Ulster) Division; Abraham Acton, 3rd Battalion, Border Regiment; and Robert Dixon, Princess Patricia's Canadian Light Infantry.

Scotland was not without its Orange heroes either. The future Grand Master of Scotland, Lieutenant Colonel Archibald Douglas McInnes Shaw was Mentioned in Despatches twice and won the Distinguished Service Order in 1918. The future County Grand Master of Ayrshire, Lieutenant Colonel T C R Moore was also Mentioned in Despatches twice.

The rank and file were not forgotten either. A number of Scottish lodges have portraits of members in uniform adorning their banners.[19] These were probably men who did not return from the war.

As in other parts of the Empire, the Order in Scotland suffered significant losses during the conflict. Some source material is available here by way of example. In Anderston District Lodge No. 13, 12 out of 52 volunteers were killed in action and the rest were wounded.[20] In Pollokshaws District Lodge No. 28, a total of 19 volunteers were killed in action.[21]

If such figures were typical, and they probably were, then some primary lodges would have been forced to close whilst others would have been severely depleted. Certainly, the first post war Twelfth procession, held in Rutherglen in 1919, attracted only 15,000 marchers,[22] a figure well down on pre-war totals.

The generous response of Orangemen to the call of military duty was only to be expected of an organisation whose ideology and ethos was so steeped in Imperialist rhetoric and sentiment. If one looks at the Orange Order beyond the restricting parameters of its contribution to sectarianism, its Imperialist credentials are revealed. In so many respects, as an international movement within the English speaking world, the Order was an adjunct of the British Empire during the Victorian and Edwardian era.

In Australia, Canada, New Zealand and to a lesser extent, South Africa, the Orange Order was a bastion of pro-British interests and traditions. Orangemen, some of them Scots-born immigrants, were to the fore in the political and religious life of these countries, particularly Canada, and were collectively resolved to maintain the British connection. For Orangemen the world over the Great War represented, first and foremost, a Protestant crusade to safeguard the freedoms established under the reign of King William III, the Prince of Orange. These freedoms were guaranteed by Britain remaining a world power at the head of a great empire.

However, as for so many individuals, groups and institutions within society, the Great War signalled the end of an era for the Order. A lot of things would not be the same again. In Australia, Canada and New Zealand, it never fully recovered from the losses it sustained during the war. The loss of so many members in the prime of their lives was a grievous blow to the Order's confidence and its power.

Political perceptions began to change as well. In time, as the countries of the Empire began to loosen their ties with the mother country, so the Order came to be regarded as unfashionable, a relic of a colonial past modern politicians wanted to forget. The Order has managed to survive in Australia,[23] Canada and New Zealand, but it has been unable to re-capture its former influence.

Although the Orange Order, worldwide, suffered considerable losses among its members in the war, the movement in Scotland recovered by entering one of the most significant periods of growth in its history. The reasons for what amounted to something of a membership boom in the 1920s are not immediately obvious but they were certainly related to the profound changes which were taking place within the fabric of Scottish society in the aftermath of the Great War.

In the immediate post war period and for much of the following two decades Scottish society experienced a considerable amount of political and social turbulence. The social problems induced by demobilisation and mass unemployment, allied to an increasingly confident and militant labour movement, presented a formidable challenge to the established beliefs and traditions of Lowland Scottish society. In such circumstances, the opportunity existed for the Orange movement to exploit fully its customary role as a bastion of conservatism and royalism at a time when society appeared to be in a state of continual flux.

That such an appeal should still prove attractive was not in doubt. Indeed, the Order's patriotic stance during the war probably encouraged a number of men and women to join the movement on the cessation of hostilities in 1918. This may have been especially true of some ex-soldiers who on being demobilised were keen to maintain in civilian life the comradeship experienced in military service with their friends who were already members of the Orange Order.

Other factors were also at work. Many ex-soldiers found it difficult to find employment upon their return to civilian life and some became very bitter, not surprisingly perhaps, that their sacrifice should go so unrewarded in a country seemingly ungrateful for their patriotism. As a Loyalist fraternity the Order was ideally placed to offer these men some solace and a limited degree of support. Although the Order was genuinely sympathetic to the sorry plight of many ex-servicemen, it also took the opportunity to exploit their situation for sectarian advantage.

This took the form of traditional militant Protestant scapegoating. It was suggested that whilst loyal Protestants were fighting for King and Country, Catholic Irish immigrants and their descendants were busily stealing their jobs from behind their backs at home. The solution to this problem was simple: end Catholic Irish immigration and there would be plenty of jobs for ex-servicemen.[24] When confronted with the misery of unemployment some ex-soldiers would no doubt have found such explanations of their predicament entirely plausible in a society so permeated by religious division.

The Orange Order played on notions of what it perceived to be Roman Catholic disloyalty and allied these to the Bolshevism it alleged was rampant in the labour movement. This correlation, termed 'an unholy alliance of Papists and Atheists', offered a post–war critique of society which however illogical it may have been, was nevertheless not entirely out of step with the prevailing attitudes held by many Scots in all social classes at this time.

Whatever reasons individuals had for joining the Order, the fact remains that membership increased dramatically during the 1920s. The two best years during this period were 1920 and 1925 as the following figures indicate:[25]

|           | 1920 | 1925 |
|-----------|------|------|
| Men       | 1588 | 950  |
| Women     | 806  | 1048 |
| Juveniles | 1751 | 760  |
| Total     | 4145 | 2758 |

Another, though less reliable, indicator of the Order's growth are contemporary newspaper estimates of attendances at the annual Twelfth processions. Although the figures quoted for the years between 1921 and 1939 are not entirely consistent, they nevertheless indicate that the Order never had fewer than 40,000 members on parade each year during this period.[26]

Part of this increase in membership is accounted for by the growth of womens' lodges and juvenile lodges. By 1924 there were about 100 womens' lodges in Scotland.[27] Ten years later the number of womens' lodges had doubled to almost 200.[28]

The Ladies Orange Association of Scotland, as it was known, had proved a success and would continue to grow in the foreseeable future. In 1929 it was permitted to elect its own Grand Mistress[29] and to all intents and purposes became an autonomous body whilst continuing to operate under the jurisdiction of the Loyal Orange Institution of Scotland.

Juvenile lodges had first been sanctioned by the Grand Lodge as early as 1875 and the first one was established in Paisley. At this time, membership was restricted to boys only. Development was somewhat slow, for by 1904 there were only about ten juvenile lodges in the whole of Scotland.[30]

However the Grand Lodge decided actively to encourage the juvenile section, with the result that a further ten lodges were established within the following year. The juveniles were then given permission to hold their own separate annual processions, under adult supervision, in 1908. In 1917 the decision was taken to admit girls also into juvenile lodges, which acted as a further boost to the overall membership of the Order.[31]

In the absence of the necessary primary sources, once again the actual membership of the Order in Scotland by the 1930s can only be estimated. Using the same calculations as before[32] and assuming there were about 350 male adult lodges, 250 female adult lodges and 100 juvenile lodges, then membership would have been in the region of 35,000. If accurate, this represented an increase of about 40 per cent on pre-war totals. It is also not too far removed from newspaper estimates of the Order's strength,[33] though these need to be treated with caution.

# Chapter 19
# 'ROME ON THE RATES'

THE Orange Order in Scotland was faced with three main issues in the immediate aftermath of the Great War, each of which contributed significantly to raising the political profile of the movement. Two of these issues, education and Ulster, had preoccupied the Order for decades, but the third issue, the rise of the labour movement, was to present a new and very difficult challenge to Orange orthodoxy. However, encouraged by its dramatic influx of new recruits, the Order was ready to fight its corner in the political arena.

The first of these issues, religious instruction in state schools, was placed very firmly back on the political agenda in 1918. In that year, the Conservative dominated coalition government passed, under wartime legislation, the Education (Scotland) Act in an attempt finally to produce one national school system for the whole country.

The schools belonging to the Church of Scotland were to all intents and purposes secularised in 1872. At that time, the Episcopalian and Roman Catholic churches decided to continue running their own schools on a voluntary basis. The funding for this came largely from within each religious community with the occasional bit of *ad hoc* assistance from the state from time to time. This situation did not last as both churches began to find it increasingly difficult to bear the financial burden their schools imposed upon them.

Under the terms of the new 1918 Act, the Episcopalian and Roman Catholic schools were incorporated into the state system. The bulk of these schools were Roman Catholic and Section 18 of the Act dealt specifically with them. In effect, Roman Catholic schools were transferred to the state sector on the understanding that a number of safeguards were met. These safeguards stipulated that only teachers acceptable to the Roman Catholic Church authorities could be appointed to teach, that Roman Catholic religious instruction was to continue to the same degree as before and that Roman Catholic clergymen be allowed full access to the schools in order to oversee and evaluate the religious content of the curriculum.

The Act effectively gave the Roman Catholic Church the power of veto on teacher appointments, in addition to guaranteeing religious instruction in their schools. However, despite the apparently generous terms of the Act, it is worth noting that the Roman Catholic authorities viewed the legislation with some suspicion at first. In the largest archdiocese, Glasgow, the schools were only 'loaned' to the local education authority until their trustees were satisfied that all of the terms of Section 18 were being fully implemented.[1]

The Act also removed almost all of the burden for maintaining and financing Roman Catholic education from the religious authorities. This was a considerable benefit to the Scottish church[2] and it was certainly the envy of its counterparts in England and Wales where Roman Catholic schools continued to be— and still are—largely funded by the voluntary contributions of the Roman Catholic community.

What was considered to be preferential treatment for the Roman Catholic Church provoked predictable outrage from sections of Protestant opinion in Scotland. The passage of the Act breathed new life into the various 'No Popery' factions in the country and indeed gave to them a certain degree of legitimacy which they had never previously enjoyed.[3] The general thrust of the militant Protestant argument was put by a Church of Scotland minister, the Rev. Fred Watson of Bellshill:

> The indignant opposition to the provision of Section 18 of the Education (Scotland) Act 1918 is that public money is being expended in educating an increasing section of the population, in the main Free Staters or their offsprings, in a faith and a loyalty hostile to the tradition and religion accepted by the vast majority of the Scottish nation...Why should we feed, clothe and educate these people who everywhere plot and plan for the downfall of Great Britain.[4]

This was old wine in new bottles but it represented a classic expression of anti-Catholic, anti-Irish tub thumping. All the traditional ingredients are there, including the suggestion of Popish plots and Irish disloyalty. It was a potent brew and amongst many working class Scottish Protestants it hit the mark.

Militant Protestants had a number of more specific objections to Section 18. The first again centred on the idea of 'betrayal'. The Act was passed under wartime legislation without any recourse to the country. This was regarded as typical of 'Rome' taking advantage whilst the country was still preoccupied with the war.

Secondly, it was argued that the Roman Catholic Church had been given preferential treatment. Some Presbyterians pointed out that when their schools were transferred to the state sector in 1872, the Church of Scotland received no safeguards at all. Thus, Presbyterian ministers did not have anything like the same degree of control over religious instruction in non denominational schools nor did they enjoy the same level of access which priests enjoyed in their schools. In addition, the Kirk had no real control over the appointment of teaching staff.

Thirdly, and perhaps most contentious of all, was the idea of 'Rome on the

Rates' which was to enjoy so much currency over the following two decades and even beyond. This grievance centred on the fact that under the terms of the Act, the state paid the salaries of all teaching staff. However, it was pointed out that many of the teachers in Roman Catholic schools were not state employees but members of religious orders who on receiving their salaries, passed them on to the Roman Catholic Church. The state could then be said to be indirectly subsidising the Roman Catholic Church. Militant Protestants were more blunt about it: 'Protestant Ratepayers' were subsidising the Roman Catholic Church.[5]

It certainly has to be acknowledged that whatever else the Education (Scotland) Act achieved, it provided militant Protestants with a golden opportunity to exploit anti-Catholic feeling over this issue. The Act effectively created a two tier education system on quite different terms. This enabled militant Protestants to argue that those terms favoured Roman Catholics at the expense of Protestants. It was all too easy to interpret the legislation as 'Rome on the Rates', particularly to a sympathetic audience.

An early test of public opinion on the education issue was the first of the triennial elections for local education authorities which were held in 1919. These education authorities had replaced the old pre-war local school boards and the elections were contested under a system of proportional representation. The largest of the new authorities was Glasgow, which was divided geographically into seven electoral divisions. A total of 45 seats were open to election.

The elections were open to both religious and political interests. The Roman Catholic Church took the initiative from the start in mobilising its vote. Through the auspices of the Catholic Union, it ensured that the maximum number of the faithful were registered to vote in each of the electoral divisions.[6] This preparation paid off since Roman Catholics topped the polls in six out of seven electoral divisions and all twelve of their candidates were successful.[7] These developments were a measure of the Church's determination to safeguard the rights it had so clearly gained in 1918.

The Orange Order was not slow either in mobilising its vote. The Grand Lodge issued a list of candidates which it considered worthy of support in each of the electoral divisions of the city. Orangemen were reminded: 'that it was of vital importance that good sound Protestant candidates should be elected who will see to it, while justice is done to every individual no matter what his religion or creed may be, that the Bible will continue to be taught in the public schools.'[8]

This statement is instructive as much for what it does not say, as for what it does say. The primary concern of the Grand Lodge in these elections was the retention of Bible instruction in state schools and not the repeal of Section 18 of the Education (Scotland) Act. Some may have expected the Order to have taken the lead within the militant Protestant constituency in the struggle to have Section 18 repealed. In actual fact, the Order's response, as a body, was much more muted than many anticipated.

Political considerations came into play. It should be remembered that the leadership of the Order was still tied politically to the Scottish Unionist Party and on an issue as sensitive as the Education Act, Orange leaders preferred backstage lobbying within the party apparatus rather than a high profile campaign which would only have succeeded in embarrassing those individuals in the Unionist establishment with Orange sympathies. There may even have been the realisation that campaigning against the Act would have been a futile gesture given the realities of post-war Scottish politics.

This is not to state that the Order in any way approved of the Act, as it most certainly did not, but it chose to fight its corner on the more traditional Orange hobby-horse of defence of Use and Wont. This had yielded electoral success in the past and it did so again. A total of five Orangemen were elected on to the Glasgow Education Authority, including four clergymen:[9] Sir Charles J Cleland, Maryhill and St Rollox; Rev. David Ness, Hillhead and Partick; Rev. James Brisby, Bridgeton and Shettleston; Rev. Victor Logan, Govan and Pollock; and Rev. John Weipers, Camlachie and Springburn.

It is not surprising that such strong Orange districts should return Orange candidates. The fact that two of the successful candidates, Cleland and Ness, were part of the traditional Orange/Tory hierarchy within the Grand Lodge merely illustrates the points made above. Cleland was the Chairman of the Glasgow Unionist Association and a Deputy Grand Master of Scotland. Following the election, he was appointed Chairman of the Glasgow Education Authority, a position he held until its demise in 1928.

Ness was minister of Whiteinch Parish Church and the Grand Master of Scotland. He represented the Orange Order on the Western Divisional Council of the Scottish Unionist Party.

Of the other clergymen elected, Brisby was, of course, already well known as a militant Protestant agitator in the city. His fellow Ulsterman, Victor Logan, was minister of the United Free Church in Bridgeton. John Weipers was also a United Free Church minister in Glasgow.[10] All three were Grand Chaplains of Scotland.

Ness stood down at the next elections, which were held in 1922, but the other four stood again and all four were again successful, as they were in 1925.[11] The Orangemen aligned themselves to the Moderate Party in these contests, 'Moderate' being a local euphemism for Conservative in the municipal politics of Glasgow. Both Brisby and Weipers took great interest in the work of the education authority, becoming members of its Committee on Religious and Temperance Instruction.

Not all Orangemen were satisfied with the Grand Lodge's somewhat tepid response to Section 18 of the Education (Scotland) Act. Amongst them was one Alexander Ratcliffe, a member of LOL 52 Edinburgh.[12] He was to become something of a bête noire to the Orange hierarchy as well as making for himself a full-time career out of anti-Catholicism.

Ratcliffe was born in Bo'ness but spent most of his childhood in Leith. He had a strict evangelical upbringing and as a young man became a deacon in a local Baptist Church. On leaving school, Ratcliffe had joined the Caledonian Railway Company as a clerk,[13] but in 1920 he formed an independent Protestant movement which he called the Scottish Protestant League (SPL). He devoted the rest of his life to this movement.

Ratcliffe's new movement made little progress until he began to publish a periodical entitled the *Protestant Advocate*. This was the first of many such publishing ventures he was to enter into in the coming years. However, the real catalyst for Ratcliffe's rise to public prominence was the education issue. In a pamphlet which he published on this subject, Ratcliffe wrote:

> When the Protestants of Scotland were fighting for their country and their Empire and those who were left at home were carrying on to keep the home fires burning, the Roman Catholics were busy with the time serving politicians framing an Act of Parliament that was to put the clock of the Reformation back and reduce Scotland to another Ireland.[14]

Like other militant Protestants, Ratcliffe regarded the Education Act as an act of 'betrayal'. In 1924, he and six other fellow travellers stood as Independent Protestant candidates in the elections held for the Edinburgh Education Authority. Only Ratcliffe was successful but his sojourn as the representative for South Edinburgh was a frustrating one. As the only militant Protestant on the Authority, he was alienated and completely impotent. He had campaigned for the repeal of Section 18 but had received no support for this from fellow members of the Authority. Similarly, when he proposed that no new Roman Catholic schools be built in Edinburgh, his motion did not even get a seconder.[15]

Disillusioned by such setbacks, Ratcliffe decided not to stand for election again in 1927, when his term expired. He was bitter and resentful at the lack of support he had received from the ministers of the mainstream churches represented on the Authority. However, he could not have seriously expected anything else. Anti-Catholicism had long since been banished to the fringes of the Kirk and the overwhelming majority of ministers in the Church of Scotland were simply not interested in such views.[16] Indeed people like Ratcliffe and his organisation were regarded as an embarrassment and quite beyond the pale.

Ratcliffe's overt militancy also brought him into conflict with the Orange Order. At first he attempted to court Orange support through the pages of the *Protestant Advocate* but he became increasingly critical of the Order's role in the life of Scotland. In 1923, he mused:

> Reformation within the Brotherhood is urgently required and what honest member of the Order can deny it? We hold Orangeism itself to be a Christian and desirable force and we are second to none in our admiration of its Christian constitution, lofty ideals and noble aims but is it at present an effective fighting force on behalf of Protestantism and righteousness?[17]

Ratcliffe had no doubts about the answers to his questions: it was certainly not an effective fighting force. As far as he was concerned the Order was rapidly degenerating into nothing better than a glorified social club. Whilst it continued to 'talk a good game', that was actually as far as it was really prepared to go in the defence and promotion of Protestant interests and values. Posturing on the Twelfth of July was all very well but in reality the Order was failing miserably to give concerned Protestants a bold and principled lead on the issues which mattered.

Ratcliffe's main objections to the Order can be summarised thus:[18]

1    The Order lacked any genuine evangelical commitment; it knew what was wrong with Roman Catholicism but failed completely to live up to the Bible based tenets of Protestantism it so fervently espoused.
2    The Order lacked political independence, being tied hand and foot to the Unionist Party; this had led to compromise and fudge on Protestant issues which had been sacrificed on the altar of political expediency.
3    The Order lacked moral discipline; in particular, the majority of the membership were intemperate whilst some were prone to violence.

These criticisms were not new and are still being made to this day but they have an added resonance coming from someone within the same milieu. They help to illustrate the growing deterioration in the relationship between Ratcliffe and the Orange leadership in the ensuing years and it was on the basis of such criticisms that Ratcliffe attempted to mount a rank and file challenge to the Orange/Tory hierarchy within the Order.

Disgusted in almost equal measure with the Kirk, the Orange Order and the Scottish Unionist Party, Ratcliffe concluded that: 'What is wanted today is a real Protestant Party in the House of Commons. A party of Protestant Christian men and women to do battle for the cause of Christ and Protestantism against the forces of political corruption and Roman Catholic plot.'[19]

Ratcliffe believed that in the Scottish Protestant League he had begun to establish the embryo organisation to achieve this objective. He decided to enter national politics in 1929 by contesting Stirling and Falkirk Burghs at the General Election of that year. The seat was well chosen, for the sitting Labour MP was a Roman Catholic, Hugh Murnin, whilst the Unionist candidate, Douglas Jamieson, had strong Orange connections. These circumstances afforded Ratcliffe the opportunity of not only opposing one of the very few Roman Catholic MPs in Scotland but also of embarrassing the Orange Order at the same time.

Ratcliffe stood as an Independent Protestant on a manifesto that was blatantly sectarian. Amongst the policies he advocated was the repeal of Section 18; the curtailment of Irish immigration; the government inspection of convents and monasteries; and the breaking off of diplomatic relations with the Vatican. In a high profile campaign he accused the Labour Party of being under the sway of 'Rome', a charge which was taken seriously enough for Ramsay MacDonald to come all the way from London to Stirling to deny.

In the event, Ratcliffe, although finishing bottom of the poll, received a credible 21 per cent of the total vote.[20] It was clear, as his Unionist opponents claimed, that his intervention in the contest only served to ensure the return of Hugh Murnin as MP. However, Ratcliffe saw it quite differently. He had been given useful publicity on a national stage and had achieved a far from derisory vote in return. This was to provide him with the platform he needed to continue the struggle.

# Chapter 20

# RISE OF THE ORANGE AND PROTESTANT POLITICAL PARTY

THE issue which really preoccupied Orangemen in Scotland in the aftermath of the First World War was the worsening political and social situation in Ireland, particularly the future status of Ulster. This was hardly surprising given the close bonds of family and kinship which existed between Orangemen on both sides of the North Channel, but it illustrates yet again the way in which the political horizons of the Order in Scotland continued to be dominated and orchestrated by events in Ireland.

The Irish Home Rule Bill became law in September 1914[1] but was put into abeyance by Parliament for the duration of the Great War. Although the government wanted to forget about Ireland, the Irish had other ideas. In fact the rule of law in parts of the South of Ireland had all but broken down and open violence had become almost commonplace. Nationalist frustration at the lack of progress towards self-determination finally boiled over in 1916 when a rebellion broke out in Dublin.

The Easter Rising, as it became known, failed in its immediate objectives. However, there was a sting in the tail. The government regarded the leaders of the rebellion as traitors and dealt with them accordingly. A number of them were executed for their part in the uprising. In so doing, the government displayed a lack of sensitivity and a level of vindictiveness characteristic of its dealings with the 'native' Irish.

The rebellion had enjoyed little support amongst the Irish people but when its leaders were executed the mood changed to one of great anger and sympathy for the victims. The government's action handed the Irish Republican movement a propaganda victory of immense proportions. It had created martyrs of the executed: martyrs for the cause of Irish freedom. It stiffened the resolve of all Nationalists to end British rule in Ireland once and for all.

On the resumption of peace in Europe in 1918 the government again turned its full attention to Ireland. It faced an insoluble problem. They could not keep the lid on Nationalist aspirations for very much longer. However, the Unionists, especially in Ulster, had already demonstrated their total opposition to any form of Home Rule. They had proved their loyalty to Great Britain and the Empire in its hour of need by the generous manner in which they had contributed to the war effort and they expected that loyalty to be repaid by the government.

Tortuous negotiations commenced between all three parties against a continuing background of escalating violence. The first stage of these talks was concluded in 1920 with the passage of the Government of Ireland Act. This set up two legislatures, one in Belfast for six counties of Ulster (Antrim, Armagh, Down, Fermanagh, Londonderry and Tyrone), and the other in Dublin for the rest of the country. The Act was a compromise which pleased neither Irish party, particularly the Nationalists, who essentially ignored it.

Further negotiations were re-opened in 1921. These talks resulted in a Treaty being concluded whereby all of Ireland was acknowledged to be a Free State with the proviso that the six counties in Ulster could opt out if they desired it. The Irish Treaty bitterly divided the Nationalist community into 'Free Staters' and 'Republicans'. The latter grouping rejected the *de facto* partition of Ireland which the Treaty implied and also the fact that the Free State would still be tied legally to Great Britain. A civil war then ensued in the South of Ireland which the government, displaying its usual heavy-handedness in all matters Irish, merely succeeded in exacerbating.[2]

There was not much rejoicing on the Unionist side either. Although partition represented a significant concession to Unionist opinion, it was only reluctantly accepted as the best deal they could get in the circumstances. It should be remembered that the point of issue for most Irish Protestants had always been the Union of Great Britain and Ireland. That is, all of Ireland. Partition was accepted because, given the realities of the situation, it represented a way of salvaging as much of that Union as possible.

Thus for those Unionists left inside the Dublin-led Free State, partition was a very bitter blow. There was particular sorrow, mixed with a great deal of anger, that the Ulster counties of Cavan, Donegal and Monaghan had been omitted from the settlement. Unionists argued that this represented an act of betrayal to the sizable Protestant population in each of these counties who had volunteered in such large numbers in the Great War, many of whom were not to return.

Indeed, the attitude of many Irish Protestants to the Treaty was that they had been betrayed by the government. Although the Treaty established a separate Parliament for the remaining six counties of Ulster, these six counties were, nevertheless, still regarded as being a part of the 'Irish' Free State.

In the event, the Unionist community in what became known as Northern Ireland exercised their right to opt out of the Free State in 1922 but the feeling that they had been 'sold out' by British politicians at Westminster was to colour their perceptions of mainland and Anglo-Irish politics for ever. It reinforced the Ulstermen in their determination to hold on to what they had and strengthened the siege mentality common to many Protestants in the North of Ireland since the time of the Williamite Wars. The old battle cry of No Surrender! was joined by a new one: Not An Inch!

Orangemen in Scotland had looked upon these events with a growing sense of bitterness and disillusionment. At a Twelfth rally in Pollockshaws in 1921, the Rev. Victor Logan thundered: '...to set Ireland free, led as she is at present, would be to set a mad dog loose.'[3]

Orangemen were becoming increasingly disgusted with what they regarded as mere posturing from Scottish Unionist MPs and senior party officials on specifically 'Protestant' issues like the Education Act and the Irish Treaty. The 'Protestantism before Politics' faction within the Orange movement was about to reassert itself, only this time with more concrete results.

That such a scenario should occur when it did was not totally surprising. The somewhat strained nature of Orange and Tory relations has already been identified. As early as 1876, Harry Long had warned Scottish Conservatives not to take Orange support for granted and attempts to form an independent political organisation were made in the late nineteenth century and again, early in the twentieth century. On both these occasions more important political factors had intervened to prevent it but this time Orange patience was finally exhausted.

Noting that a Conservative-dominated government had introduced both the Education Act and the Government of Ireland Act, the Grand Orange Lodge of Scotland withdrew its official representation from the Western Divisional Council of the Scottish Unionist Association as a protest in January 1922. The following month, under the direction of the Grand Lodge, the Orange and Protestant Political Party (OPPP) was formed in Glasgow.[4]

Although it is evident that the Grand Lodge supported the formation of the OPPP, it is interesting to speculate on just how much this was a response to rank and file pressure from within the Order itself. Many ordinary members would have been deeply unhappy with a leadership seen to be acquiescing with political allies who were perceived to have sold Irish and Scottish loyalists down the river. In these circumstances, the formation of the OPPP, under Grand Lodge supervision, could be considered as something of a 'damage limitation' exercise undertaken by a leadership fearful of alienating themselves too much from the traditional Conservative and Unionist establishment.

This explanation is offered in the knowledge that during its short life there appears to have been no occasion where the OPPP actually opposed the Unionist Party in an electoral contest. This would indicate that some sort of deal may have been struck between them. In addition, there would also be occasions where the OPPP instructed its members and supporters to vote Unionist.

So why was the OPPP formed? The formation of what appeared to be a separate political party probably did just enough to appease the resentment that many rank and file Orangemen felt for the Scottish Unionist Party at this time whilst enabling the Grand Lodge to channel that resentment in a more constructive direction than might otherwise have occurred had it done nothing at all.

It is probable that another factor in the decision of the Grand Lodge to set up the OPPP was as a response to the challenge offered to its authority over the rank and file by maverick militants like Alexander Ratcliffe and his Scottish Protestant League whose very existence was not only an irritation but also a serious threat to Orange unity.

It is also likely that whilst they would have been reluctant to sever completely their ties with the Scottish Unionist Party, most Orange leaders would have been keen to make some sort of protest over the government's apparent indifference to Protestant interests. Pressure may also have been exerted by the Irish Grand Lodge for them to do 'something'. By actually setting up their own political movement, Orange leaders in Scotland were again firing a warning shot across the bows of Unionist Party complacency. It was sabre rattling, but at least this time it had surpassed mere rhetoric.

As in so many other aspects of Orange historiography, primary source material relating to the development of the OPPP remains elusive. Thus, important factors such as the party's actual membership or its relationship to the Orange Order remain open to question. However, as some facts are added to what is hoped to be educated guesswork, a picture does begin to emerge of the aims and philosophy of the new party.

Membership of the Orange and Protestant Political Party was open to all Orangemen and women and probably other Protestants who were not actual members of the Orange Order. It is unlikely that anyone other than a militant Protestant would have sought membership or been eligible for membership. It is probable that local branches of the party were based on the District Lodge structure of the Order and consequently both local and senior officials of the party would have been exclusively Orangemen.

The President of the OPPP was one James Rice. He was a well known figure in Orange circles being the then Grand Secretary of Scotland. Within the party structure four major committees were established to look after respectively: Ulster, Education, Finance and Propaganda.[5] It is instructive and not at all surprising that Ulster and Education should be the two main political issues deemed important by the new party.

The public launch of the OPPP did not occur until October 1922. Its inaugural meeting was held in the St Andrew's Hall, Glasgow, and was addressed by the Imperial Grand Master of the Orange Order, Sir Joseph Davidson. He pointed out that the essential aim of the OPPP was to give political expression to the principles of the Orange Order.

Davidson stated that the party was pledged to support:

...their Orange and Protestant brethren and the Parliament of Northern Ireland and to support candidates for Parliament who were prepared to stand by Ulster and its loyal Protestant people; to promote the election to municipal and parish councils and education authorities, men and women of good Protestant character who were able and willing to serve solely in the public interest and who would support economy and efficiency of administration and to maintain religious and temperance instruction in the schools.[6]

It should be understood from the tenor of these remarks that members would not necessarily be precluded from continuing to support the Scottish Unionist Party provided its candidates were men and women of 'good Protestant character' who were prepared to 'stand by Ulster and its loyal Protestant people'. Although most Orangemen had come to believe that such people were thin on the ground within the official Unionist establishment, it would seem that the umbilical cord between the Orange Order and the Scottish Unionists had not been completely severed.

This was probably the intention of the Grand Lodge when it set up the OPPP. The party was, in effect, no more than a pressure group still operating within the normal parameters of Scottish Unionism. It intended to work with the Unionists rather than against them even if their actual relationship appeared somewhat opaque.

If the OPPP's relationship with its erstwhile political allies appeared ambiguous then there was no such prevarication in identifying Socialism as its principal political enemy. The Orange Order regarded Socialism as atheistic in character and undemocratic in philosophy. For both reasons, Orangemen were encouraged to oppose it.

At a Twelfth rally held in Ardrossan in 1924, Matthew Munn, a Deputy Grand Master of Scotland made the official Orange attitude abundantly clear: '...they could not be allied politically to Socialism and Communism and at the same time be true to Orangeism which stood for liberty and loyalty.'[7]

Within the confines of Scottish politics, there was an added dimension to all this. Orange leaders continually expressed the view that the various Socialist parties and organisations, including the trade unions, were completely dominated and run by Roman Catholics. Indeed the criticism went further, that not only were they run by Roman Catholics, they were run *for* Roman Catholics. The Order saw a political conspiracy emerging between Socialists and Roman Catholics, the object of which was the overthrow of the country's established 'Protestant' traditions and institutions.

The OPPP did not contest the General Election of 1922. It advised its members and supporters to vote for suitable Scottish Unionists or National Liberals. The following year another General Election was held which was notable as the only occasion when the OPPP actually contested a Parliamentary seat. It stood in the constituency of Motherwell and Wishaw. Even more notable was the fact that its candidate, one Hugh Ferguson, won the seat.

The OPPP's electoral success in Motherwell and Wishaw was a remarkable achievement and is worthy of some explanation. There seems little doubt that a unique blend of socio-religious factors in the constituency combined to produce what was a sensational result.

Part of the explanation may well have been connected to the struggle which was taking place at this time between the hierarchy of the Roman Catholic Church and the Labour movement in Lowland Scotland for the hearts and minds of the 'faithful', a struggle which became especially acute in Motherwell and Wishaw following the election of a Communist MP, J F W Newbold, in 1922.

Contrary to the opinions held by the Orange Order, the Roman Catholic Church was deeply suspicious of the political left, although it was acknowledged that the Labour Party and Independent Labour Party, as well as various other Socialist groupings, had become the principal beneficiaries of mass Roman Catholic support following the decline of the Liberal Party.[8] Church leaders were aware that in Motherwell and Wishaw, a constituency with one of the largest concentrations of Roman Catholic voters in the country, a large number of the laity had defied Church teaching and voted for a Communist.

Whether by calculation or divine intervention, the response of the Church to the challenge presented to its moral authority was swift indeed. During an industrial dispute at the nearby mining village of Carfin, the local priest asked some of the striking miners amongst his flock to errect a grotto, later dedicated to Our Lady of the Rosary. The miners complied and within a very short time the waters of the grotto were said to possess miraculous properties. Soon the grotto became a place of pilgrimage for thousands of pious Roman Catholics from all over Scotland, and in the summer of 1923 over 250,000 people visited Carfin.[9]

It was against this background of Roman Catholic devotion and piety that the electoral contest of 1923 in Motherwell and Wishaw was fought. It was clear that Newbold was going to have a major battle on his hands to retain his seat. In addition, he also had to contend with the opposition of a local populist, one Hugh Ferguson, who had fought the seat twice before, improving his vote each time.

Hugh Ferguson was born in 1863. His early life had been spent in the army and although he was too old for military service during the First World War, he had been very active in recruitment. He had also spent 19 years of his life as a miner in the local pits and was proud of the fact that he had been able to save £350 with which to start his own business as a scrap metal dealer. Brought up in the strict Plymouth Brethren sect, Ferguson also joined the Orange Order.

Ferguson turned his attention to politics, becoming a local school board member, councillor and Baillie in his home town of Motherwell. He then stood as an Independent Conservative for Motherwell and Wishaw in the General Election of 1918 but finished bottom of the poll with ten per cent of the total vote.[10] 'Hughie', as he became known locally, stood again for Parliament in 1922 and this time finished second to Newbold, who won the seat for the Communist Party. Ferguson captured 29 per cent of the total vote and finished well ahead of both Liberal candidates.[11]

Ferguson had built a solid reservoir of support in a constituency which had a strong Orange tradition. His election agent, one Ephraim Connor, also an Orangeman, estimated the local 'Orange Vote' to be between 3,000 and 4,000.[12] Although this estimate seems exaggerated, nevertheless there was a significant Orange presence in the area.

Yet another General Election was called in 1923. The contest in Motherwell and Wishaw would be fought between the Communist Party, the Liberal Party and, for the first and only time in a national election, the Orange and Protestant

Political Party. Ferguson's decision to fight officially under the colours of the OPPP was a gamble, but Connor had no doubts about the outcome:

...at the last General Election, Baillie Ferguson polled 7,214 votes, with the official Unionist Associations against him supporting the National Liberal, Captain Colville, who polled 3,966 votes, over 3,000 of which were Unionist voters but on this occasion, the Orange and Protestant and the Unionist Parties have come close together in support of Mr Ferguson and the likelihood is Mr Ferguson and not Mr Maxwell, the Liberal, will be the future MP for this division.[13]

Connor's optimism was justified, as the official result confirmed:

| | | |
|---|---|---|
| Hugh Ferguson (OPPP) | 9,793 | 42.0% |
| J F W Newbold (Communist) | 8,712 | 37.4% |
| J Maxwell (Liberal) | 4,799 | 20.6% |
| **Majority** | **1,081** | 4.6%[14] |

There were, perhaps, four main reasons for Ferguson's remarkable victory at Motherwell and Wishaw. The most important was the fact that Ferguson benefited from official Unionist backing in 1923, a situation denied to him in the election of the previous year. His nomination this time had been seconded by Thomas Muir, President of the Motherwell Unionist Association, and he was publicly supported by the ex-Unionist MP for the constituency, R W R Nelson, the candidate who defeated Ferguson in 1918. Ferguson's endorsement by senior party figures in the area would have encouraged a number of Unionist waverers to vote for him this time, and in a constituency as tight as Motherwell and Wishaw, this was not without electoral significance.

Tactical voting by Liberals would have played a part as well. It is quite probable, as Connor suggested, that a number of National Liberal votes would have gone to Ferguson as the only pro-government candidate in the contest.[15] In addition, since Maxwell's vote was reduced, it is possible that some of his support also went to Ferguson as the candidate most likely to unseat Newbold. Since both the Liberals and the Unionists would have regarded the defeat of the sitting Communist MP as a priority, Ferguson must have benefited from this strategy.

Personal and religious factors were also important in Ferguson's success. Despite being a controversial character, 'Hughie' had a large following in the area built up over a number of years. He had demonstrated obvious commitment to the constituency by serving as a school board member, councillor and magistrate. He was ideally placed to be the recipient of any sectarian 'fall out' arising from the remarkable events at the Carfin Grotto. In a constituency long accustomed to Orange and Green antagonism, Ferguson possibly benefited from a solidifying of the 'Protestant' vote.

Ferguson's tenure as the MP for Motherwell and Wishaw was short but controversial. He was able to prevent a Corpus Christi procession from taking place at Carfin in 1924 by invoking an obscure piece of legislation at Westminster which had not been enacted for almost a century. However, as explained in the next chapter, this calculated piece of vindictiveness backfired on him, for his intervention only prompted Roman Catholic interests at Westminster into action. They were determined to remove all remaining anti-Catholic legislation from the statute books and largely succeeded with the passage of the Roman Catholic Relief Act in 1926.[16]

By this time Ferguson had lost his seat. Another General Election had been held in October 1924. In Motherwell and Wishaw, the Communists decided not to contest, as did the Liberals. Hughie's sole opponent was the Labour Party candidate, one James Barr.

The selection of Barr was an astute move by the Labour Party since, as a minister of the United Free Church, he was ideally placed to appeal to moderate Protestants. It also gave Roman Catholics the opportunity of voting for a Labour candidate who had solid Christian credentials.

This combination of factors produced a not unexpected result:

| | | |
|---|---|---|
| James Barr (Labour) | 12,816 | 52.1% |
| Hugh Ferguson (OPPP) | 11,776 | 47.9% |
| Majority | 1,040 | 4.2%[17] |

Just as tactical voting had played a part in Ferguson's victory in 1923, so it played a part in his defeat a year later. During the campaign, Ferguson had constantly alluded to Barr's alleged 'Communist' support as his main electoral strategy. After all, he could scarcely accuse Barr of being anti-Protestant. However, he did accuse Barr of splitting the religious (i.e., Protestant) vote in the constituency.

In the event, Ferguson actually increased his share of the vote but not by enough to win in a two-sided contest. The key to his defeat was probably the decision taken by Liberal voters to back Barr as the more acceptable candidate of the two. Having played a major part in disposing of an 'extremist' in 1923, Liberals repeated the act in disposing of another, a year later.

# Chapter 21

# RAPPROCHEMENT
# WITH THE UNIONISTS

THE election of Hugh Ferguson was the single major achievement of the Orange and Protestant Political Party. However, the Party's independence was again seen to be compromised when Ferguson took the Conservative and Unionist whip upon his arrival at Westminster. Following his defeat in 1924, the OPPP appears to have tottered on for another couple of years[1] but in reality it had become a spent force.

The OPPP had never really enjoyed the wholehearted support of either the Grand Lodge or the movement and thus it always lacked any real sense of purpose or organisation. It had also become clear by the mid 1920s that the terms of the Irish Treaty, the midwife of the OPPP, were far from being the sell-out of Ulster Protestantism many Orangemen had predicted it to be. Lacking direction and genuine commitment, the Party was on a hiding to nothing and its situation became terminal following the election of a new Grand Master in 1925.

The new leader of Scotland's Orangemen was Lt. Col. Archibald Douglas McInnes Shaw, a man firmly entrenched in the Scottish Unionist establishment. Born in Glasgow in 1895, he became a partner in his father's engineering business and later served with distinction in the Great War, where he was Mentioned in Despatches on two occasions. He was awarded the DSO in 1918. An ardent Unionist and devout Presbyterian, Shaw entered municipal politics after the war and was elected a Councillor for the Maryhill ward of Glasgow in 1921.

Shaw then decided to pursue a career in national politics. His first attempt was at a by-election in Paisley in 1923 but he was unsuccessful. A year later he stood in Lord Blythswood's old seat of West Renfrewshire at the General Election and was duly elected as its MP. In so doing, Shaw became the second Orangeman this constituency had returned to Westminster and his success heralded a new chapter in Orange/Unionist relations in the country at large.

It is quite probable that Shaw would have been deeply unhappy at the Order's attempt at political independence in forming the OPPP and his elevation to the office of Grand Master in 1925 was almost certainly the Party's death knell. Indeed it is possible that the demise of the OPPP was a condition of his accept- ance of the Order's leadership. Alexander Ratcliffe was in no doubt about this point: the OPPP was killed off at the insistence of the traditional Tory establish- ment re-asserting themselves within the hierarchy of the Grand Lodge.[2] It is difficult to disagree with this assessment, given the Order's future political direction.

Shaw's stewardship of the Orange Order through the socially turbulent dec- ades of the 1920s and 1930s was characterised by his attempt to steer Orangemen more towards their religious obligations and away from political controversy. His attitude was summed up in remarks he made at a Twelfth rally at Cambuslang in 1927, when he appealed: '...very strongly to those who would associate the Order with politics not to do so. By making the movement political, they would rob the Order of a great deal of its strength.'[3]

Shaw continued in this vein when, at a similar rally at Kirkintilloch a year later, he bemoaned the growing secularisation of Scottish society and he urged all Orangemen to: '...do their best to maintain the traditions of the Church of Scotland.'[4]

Speaking at Whiteinch in 1934, he asserted that there were far too many 'Twelfth of July' Orangemen and that it was their duty as good Protestants to become much more actively involved in the life and work of their churches since this was the only true way to defend and maintain the faith.[5]

There was a curious paradox to Shaw's leadership of the Order during this period. He led what was in essence a politico-religious organisation yet he at- tempted firmly to separate these twin pillars of Orange ideology. His attitude can be partly explained by his utter determination to distance the Order as much as possible from the controversies and excesses of rival militant Protestant organisa- tions like the Scottish Protestant League and later the Protestant Action Society. It can also be partly explained by his own personal beliefs regarding legitimate political activity.

Shaw was an establishment Scottish Unionist to his bootstraps. He believed that it was so 'natural' for Orangemen to support unquestioningly the Scottish Unionist Party, that the act of doing so in itself was 'unpolitical'. In 1935 he spelled this out at an Orange gathering: 'If there were people in their Order who simply wanted to make political propaganda out of their Protestant faith, let them get out of the Order.'[6]

Shaw was attacking here the extreme politics of the Scottish Protestant League and the Protestant Action Society but it was precisely this attitude which militants like Ratcliffe found so sickening. To him it smacked of blatant hypocrisy and was a betrayal of the true interests of ordinary working class Orangemen. Ratcliffe regarded Tory grandees like Shaw as compromisers who had the gall to expect the rank and file to go on supporting the Unionists almost as a duty but receive nothing but platitudes in return.

However true such comments may have been in regard to other establishment

Unionists with Orange credentials, it would be inaccurate to suggest that Shaw was in any way 'soft' on Popery. Rather he preferred to go about his business in a more discreet manner. Indeed it was not long before his commitment to 'Protestantism before Politics' was put solidly to the test. The catalyst was Hugh Ferguson's action in preventing the Corpus Christi procession at Carfin in 1924.

Corpus Christi processions were not new in Scotland and in fact one had been held at Carfin since 1916.[7] The erection of the grotto in 1923 had made this small mining village a place of pilgrimage for thousands of Roman Catholics in Scotland. Up to this time the procession had been held in private church grounds, but the huge interest in the grotto had occasioned a public procession through the streets of Carfin in 1923.

The Roman Catholic authorities intended to repeat the public celebration again in 1924 but were astonished when told by the local police that they could not do so. When asked why, they were courteously informed that such a large public procession would cause major traffic congestion.[8] However, when the local priest started to query this explanation, he was then told that a public procession would, in fact, be illegal under Section 26 of the Roman Catholic Emancipation Act of 1829.[9] The procession did not take place.

This prohibition caused considerable anger amongst Roman Catholics and their case was taken up in Parliament by the Conservative MP for Ormskirk, Francis Blundell. A series of pertinent questions were asked by Blundell in the House of Commons during the month of July to which he received somewhat evasive answers. At first, Scottish Ministers reiterated the original explanation offered by the local police that the procession had been prohibited due to expected traffic congestion in Carfin and the surrounding area. When Blundell pointed out that this consideration never seemed to prevent other processions from taking place, including those of the Orange Order, he was then informed officially that Corpus Christi processions were illegal under the 1829 Act.

The Labour MP for Glasgow Gorbals, George Buchanan, wanted to know who was responsible for invoking the legislation. Again, Ministers were evasive and would only state that the police had acted on advice from a 'higher authority'. It was at this point that Ferguson admitted that he had sounded out the Scottish Secretary on his views regarding the legality of Corpus Christi processions. When it was clear to Ferguson that the Scottish Secretary was not prepared to do anything about the matter, he took the necessary legal action himself to have it prohibited.[11]

Ferguson boldly defended his action in the House of Commons. During the ensuing debates on the issue he mischievously asked the Scottish Secretary whether he was aware that the carrying of the Host in public procession was against the law and whether he intended to make arrangements for prosecuting the Roman Catholic authorities accordingly.[12] On another occasion, he alleged that bottles of water from the grotto were being sold at five shillings each and he again demanded the prosecution of the Roman Catholic authorities, this time for 'fraud'.[13]

In August 1924 Blundell introduced a Roman Catholic Relief Bill, designed to give Roman Catholics in the country a level of civil and religious equality on a par with every other citizen. Due to a variety of circumstances, the Bill never got to the stage of a third reading that year. Attempts continued to be made to introduce the legislation and in March 1926, Dennis Herbest, the Conservative MP for Watford, introduced a Private Members Bill to 'provide for the further relief of his Majesty's Roman Catholic subjects'.[14]

The Bill received its third reading in December 1926 and was the subject of some heated debate involving the small minority of MPs who opposed it. Orange MPs were well to the fore within this group. The Bill was subjected to a number of proposed amendments, including one from Sir Alexander Sprot, the Unionist MP for North Lanarkshire, who moved that Scotland be exempted from its terms altogether. He was seconded, not surprisingly, by Archibald McInnes Shaw, Unionist MP for West Renfrewshire.

In moving the amendment, Sprot, who was not an Orangeman, pointed out:

> In the West of Scotland we have a large number of Roman Catholics and a large number of immigrants from Ireland. The numbers are increasing from day to day and this influx of Roman Catholics and Irish constitutes one of the problems to be dealt with in Scotland. It is one of the problems which all bodies, the civil authorities and everybody else, have to keep in mind.[15]

In Sprot's mind the terms 'Roman Catholic' and 'Irish' still seemed to be synonymous and they constituted a 'problem' to be dealt with. In actual fact, the real numbers of Irish immigrants coming into Scotland at this time were nothing like as high as they had been in the nineteenth century. Sprot was being disingenuous on this point when what he was really concerned about was what he regarded as the failure and lack of will on the part of the Scots-born descendants of these immigrants to assimilate themselves fully into the fabric of Scottish society. He believed the Bill, if enacted, would lead to an increase in sectarian friction between the immigrant Irish or their descendants and the native Scots.

Shaw, in seconding the amendment, preferred to play down this aspect of the Bill's potential. He chose to focus on the religious impact of the Bill and he included in his comments some special pleading for the Orange Order:

> We feel that more time should be given to allow Presbyterian opinion in Scotland to get more knowledge of this subject and I hope the House will therefore allow Scotland to remain out of this Bill for the time being. The Honourable and gallant Member who moved the amendment has mentioned the fact that there are a number of Orangemen in Scotland. They are a very gallant and law abiding people but they feel that there is more in this Bill than meets the eye...[16]

The House of Commons remained unimpressed by the arguments put forward by Sprot and Shaw and their amendment was soundly defeated by 200 votes to 22 votes.[17] The collective mind of the victors was probably summed up by the new Labour MP for Motherwell and the man who put Ferguson to the sword, the Rev. James Barr, when he pleaded for Scotland not to be seen is as 'the last refuge of bigotry and injustice'.[18] The various other amendments intended to water down the Bill were also defeated and consequently it was carried without a division. The Roman Catholic Relief Act became law on 15 December, 1926.[19]

Five Scottish Unionist MPs and one Scottish Liberal MP voted for Sprot and Shaw's amendment.[20] Of these, only one, Lt. Col. T C R Moore, was an Orangeman. Of the other MPs who voted for it, seven represented Ulster constituencies and nine represented English constituencies. Some of the Ulster MPs were Orangemen and all of the Ulster and English MPs were Unionists or Conservatives.

For the Orange Order, history had repeated itself. Just as its opposition to Roman Catholic relief had been defeated in 1829, so it happened again about a century later. However, this latest defeat was more keenly felt within the movement in Scotland. After all it had been a Scottish Orange MP, Hugh Ferguson, who had initiated the action which led to the Bill being drafted in the first place and it was a Scottish Orange MP, Archiebald McInnes Shaw, who had jointly led the fight against it becoming law.

It was perhaps ironic that at a time when Orangeism had already been confined to the margins of Scottish Unionism, the actual number of Scottish Orange MPs in the Party was at an all-time high. At the beginning of the 1920s relations between the Order and the Party had all but broken down,[21] yet less than a decade later, four Scottish Unionist MPs either had been or were members of the Loyal Orange Institution of Scotland. Although this was, in reality, still a very small percentage of the total number of Unionists in Parliament, it was testimony to the fact that the Order was not yet a spent force in the political life of the country.

Part of Shaw's contribution has already been noted. It may be of interest to look briefly at the careers of the other three Scottish Orange MPs to see if any conclusions can be drawn regarding their political outlook and behaviour.

## (i) Lt. Col. Sir John Gilmour

In terms of social and political prestige, Sir John Gilmour was the Loyal Orange Institution of Scotland's most significant recruit. A military man with a long and distinguished record of public service, he was a well known figure in the national life of the country during this period. It was said of him that:

> ...his urbanity and tact, his gentlemanly bearing, his courtesy and affability and his ready accessibility made him personally liked by both political friends and foes. Under his regime, marked by wise and prudent administration, the interests of Scotland were well and zealously looked after.[22]

Gilmour was born into the minor aristocracy in 1876 and like so many of his class pursued a military career. An officer in the Hussars, he later raised and trained for active service the Fife and Forfar Unit of the Imperial Yeomanry, becoming its Lieutenant-Colonel. The Unit was involved in particularly severe fighting during the South African War for which Gilmour was Mentioned in Despatches on two occasions. He later saw service in the Great War serving at Gallipoli, Egypt and Palestine.

In 1920, he succeeded to the baronetcy, by which time he had ventured into politics. A member of Fife County Council between 1901-10, his first attempt at national politics was unsuccessful when he stood for the constituency of East Fife in 1906. However, he was later elected the MP for East Renfrewshire in 1910 and held the seat until 1918. Following a boundary change that year, he then stood for the Pollock division of Glasgow and was elected. He held this seat until his death in 1940.

It was during his time as MP for Pollock that Gilmour joined the Orange Order. He became a member of a local lodge, LOL 172,[23] probably some time around the early 1920s. Needless to say he quickly assumed high office in the movement and was appointed an Honorary Deputy Grand Master of Scotland.[24]

Gilmour held several minor government posts before being appointed the first Secretary of State for Scotland in 1926. He held this post until 1929 and was responsible for the reform of local government in Scotland. He was then promoted to Minister of Agriculture and Fisheries in 1931. A devout Presbyterian, Gilmour was Lord High Commissioner of the General Assembly of the Church of Scotland between 1938-39.

Gilmour had a number of interests outside politics and religion. He had been a member of the Royal Commission on Horse Breeding in 1910 and was a Director of the Highland Agricultural Society. He was also a Director of the Caledonian Railway Company. He was awarded a number of academic honours during his lifetime and was made a Freeman of Glasgow. Gilmour was also a Member of the Royal Company of Archers.

When Gilmour died in 1940 his funeral was held in the small Fife town of Largo where the service was conducted by the Moderator of the Church of Scotland. Two memorial services were also held for him, one in Edinburgh at St Giles Cathedral and the other in London.[25]

## (ii) Lt.Col. Thomas C R Moore

Thomas Cecil Russell Moore was born in County Tyrone in 1888 and was educated at Trinity College, Dublin. He pursued a military career, joining the Regular Army in 1908. As a career soldier his war service was extremely varied. He served in France 1914-16; Ireland 1916-18; and Russia 1918-20. Moore was Mentioned in Despatches on two occasions and was also decorated by the White Russian government in exile. He was awarded the OBE in 1918 and the CBE in 1920.

Between 1923-24, Moore was attached to the Ministry of Home Affairs in the Northern Ireland government and this experience may have stimulated his appetite for a political career. He decided to enter national politics but was initially unsuccessful when he stood at Coatbridge in 1924. However, he finished a very close second, trailing the Labour candidate by only 57 votes. This may have encouraged him, for he retired from military service the following year.

Moore was elected that same year as the MP for Ayr Burghs and held the seat until he retired in 1964. Politically, he was a hard-line right wing Conservative whose well known views on law and order put him very firmly in the 'hangers and floggers' tradition of the Party. He was equally uncompromising in his attitude towards Socialism and was an almost fanatical anti-Communist. His strident anti-Left views were no doubt a legacy of his experiences during the Russian Civil War.

Moore's commitment to the Orange Order was in little doubt either, given the frequency of his appearances at Twelfth demonstrations in Scotland during the 1920s and 1930s. He was for a time the County Grand Master of Ayrshire[26] and seems to have been a popular enough figure amongst the rank and file of the movement. Of course, as an Ulsterman, Moore may already have had family connections with the movement and probably joined the Order in Ireland.

During his long Parliamentary career Moore sponsored a total of nine Acts of Parliament including the Slaughter of Animals Act and the Architects Registration Act. He was an enthusiastic supporter of animal rights and was associated with all of the leading animal protection societies in the country. He was a Trustee of the RSPCA.

Moore was a Fellow of the Royal Incorporation of Scottish Architects and a Director of the General Accident Assurance Corporation. He was a Freeman of the City of London. Moore was knighted in 1937 and awarded a baronetcy in 1956. He died in 1971.

### (iii) William P Templeton

William Paterson Templeton was born in the Mile-End district of Glasgow in 1876. He became a wood turner to trade and worked as such for a time in Falkirk. Being rejected for active military service during the Great War, he acted as an examiner of shells at Parkhead Forge in Glasgow. He then moved to Edinburgh to perform similar work in the munitions industry. It was while he was in Edinburgh that he became the secretary and organiser of the Unionist Workers' League in 1919.

Originally a Liberal Unionist, Templeton unsuccessfully stood for Parliament in Ross and Cromarty in 1911. He later stood as a Unionist in Banff in 1924 and was elected. He held the seat until defeated in 1929. He next contested the Shettleston by-election in 1930, caused by the death of the Labour Minister, John Wheatley. Although he was unsuccessful, he put up a good show and drastically reduced the Labour majority to only 396 votes.

Templeton then stood for Coatbridge in 1931 and defeated the sitting Labour MP. Although he retired from public life in 1935, he had the distinction of being the only Unionist MP to represent this solidly working class and predominantly Roman Catholic constituency in the inter-war period. His success in 1931 was largely due to the support he received from the Liberals, who did not put up a candidate.

Templeton was a member of 'True Blues' LOL 232, which met in Bridgeton,[27] although he may only have joined the Order at the time he contested the Shettleston by-election or shortly after. He was certainly a fairly regular attender at Twelfth demonstrations during the 1930s which would have gone down well with the sizable number of Orange voters in both Shettleston and Monklands. Templeton died in 1938.

There are obvious similarities in the profiles of Shaw, Gilmour and Moore. All three were military men who had each served with distinction in either the South African War or the Great War or both. All three reached the rank of Lieutenant-Colonel. Both Shaw and Gilmour were devout Presbyterians and both had served in local government. All three had successful business interests outside Parliament and all three were knighted. Of the three, Moore was probably more of a populist.

Templeton was perhaps the odd man out in that he was born into more humble circumstances and never attained either the political or social prestige of his colleagues.

A more difficult comparison to make is the level of each man's personal commitment to the principles of Orangeism in practice. As Grand Master of the Loyal Orange Institution of Scotland, Shaw's commitment is not in doubt. He led the movement from the front and his membership of it was not a secret to anyone. It is much more problematical to judge what membership of the Order actually meant to Gilmour, Moore and Templeton.

In the absence of primary sources, reliance has to be placed on public indications of Orange sentiment being expressed by the individuals concerned. One indicator is attendance at the annual Twelfth processions and rallies. It is clear from the evidence here[28] that both Moore and Templeton were fairly regular participants at these events and on occasion even made speeches from the platform. However, Gilmour does not appear to have attended a single procession.

Another indicator is parliamentary activity, though it has to be acknowledged that the opportunities for taking a specifically Orange line on any issues in the House of Commons were really few and far between. However, there were perhaps two such opportunities during the period under review. The first was the Roman Catholic Relief Bill of 1926. Shaw seconded the amendment which would have removed Scotland from the terms of the Bill and he was supported by Moore. Gilmour neither spoke on the issue nor voted on it. Perhaps he was not in the House during the debates.

The second opportunity arose during a debate on Scottish Home Rule in 1932.[29] A number of Scottish Unionists, including Lord Scone and Sir Robert Horne, made long speeches expressing their disquiet at the perceived failure of the Irish in Scotland to assimilate fully into Scottish society and indicating their fear of an Irish takeover should Home Rule become a reality in Scotland. This was certainly an issue dear to Orange hearts but there was a deafening silence during the debate from Gilmour, Moore and Templeton. Of course, they may not have been present, but this is unlikely.

Yet despite what appears to have been a marked reluctance at times to put their heads above the parapet, it should be remembered that men like Gilmour and Moore did not have to be associated with the Orange Order at all. This was especially true of Gilmour. The fact that they chose to be associated with the Orange movement must have been an indication of at least some level of commitment to the cause. Membership must have meant something to them, otherwise there was no reason to bother at all. After all it is extremely doubtful if their membership was an essential factor in any of them being elected, although here perhaps, Templeton may have derived some benefit. It is also worth bearing in mind when discussing this question that there were a number of other Scottish Unionist MPs and Parliamentary hopefuls who held similar views on politico-religious issues but had refrained from having anything whatsoever to do with the Orange Order.

The participation of Gilmour, Moore and Templeton, no matter how nominal it may have appeared, was a major factor in keeping the Orange Order tied politically to the Scottish Unionist Party in the inter-war period.

# Chapter 22

# ORANGEISM AND THE SCOTTISH LABOUR MOVEMENT

THE relationship between the Orange Order and the Labour Movement in Scotland was and continues to be complex and problematical. As suggested,[1] stereotypical conclusions and simplistic sloganising need to be abandoned if an approximation of the truth about this issue is to be successfully arrived at. Of course, it is clear from the evidence looked at so far that many working class Orangemen in Scotland did vote Unionist but it is also apparent from the same evidence that increasing numbers were beginning to vote Labour as well. In addition, Orangemen at the workplace were unionised and were caught up in the normal struggles of workers in employment.

Orangemen, unlike some academics, political theorists and sociologists, live in the real world. If there were and continue to be apparent contradictions in the political and social behaviour of Orangemen then they were and are prepared to live with these contradictions. It may be untidy, it may not 'fit' the sociological framework of some intellectuals, but that is the way it is. Orangemen, in common with most working class people, live a life of contradiction and there is nothing especially deviant about it.

In everyday life Orangemen did mix and continue to mix with Roman Catholics, both in the workplace and outside of it. They may even mix socially, and friendships between individual Orangemen and Roman Catholics are most certainly not uncommon in Scotland. However, these relationships do not stop Orangemen from participating in sectarian behaviour whether it offends their Catholic neighbours or not. Sectarianism, from whatever quarter, is an ugly beast but in Scotland at least its worst effects have more often than not been mitigated by the judicious application of common sense, good humour and contemptuous indifference from its intended victims.

Orangeism as a coherent political philosophy was ill-equipped to deal with the profound changes about to affect Scottish society in the aftermath of the First World War. Orangemen at the sharp end of the new social arrangements were required to readjust their thinking and behaviour in a number of key areas of every day life. Traditional political and religious attitudes were seriously challenged, even compromised, in the wake of the steady advance of Labourism. The Great War signalled the beginning of the end of the British Empire and with that, the relevance of much Orange ideology and rhetoric. Whilst sectarianism would remain as a badge of cultural identity for most Orangemen and some like minded working class Protestants in general, there was the growing realisation that their economic and social advancement in society depended more on the political left than it did on the political right.

One result of the outbreak of war in 1914 was the boom it created in certain sectors of the economy, particularly those industries most directly involved in the production of armaments for the war effort. On Clydeside, the industries which benefited most were engineering and shipbuilding, both of which were regarded as the domain of a skilled or semi-skilled and predominantly Protestant workforce. Many workers in these industries were given exemption from military service, and although the Orange Order was keen for its membership to volunteer for active military service, it was quite probable that a significant number of Orangemen would have continued to work in the engineering shops and shipyards for the duration of the war.

In order to prosecute the war effort more successfully on the home front the government felt obliged to increase both the supply and productivity of the labour force. This was to have serious local consequences for the engineering and ship-building industries on Clydeside. The government's aim brought it into direct conflict with traditional working practices long established and hard won by the trade unions. In 1915 the government passed a series of measures which severely curtailed the rights of trade unions, including the right to strike. Equally contentious was the introduction of what came to be known as 'dilution' whereby unskilled labour, including that of women, was permitted to perform tasks which were previously reserved for skilled men.

Although the trade union leadership accepted these restrictions as being in the national interest, they were bitterly resented by sections of the rank and file. Hostility was particularly prevalent on Clydeside with its high concentration of munitions work. This led to the formation of the Clyde Workers' Committee, an unofficial shop stewards movement, opposed to what it perceived as a government attack on long established rights and privileges at the workplace and on the working class in general.

The legend of 'Red Clydeside'[2] has been partly constructed on the efforts of these militant trade unionists. Many of the leaders of this movement were indeed Marxists drawn from political groups like the Socialist Labour Party or the syndicalists. They regarded industrial struggle as a means to an end, the end being social revolution. However, not all of the leaders of the Clyde Workers' Committee were out-and-out revolutionaries and certainly not the vast majority of the led. Rather, some merely wished the restoration of lost craft status.[3]

In 1915 the movement led a strike which eventually involved about 8,000 engineering workers. That same year, a rent strike erupted in Glasgow against profiteering landlords. This struggle was also centred in the shipyard districts of Govan and Partick as well as the engineering district of Parkhead in the east end of the city. The rent strike was mainly organised by women but does not seem to have taken on a particularly political temper.

Indeed, the rent strike was characterised partly by the adoption of slogans taken from Orange terminology such as 'No Surrender!'[4] This identification with the rhetoric of Orangeism was probably not a coincidence. The strike was largely centred in the Orange strongholds of Govan and Partick and if pictorial evidence is anything to go by, it was not the Red Flag which was hung out the windows of striking rent payers but the Union Flag. According to one account: 'one local woman who remained a life long Tory and Orange leader is reported to have played a prominent role in mobilising local tenants borrowing a fishmonger's bell as the alarm against the approach of the enemy.'[5]

Whatever the motivation of the leaders of the industrial unrest on Clydeside in 1915, the dispute was primarily directed against the dilution of craft status. Since Orangemen must have been reasonably well represented amongst the workforce in the munitions industry it is interesting to speculate on whether their presence was a significant factor in ensuring that the militancy exhibited did not take on a more revolutionary character than it did. Defending craft status and privilege was one thing but Orangemen as individuals or taken as a collective entity would have been strongly opposed to any attempt made by militant Socialists to impose 'Bolshevik' solutions on the Clyde.

The Orange Order in Scotland was not opposed to official trade unionism. It was opposed to unofficial trade union activity along the lines of that represented by the Clyde Workers' Committee. This situation created a great dilemma for Orange workers.

Orangemen were traditionally tied politically to an ideology embracing notions of what may be termed Protestant Unionism. This philosophy was based on class collaboration, Protestant unity and patriotism. It was held together economically by the continuance of Empire trade and the perceived benefits this brought to Scottish workers.

However, this adherence was doomed to failure in the long run given the contradictions inherent in capitalist relations of production, such as the inevitability of periodic bouts of unemployment or lay offs. In the 1920s and 1930s there was a growing awareness amongst Orange workers caught up in workplace struggle to improve conditions or safeguard trade practices that their material interests were better served by supporting an organised and official labour movement.

This development did not happen overnight but it did occur gradually during the inter-war years. This process illuminated the latent tension existing within the Orange movement between a leadership tied to the Unionists and supporting a pluralist conception of industrial relations and a membership largely composed of urban industrial workers continually facing the hardships, privations and uncertainties prevalent in an economic system prone to episodes of crisis.

The Orange response to the widespread industrial militancy which character-ised post war society can be examined by focusing on two specific disputes which occurred in 1919: the demand for nationalisation of the mining industry and the 40 Hours Strike

The 40 Hours Strike of engineering workers and related trades on Clydeside was instigated by the still unofficial Clyde Workers' Committee. It began in late January 1919 and would last for approximately two weeks. The main demand of the strikers was for a 40 hour week. Prior to 1914, the average weekly hours for engineering workers was 54 hours. The strike was centred in and around Glas-gow and involved some workers in industries related to engineering. It had some support from the Scottish Trade Union Congress but the dispute remained unofficial.[6]

From the outset there was less than unanimous support for the dispute from the workforce. A number of engineering shops and shipyards came out but the strike was not solid. However, the strikers were well organised and moti-vated. Their militancy eventually led to confrontation with non-strikers and the authorities.

The dispute took a particularly serious turn when strikers clashed with the police in the centre of Glasgow. This incident has passed into labour folklore as the George Square Riot or 'Bloody Friday'. The government was sufficiently alarmed by these events to send in the military to Glasgow to ensure that order was fully restored.

A crucial allegation made against the Clyde Workers Committee and others was that workers were being intimidated into joining the strike. There certainly was mass picketing of a number of major engineering firms and shipyards in the city.[7] These tactics alienated large numbers of workers who were otherwise quite sympathetic to the basic demands of the strikers. This view was encapsulated in a resolution passed by workers at Alexander Stephen's of Linthouse:

> that the unofficial strike committee are not authorised to act on our behalf; repudiate their action in calling a strike; uphold the decision of the Minister of Labour not to negotiate with them and in view of us having been forcibly kept from work by them, we call upon our executive to negotiate with the Minister of Labour for a settlement of this dispute.[8]

Similar anti-strike resolutions were passed by workers employed in some of the largest engineering firms on Clydeside including Howden's in Kinning Park, Babcock and Wilcox in Renfrew and the North British Locomotive Works in Springburn.[9]

Following the disturbances in George Square, anti-strike feeling intensified and became organised. A group calling itself the Patriotic Workers' League was established in the shipbuilding district of Whiteinch. It was apparently composed of 'loyalist' workers who were pledged to: '...stand by the representatives of the trade unionists of the country and to use our influence to maintain law and order.'[10]

The aim of the Patriotic Workers' League was to regain control of the trade unions from 'extremists' by ensuring the election of shop stewards who had a more conciliatory approach to industrial relations. This was a clear challenge to the Clyde Workers' Committee. Within a short period of time branches of the Patriotic Workers' League were organised in Govan, Yoker, Partick and Maryhill.[11]

During the second week of the dispute a large anti-strike meeting was held at Whiteinch Public Hall. It passed the following resolution:

> that this meeting of Whiteinch shipyard workers condemns the present strike agitation with the methods of mass picketing; that we express ourselves in favour of the movement for a shorter working week with no reduction in wages; that we return to work tomorrow and leave our official trade union leaders to secure in a constitutional way, our demands.[12]

One of the main speakers at this meeting was none other than the Grand Master of the Orange Order in Scotland, the Rev. David Ness. Of course, as minister of Whiteinch Parish Church, Ness may have considered it his duty to attend a meeting of such critical importance to the local community which he served but it is much more likely that his presence signified what was a directly political stance in the dispute. It is probably more than mere coincidence that Whiteinch became a centre of anti-strike sentiment.

Whatever Ness's actual relationship was to the anti-strike movement, there is little doubt that the resolution passed by the shipyard workers of Whiteinch would have reflected the views of the Orange Order on this dispute. Whilst supporting the strikers' central demand for a shorter working week, Orangemen both at Grand Lodge and rank and file level were utterly opposed to the way the dispute was being conducted. The fact that the strike was instigated and predominantly led by known Marxists was enough in itself to guarantee Orange hostility.

This opposition had important consequences for the eventual success of the dispute. The anti-strike movement appears to have been solidly rooted in those districts of Glasgow which had a sizeable Orange presence. It cannot be just coincidence that a number of anti-strike resolutions passed by workers during the dispute occurred in firms located in districts like Kinning Park and Springburn. In addition, the establishment of branches of the Patriotic Workers' League in such districts tends to support this theory. The Patriotic Workers' League may not have been a specifically Orange organisation as such and whilst its actual relationship to the Order remains unclear, it clearly enjoyed the support of Orangemen in its aims.

Whilst it most certainly is not being suggested that Orangemen as a collective and organised body broke the strike, this being due much more to an absence of strike pay and increasing apathy amongst the workforce, it is being suggested that the relative strength of the Orange movement in certain firms and districts of the city played a significant part in its eventual defeat.

Although the 40 Hours Strike was defeated, industrial militancy continued. Early in 1919 the Miners' Federation led by its left wing leader Robert Smillie came out with a set of demands which included a six hour day, a 30 per cent increase in wages and the nationalisation of the industry. With strike action threatened, the government prevented immediate industrial action by setting up a Commission presided over by a judge, Sir John Sankey, to consider the miners' demands and the future of the industry in general.

A national and official dispute of this type in the coal mining industry posed extreme difficulties for the leadership of the Orange Order in Scotland, given the strength of the Orange movement in the coalfield communities. The Grand Lodge was required to tread carefully on this issue for fear of alienating a substantial part of the Order's membership whose material interests and those of their families were at stake in the dispute. Just how sensitive Orange leaders were was highlighted by a quite extraordinary incident which occurred during the speeches at the Twelfth rally held that year at Rutherglen.

Acknowledging the ongoing dispute in the mining industry, the Order proposed a resolution expressing the hope that the government would at an early date bring forward legislation which would enable all classes to work in harmony for their mutual benefit and the prosperity of the country.[13] The absence of any criticism of the miners or their demands is noteworthy. However, it was at this point that some dissension appeared on the platform when one of the guest speakers invited to address the rally, J Buyers Black, interrupted the proceedings by proposing an addendum to the resolution.

Without any apparent prior notice to the Grand Lodge officers present, Black proposed: 'a request to the government to offer determined resistance to the attempted domination of the country by the miners and protests against the proposal to nationalise the coal mines and against the principle of direct action.'[14]

The Grand Master, the Rev. David Ness, immediately announced to the meeting that he would not accept Black's addendum and the resolution in its original form was unanimously adopted as submitted by the Grand Lodge. To give any official credence to Black's comments would have been disastrous for the Order and Ness knew it. There was little doubt that most of the miners were in favour of nationalising the industry and whatever the private thoughts of Ness and other Orange leaders were concerning this dispute, discretion was required with public comment.

For his part, Black, a future Unionist candidate for Bridgeton, seriously misjudged the situation.[15] He assumed that he could address an Orange gathering and simply churn out the party line without equivocation. In taking Orange support for granted he displayed a shocking lack of political acumen on an issue of such grave importance to many ordinary Orangemen and their families. In addition, he seriously embarrassed Ness and the other Grand Lodge officers present.

The difference in Orange attitude to the two industrial disputes under review is primarily explained by the Order's acceptance of a pluralist conception of industrial relations. In this framework, peace is regarded as normal and conflict is regarded as abnormal.

When trade unions pursue their demands through established constitutional mechanisms such as collective bargaining under the direction of elected and re-sponsible officials, the Order is usually unconcerned. However, when these mechanisms are bypassed and conflict arises it is because subversive elements or other malcontents have captured the trade union machinery for their own political ends. This was certainly the Grand Lodge appraisal of the 40 Hours Strike. That dispute was considered 'political' whereas the mining dispute was conducted through normal channels and therefore considered as 'legitimate'.

The changing political landscape of Scotland in the aftermath of the First World War was confirmed by the Labour Party's sensational electoral break-through in 1922.[16] The emergence of popular Socialist parties capable of winning electoral contests and of participating in, or themselves forming, the government of the country sent shock waves down the corridors of the Grand Orange Lodge of Scotland. Putting its minor deviant adventure with the Orange and Protestant Political Party behind it, the Orange leadership pulled up the drawbridge and stood four square behind the Scottish Unionist Party in opposing the Socialist challenge.

The issue was not as cut and dried for the rank and file as it was for the Grand Lodge. Ordinary Orangemen at the sharp end of the social and economic upheavals of the 1920s and 1930s were forming different, and, on occasion, contrary per-spectives from those held by their leadership. There developed during this period something of a struggle between Orange leaders on the one hand and the Labour Party and Independent Labour Party (ILP) on the other for the political souls of Orange workers and working class Protestants in general.

Between 1920 and 1939 unemployment never fell below 10 per cent of the available working population. The worst years occurred between 1931 and 1935 when the unemployment figure never fell below two million. The old traditional industries, such as textiles, iron and steel, shipbuilding and coal mining, started their long decline. As an example, the number of miners decreased from 1,250,000 in 1920 to under 800,000 by 1939. During the peak years of 1931-33, 35 per cent of miners; 43 per cent of cotton operatives; 48 per cent of iron and steel workers; and 62 per cent of shipbuilders were out of work.[17]

The consequences of this decline in an area like Clydeside and West Central Scotland where the iron and steel, shipbuilding and coal mining industries were so heavily concentrated, interdependent and labour intensive, were utterly devastating to the communities involved. The dislocation caused was perhaps most acutely experienced by skilled workers to whom the tragedy of unemployment was as much a pyschological blow, given their sudden loss of dignity and status within the community, as it was an economic one, which plunged them and their families into financial insecurity.

Many Orange workers and their families faced with these grim realities in their everyday lives increasingly turned to the Labour Party and the ILP as the best hope of mitigating their difficulties. However, this should not necessarily be regarded as a sign of ideological support for Socialist principles. Rather, it was more often than not a purely common sense response to the political realities of their situation.

This was an important point and one which seemed beyond the ken of the Grand Lodge to contemplate seriously. Orange leaders remained reluctant to deal honestly with the conflict confronting rank and file Orangemen between an ideology predisposed towards class collaboration and Protestant unity and their material interests which were so closely bound up with concepts of class unity and religious co-operation. Ordinary members of the Order could see nothing intrinsically wrong with giving their vote to a party committed to policies of full employment, social welfare and a free health service. For many Orangemen voting Labour was, and still is, an act of self defence given the normal state of their socio-economic conditions.

It is, of course, impossible to quantify how many Orangemen decided to vote Labour or ILP in any one constituency or ward in any given national or local election. One cannot analyse precisely what one cannot possibly know. However, given the strength of the Labour vote in the industrial belt of Scotland, it is difficult to escape the conclusion that some of it did come from members of the Orange movement as well as from other more likely and sympathetic groups and individuals in society.

The ILP was certainly in no doubt about this point. In its official newspaper *Forward* it was claimed that:

> there are literally thousands of Orangemen who are members of the Labour Party and there is a large number of Orangemen who are members of the ILP and these men will doubtless be anxious to know exactly wherein their Protestant faith conflicts with the principles and programmes of the Labour Party and the ILP.[18]

This statement was made in relation to a report which *Forward* carried over the alleged expulsion of an Orangeman from his lodge in Irvine because he had joined the ILP.[19] The newpaper asked the Rev. David Ness for an explanation of the Order's conduct over this affair but not unexpectedly none was forthcoming. It is doubtful if *Forward* was one of the Grand Master's favourite reads! The claim that thousands of Orangemen were members of the Labour Party and that large numbers were members of the ILP must be treated with caution. Whilst *Forward* would have been keen to publicise the support the Labour parties were receiving from such an unexpected quarter, it almost certainly exaggerated the extent of that support for propaganda purposes. Orangemen may have been willing enough to vote Labour or ILP but joining these political parties was something else entirely. It is doubtful if there were very many Orangemen who followed the example of their brother in Irvine.

Orange leaders characterised all Socialists of whatever hue as Marxists. They played the 'Bolshevik card' for all it was worth.[20] The very real distinctions in Socialist thought as represented by the Labour Party, the ILP, the Fabian Society or the Communist Party of Great Britain were quite deliberately ignored by a Grand Lodge which chose to see them all as dangerous 'Reds' hell bent on destroying the established customs and institutions of British society.

This simplistic analysis suited the Orange/Unionist establishment in the Grand

Lodge well. Stereotyping all Socialists as Marxists or Bolsheviks enabled Orange leaders to argue that membership of Socialist parties and organisations was incompatible with membership of the Loyal Orange Institution of Scotland. It was pointed out that the basis of Marxism was atheism and so as a member of an avowedly Christian society, no Orangeman could contemplate membership or support of any Socialist party. Socialists were to be regarded as disloyal.

Socialists were disloyal because they wanted fundamentally to change the British Constitution which Orangemen considered to be essentially Protestant in character and essence. From this it was argued that Socialists were anti-Protestant. Because they were considered to be anti-Protestant, they were therefore also anti-Monarchist and anti-Imperialist. Thus, they were essentially anti-British. To sum up the Grand Lodge view, Socialism was an ungodly, anti-democratic, foreign ideology completely at odds with British character and sentiment.

Orange leaders were also quick to stress what they saw as the similarities between the totalitarianism of the Soviet Union and the totalitarianism inherent in the Papacy. Both regimes were considered to be anti-democratic and anti-Christian in theory and practice. Here again the establishment of democracy was being equated with Protestantism. Wasting little energy in worrying about the logic of such a scenario, Orange leaders argued that Marxists and Papists were in league in a revolutionary conspiracy designed to overthrow the British state.

This 'unholy alliance' as it was termed was another manifestation of the Order's fixation with 'Popish plots', only this time the Jesuits had Reds in the bed with them. However, it does have to be acknowledged that the Labour Party and the ILP seriously courted Roman Catholic support.

Both the Labour Party and the ILP had looked favourably on the Education (Scotland) Act of 1918 with its committment to state funding of Roman Catholic education and self government for Ireland. Neither of these particular policies would have endeared these parties to the average Orange voter. In addition, there is evidence from Glasgow which suggests that the Labour Party deliberately cultivated links with specific groups from within the Roman Catholic community for political ends.[21]

The effects of any specific policies on the overall view which ordinary Orangemen entertained about the Labour Party and the ILP probably remains inconclusive if voting behaviour over the period under review is anything to go by. No clear pattern can be determined in those local authority wards or Parliamentary constituencies known to contain a significant Orange presence.

A review of local election results in Glasgow between 1921 and 1939 underlines this point.[22] In Govan and Kinning Park, for example, Labour regularly won Council seats despite these districts containing some of the numerically largest Orange Lodges in the country. On the other hand, Orangemen were themselves able to win Council seats in districts with a much lower Orange profile. The success of Jonathan Harvey[23] in defeating the sitting Labour councillor in Kelvingrove in 1931 was notable.

In looking at national politics a similar lack of consistency emerges. Govan remained a Labour stronghold throughout the inter-war period. Bridgeton, another district renowned for the fervour of its Orangeism, returned an ILP MP throughout the period. Indeed in James Maxton, the constituency regularly returned one of the most left wing MPs in the country. In the 1935 General Election his Unionist opponent was none other than the Grand Master, Lt. Col. A D McInnes Shaw, but even he was unable to unseat Maxton in 'Loyal Brigton'.

The continual success of Maxton in an area like Bridgeton begs the question as to how many Orangemen were prepared to vote for him, at least on those occasions he was not opposed by the Grand Master of the Orange Order. If some were willing to vote for Maxton, and it is likely that some did, then it must be assumed that more moderate Labour candidates would have also enjoyed Orange support in other constituencies.

There is another way of looking at this question. If some Orangemen were voting Labour or ILP then they were obviously not voting Unionist. All that the various local and national election results at this time seem to indicate again is the limited extent to which the so-called 'Orange vote' delivered electoral success for the Scottish Unionist Party.[24]

Whilst the Orange strongholds of Bridgeton and Govan were returning Labour and ILP MPs with monotonous regularity, other working class districts of Glasgow with a smaller but still significant Orange presence did manage to elect Unionists from time to time. Maryhill was captured by the Unionists in 1924 and 1931. Partick elected Unionists in 1923, 1931, and 1935. Springburn returned a Unionist in 1931.[25]

How electorally significant the 'Orange Vote' was in these particular contests is open to speculation. What happened to it when the seats returned to form and voted Labour or ILP? The 'Orange Vote' was never large enough in any one single constituency in Scotland solely to decide the outcome of any electoral contest. Of course, it could be a significant factor amongst others in determining an outcome in some constituencies at certain times in particular circumstances, for example, Motherwell and Wishaw in 1923 and Coatbridge in 1931, but that is all that can really be said of it. It was and remains a purely episodic phenomenon.

Whilst a majority of Orangemen probably continued to vote Unionist during the inter-war period, it was apparent that there were already an indeterminate number who were prepared to vote for the Labour Party or the ILP. This was despite the protestations and dire warnings of Orange leaders. By the 1930s it was quite clear that Labour was committed to social democracy and not Marxist revolution. Whatever else Ramsay MacDonald and the other Labour leaders were, they most certainly were not Bolsheviks! The Labour Party was obviously constitutionalist in character and many Orangemen have taken the view that a vote for it was not an act of betrayal. Of course, other Orangemen who voted Labour quite probably did not even bother to think too much about these considerations. If their behaviour was contradictory then too bad. They were prepared to live with that.

In looking at the relationship between Orangeism and Socialism, a curious paradox emerges which has already been suggested.[26] Orangeism with its accent on brotherhood, mutual aid and communal solidarity can be viewed as a perverse manifestation of some of the central tenets of Socialism. It mirrors traditional working class values at the same time as it does so much to negate them. That is the paradoxical situation in which the typical working class Orangeman finds himself. It may help to explain his social and political behaviour.

# Chapter 23

# RISE OF MILITANT PROTESTANTISM IN THE 1930s

THE sectional, ethnic and religious divisions characteristic of so much working class experience in the Central Lowlands of Scotland came suddenly to the boil during the Depression years with the rise of militant Protestant parties in the municipal politics of Glasgow and Edinburgh. The success of the Scottish Protestant League (SPL) in Glasgow and the Protestant Action Society (PAS) in Edinburgh was essentially a reaction to the disillusionment many people felt at the inability of the existing and traditional parties to deal effectively with their problems. Ordinary people at the sharp end of economic recession are not often interested in the myriad and complex issues surrounding their plight, they simply want something done about it, and fast.

The militant Protestants offered simplistic arguments and easy solutions and the type of populist sloganising and rhetoric they indulged in won the support of some people living in often desperate socio-economic conditions. Their success, albeit brief, was a local by-product of the times but it was also symptomatic of the sectarian tensions underlying Scottish society. The Orange Order, the traditional repository of militant Protestantism in Scotland, viewed the emergence of the SPL and the PAS with a well founded sense of apprehension.[1]

In 1920 Alexander Ratcliffe moved the focus of the SPL's attention to Glasgow as he believed this would provide a more fertile ground for planting his ideas and engaging in his activities. His recent experiences on both the Edinburgh Education Authority and during the election campaign in Stirling had convinced him that whilst an outright and blatant appeal to sectarian emotions could win him votes, it was probably not enough to secure him lasting electoral success. When he decided that the time was right for the SPL to contest Council seats in Glasgow, Ratcliffe was careful to include a strong populist element in his programme.

Ratcliffe's preoccupation with the repeal of Section 18 of the Education (Scotland) Act of 1918 was still well to the fore as were his demands for the ending of Irish immigration and the compulsory government inspection of convents and monasteries, but these concerns were allied to other policies designed to attract wider voter appeal, including an end to rent and rates increases and opposition to cuts in social services. Ratcliffe also focused on standards of conduct in public service. He argued for a reduction in Council salaries and for an end to what he termed 'free feeds' and the expenses-paid junkets indulged in by some city councillors.

Ratcliffe calculated that such a programme would appeal to both working class and lower middle class voters. His calculations were correct. He undoubtedly struck a chord with many voters in criticising the social activities of some councillors, especially at a time of financial hardship for so many people in the local community.[2] Of course Ratcliffe hoped to benefit from Protestant working class support and in so doing take votes away from the Moderates.[3] However, the programme of the SPL was to the left of the Moderates on socio-economic issues and it seems that Ratcliffe also hoped to attract Protestants who normally voted Labour. On this point, the Conservative press was in no doubt as to where the ideology of the SPL originated: 'the SPL was…presenting what is essentially a Socialist case wrapped up in the vestments of religion.'[4] Although it is an exaggeration to depict the SPL as in any real sense Socialist, the statement did accurately reflect the views of a section of the Unionist Party and in particular, its Orange 'tendency'.

Ratcliffe's optimism in moving his operations to Glasgow was fully rewarded in the ensuing years. Between 1931 and 1933, the SPL won a total of seven seats on Glasgow City Council:

| 1931 | Alexander Ratcliffe | Dennistoun |
|------|---------------------|------------|
|      | Charles Forrester   | Dalmarnock |
| 1932 | Robert Crosbie      | Kinning Park |
| 1933 | Edith Fairbairn     | Govanhill  |
|      | Angelina Selby      | Cathcart   |
|      | Archibald Jackson   | Dennistoun |
|      | Francis McGhee      | Camphill   |

The evidence from its electoral contests suggests that the SPL took about twice as many votes from the Moderates as it did from Labour.[5] Its best electoral performance was in 1933 when it took an impressive 33 per cent of all the votes cast in the election and won four seats. This was a great improvement from the previous year when it managed only 11.7 per cent of the total vote and won just one seat.[6] Of the seats won by the SPL, Dalmarnock, Dennistoun and Kinning Park were predominantly artisan wards with a significant Orange presence. The Order was a great deal weaker in lower middle class Cathcart and almost non-existent in Camphill and Govanhill.

By the time of Ratcliffe's greatest electoral triumph, relations with the Orange Order had all but ceased to exist. From his new power base on Glasgow City Council, he stepped up the level of his attacks on the Orange leadership and its links with the Unionist establishment. His disgust with what he perceived as the Order's utter failure to either defend or promote Protestant interests reached new heights. In his newspaper he pointed out: 'During the two years I have been on Glasgow Town Council, the Orange members on the Council have been dumb on every question pertaining to the Protestantism and Orangeism of Scotland.'[7]

Prior to the 1933 election, there were about eleven Orangemen on the city council, all members of the Moderate Party. Of these, Rateliffe was especially critical of the four who sat on the Education Committee for their refusal to support his motions against the 1918 Education Act.[8] Two of these Orange councillors were Church of Scotland ministers and Grand Chaplains of the Orange Order, the Rev. Robert Daly and the Rev. Peter Cowan of Maryhill Old Parish. When they and the two other Orange councillors on the Education Committee lost their seats at the election,[9] Ratcliffe could not contain his pleasure. Indeed, he boasted that the SPL had been instrumental in their downfall and he expressed his delight that the overall number of Orange councillors had been reduced in the election from eleven to six.[10]

Ratcliffe had become almost as hostile to the Orange Order as he was to 'Rome', but his constant barrage of criticism was already damaging the somewhat fragile unity and morale of his own movement. Orangemen like Councillor Robert Crosbie in Kinning Park were put in an intolerable position by these outbursts, and a year after his electoral success, he resigned from the SPL. His resignation should have acted as a warning to Ratcliffe but he seemed oblivious to the storm clouds which were gathering around him.

Another warning was the electoral contest in the Shettleston and Tollcross ward in 1933. Here, one James Crawford stood as an Independent Protestant against the SPL after standing and almost winning the seat for it the previous year. Crawford's intervention split the Protestant vote and prevented the SPL from having any chance of victory. Crawford was an Orangeman and was sponsored by a group calling itself the Shettleston Protestant Club. This group was in all probability a cover for local Orangemen out to spoil the electoral chances of the SPL and it indicates just how bad relations had become between the two bodies in parts of the city.

In fact, the SPL was beginning to disintegrate. This was primarily due to Ratcliffe's inability to get on with people, delegate authority or listen to advice. In 1934 Councillors Selby and McGhee resigned, the former implying that Ratcliffe was a virtual dictator. Forrester had also resigned in somewhat controversial circumstances.[11] Another blow was the resignation of the Honorary President of the SPL, Lord Scone, apparently sickened by Ratcliffe's never ending torrent of abuse directed against the Unionists.[12]

The writing was on the wall for Ratcliffe and the *coup de grâce* was delivered by one Matthew Armstrong, Kirk elder, Orangeman and Justice of the Peace. He stood against Ratcliffe in the municipal election of 1934 and in a close contest defeated him by a majority of 341 votes in Dennistoun. Ratcliffe had been outmanoeuvred. Armstrong stood as an Independent Moderate, thus guaranteeing Moderate support,[13] and was backed by the considerable number of local Orangemen in the ward. Both the Labour Party and the Independent Labour Party stood down and it is likely that Armstrong benefited from at least some of their support as the lesser of two evils. Labour voters may have disliked Armstrong but they detested Ratcliffe.

Ratcliffe's defeat in 1934 signalled the end of the SPL as an effective and coherent force in the promotion of militant Protestantism. As far as the leadership of the Orange Order was concerned it was a case of good riddance. For them, the rise to prominence of Alexander Ratcliffe and the SPL had been a profound embarrassment. Apart from any personal dislike they may have harboured for Ratcliffe as an individual, they regarded his movement and his leadership of it as a direct challenge to their own authority over the Orange rank and file.

Despite the manoeuverings and misgivings of Orange leaders, it is clear that ordinary Orangemen must have supported the SPL at grassroots level, either as members or voters or both. That is why the Grand Lodge refrained from openly or publicly criticising the SPL. This was hardly surprising. Such a tactic would have been very risky. Open criticism of such an overtly 'Protestant' organisation which in the tradition of Harry Long put 'Protestantism before Politics' would have seemed like treachery to rank and file Orangemen. For ordinary Orangemen the sectarian populism embodied in the programme of the SPL was what Orangeism should be all about and the Grand Lodge would have had some explaining to do if it intimated anything to the contrary.

The dilemma for the Orange leadership was that the SPL was clearly supported by many Orangemen. It was also identified, at least in the collective mind of the general public, as an 'Orange' organisation and yet it was led by what the Grand Lodge considered to be an egotistical and independent maverick totally outwith their sphere of influence. Ratcliffe was more than just a loose cannon, he represented an entire army which could be just as hostile to the Orange Order as the Church of Rome. The fact that he was successful exacerbated the Grand Lodge's difficulties.

In such circumstances the Grand Lodge could do nothing else but move with extreme caution. It continued to urge the membership to support Moderate Party candidates, some of whom were of course Orangemen, whilst adopting a somewhat muted position in regard to SPL candidates. Officially, the Order neither helped nor hindered the SPL. Orange leaders essentially abdicated their responsibilities in this delicate matter and left it to the membership to decide the best voting tactic to adopt in the light of local circumstances.

The high profile of Ratcliffe and the SPL had other negative repercussions for the Orange Order. It cannot be mere coincidence that sustained attacks on Orange processions re-appeared in Glasgow at precisely the same time as the SPL was winning seats on the city council.[14] The electoral success of the SPL had obviously raised sectarian tension and it seems that the Order bore the brunt of the anger, frustration and offence which many working class Roman Catholics must have felt at this time. It mattered nothing to them that relations between Ratcliffe

Local Identity: Renfrew Town Hall

and the Orange leadership had completely broken down.[15] Such nuances in militant Protestant circles went unrecognised.

These attacks were a reflection of the way in which sectional religious loyalties could be exploited in the troubled decade of the 1930s. Although the odd incident had continued to be a minor feature of Orange processions in Scotland since their re-introduction in the 1870s, the level and scale of the violence exhibited between 1931 and 1935 was of a much more serious and concerted nature. In 1931 and 1932, processions were attacked at various points along their routes.[16] In 1933, several affrays were reported from different districts of Glasgow. The main trouble spots were centred in the east end of the city and at Garngad, where the police had to make a baton charge to restore public order.[17]

The Grand Lodge, no doubt mindful of what had happened in 1857, were extremely concerned about these disturbances which were a serious threat to their aspirations towards respectability. The disturbances also represented a major embarrassment for an organisation which liked to be seen as supporting good citizenship and respect for law and order. This well-founded unease prompted the Grand Master, Lt. Col. McInnes Shaw to remind Orangemen that:

We want to maintain the dignity of our Order. The only way we can do that is by showing an example to other people. If we...allow our feelings to run away with us, it gives the opposition a chance to point the finger and say that is the behaviour of the Orange Order.[18]

It had been a principal aim of Shaw whilst Grand Master to steer the Order away from 'political controversy' of all kinds[19] and it was therefore particularly galling for him and other senior Orange officials that the movement was being brought into disrepute in this way because of the activities of some whose behaviour was completely outwith their control. However, although there were again serious street disturbances during 'The Walk' in Glasgow in 1935,[20] that was the last year that the level of violence exceeded the norm. By that time, Alexander Ratcliffe was already a spent force in Glasgow politics.

It remains a curiosity that at the time the Scottish Protestant League was disintegrating in Glasgow another militant Protestant movement was emerging in Edinburgh which would become even more successful than its West of Scotland counterpart. Why such an organisation should have done so well in the capital city of Scotland still requires a satisfactory explanation.[21]

However, an attempt has been made at such an explanation:

The rise of Protestant Action owed more to the angry eloquence of its leader, John Cormack, than to the prevailing political situation or previous sectarian unrest. For a brief period, he showed that even in the absence of deep and readily understood divisions, a city or community can almost be torn apart by the sudden emergence of a charasmatic individual who can move people to deeds which they would never normally contemplate.[22]

John Cormack was born in 1894 into a strong Baptist household. As a young man he joined the Army and served with the Argyll and Sutherland Highlanders during the First World War. More significantly for his future career, he also served in Ireland during the civil war of 1922-23. It may be that his experiences in Ireland served to fuel the anti-Catholicism he probably acquired in his childhood.

On retiring from the Army in 1923, Cormack found employment in the general post office in Edinburgh. However, an increasing amount of his spare time was being devoted to militant Protestant activities.[23] He had joined Ratcliffe's Scottish Protestant League and another group, the Edinburgh Protestant Society. He soon became disillusioned with both, regarding them as mere talking shops. Cormack was already developing his own ideas about combating 'Rome' and had embarked on a part time career of public speaking at the Mound in Edinburgh. Like Harry Long before him, Cormack railed against the perceived errors in Roman Catholic doctrine and the political machinations of the Vatican.

Cormack was making a name for himself and developing a loyal following. When he lost his job at the post office, he decided to make anti-Catholicism a full time career. In 1933 he and a number of other like minded individuals formed the Protestant Action Society.[24]

Cormack was determined from the outset that the Protestant Action Society (PAS) should be different from other militant Protestant organisations. The key to his vision was in the title chosen for the new society. The emphasis would be on 'action', aggression and high profile activities as opposed to reasoned argument, literature and compromise.

The political programme of the PAS was blatantly sectarian. It included the repeal of Section 18 of the Education (Scotland) Act of 1918; the expulsion of all Roman Catholic religious orders from Scotland; an end to Catholic Irish immigration into Scotland; an end to Roman Catholics holding commissions in the armed forces; and an end to Roman Catholics holding positions of authority in the judiciary.

Cormack's reasoning was quite unapologetically simplistic: 'As Romanists deal with Protestants in countries where they have full power, so we shall deal with Romanists in this country.'[25]

At the local level the PAS proposed the creation of a programme of public works as a solution to the unemployment problem in Edinburgh. Cormack entertained simple views on this particular issue. He equated levels of Catholic Irish immigration into Scotland to the local unemployment rates. End the former and the latter would be solved. Until such time as this happened, the PAS would encourage the promotion of policies designed to discriminate positively in favour of Protestants in employment, particularly in local government administration and direct labour works.

To sections of the electorate in desperate economic straits, it did not matter whether Cormack could justify any of the assertions underlying his programme. He offered simple solutions to complex problems. When he stood in the municipal elections of 1934, he could be assured that his simplistic scapegoating of the Roman Catholic community would win him some support. However, even he must have been surprised at just how much support would come his way in the ensuing years.

Cormack won the North Leith ward in 1934. Edinburgh's port elected a further two PAS councillors a year later. Its best electoral year was 1936 when it won 32 per cent of the total votes cast and gained a further six seats. This gave the PAS nine councillors on Edinburgh City Council.[26] The PAS seems to have gained the support of voters from both the Moderate Party and the Labour Party.[27]

The election of these councillors occurred against a background of extreme sectarian tension which had been orchestrated almost entirely by Cormack and the PAS. He had been true to his word that the accent of the movement would be on action. A major tactic of the PAS, designed to attract maximum press attention, was to disrupt the meetings of those perceived to be its opponents. An example of this occurred in 1935 when a large crowd of PAS members and supporters heckled and jostled guests arriving at the City Chambers for a reception marking the international meeting in Edinburgh of the Catholic Young Mens' Society.[28]

For Cormack such events were opportunities to be exploited in his campaign against 'Rome on the Rates' and were therefore fair game for a protest. A year later, he mobilised some 3,000 supporters to barrack a meeting of the Catholic Truth Society. The ensuing fracas required the presence of mounted police with batons drawn to restore order. This incident led to Cormack being arrested on a charge of breach of the peace.

Seizing the opportunity this offered, Cormack refused to pay the fine imposed on him and was consequently sentenced to 60 days' imprisonment. He only spent one night in gaol as his fine was paid by a sympathiser.[29] With this spell of self-imposed martyrdom under his belt, Cormack's popularity as a Protestant folk hero soared.

Cormack's greatest stunt occurred later in 1935 when a Roman Catholic Eucharistic Congress was held in Edinburgh. This event included in its programme an open air religious service on private property owned by the Roman Catholic Church. This purely religious occasion was marred when a hostile mob estimated at about 10,000 encircled the grounds shouting abuse and making threatening gestures at the participants. Special coaches bringing women and young adults to the service were stoned by demonstrators. Sporadic violence then erupted between the demonstrators and the police who were trying to restore some order.[30] This disgraceful behaviour led to a climate of sectarian hatred previously unknown in Edinburgh in modern times. In certain districts of the city, the local Roman Catholic community appears to have been on something of a red alert in the defence of their priests and church property, as well as themselves. It was fortunate for the future of community relations that the PAS ran out of steam as suddenly as it had appeared and that the Roman Catholic community did not rise to the bait.

The official attitude of the Orange Order to the PAS was one of ambivalence. Although Cormack's relationship with the Order was problematical he was on a much better footing with it than Ratcliffe had been. This was primarily due to the fact that Cormack was not anything like as critical or scornful of the Order as the leader of the SPL, either in print or speech.

In fact, Cormack only joined the Orange Order in 1933, becoming a member of a local lodge 'True Blues' LOL 188 in Portobello just as his own movement was about to take off.[31] He resigned from the Order three years later, concluding that it was another of the 'talking shop' organisations he had been so critical of in the past.[32] By this time, the PAS was almost at its zenith.

Another reason why Cormack enjoyed better relations with the Orange Order than Ratcliffe was the Order's relative weakness in Edinburgh and the Lothians. It therefore posed little threat to Cormack's dominance of militant Protestant activity in the region. On the other hand because the Order was so weak it did not feel it was in competition with or threatened by the PAS

At its height in the mid 1930s, the PAS had a membership of 8,000.[33] By comparison, it is doubtful if the Orange Order had 800 members in the entire East of Scotland at this time. In putting Cormack's level of local Orange support in perspective, it is worth noting that whilst there were approximately 250 Orange

Lodges in the West of Scotland, there were no more than 15 Orange Lodges in Edinburgh and the East of Scotland. The 'Orange Vote' in Auld Reekie was negligible.

Rather, the evidence seems to suggest that the activities of the PAS actually encouraged the development of the Order in the region. Thus, Midlothian District No. 52 was established in 1936. It was initially comprised of Cormack's own lodge, LOL 188, a Musselburgh lodge, LOL 252 and a ladies lodge in Leith.[34]

Although small in number, there is little doubt that most Orangemen in the Edinburgh area would have supported the PAS notwithstanding the reservations of the Grand Lodge. There is also little doubt that the activities of the PAS, both at the individual level of acts of personal violence and at the more elaborate level of stage-managed demonstrations and protests, would have been as much an embarrassment to Orange leaders and officials as the activities of the SPL had been in Glasgow.

Yet, as with the SPL in Glasgow, the Grand Lodge drew back from criticising the PAS by name and for the same reasons. The pragmatic approach undertaken underlined its fear that any criticism of such 'good Protestants' would alienate some of the membership and thereby cause dissension in the ranks. Its adoption of this tactic was probably the beneficial given that the Order emerged from the disintegration of the SPL and the PAS in one piece.

As one historian has argued:

> The Order has always had a tendency to distrust populists...It has usually been led by cautious men who defer to nobody in their anti-Catholic views but who have come up through a very formal bureaucratic structure and who are content to manifest their hostility to the Church of Rome in backstage lobbying and ritual marches rather than in dramatic political ways.[35]

Whilst this analysis is certainly correct, it actually goes deeper than this. The Orange Order regards itself as the sole repository of militant Protestantism in Scotland, with two centuries of experience in this field.

It does not take kindly to 'Johnny come lately' rivals who attempt to muscle in, as it were, on its chosen sphere of activity. The Order has managed to carve out a niche for itself as an established part of Protestant working class culture and this lends it almost a kind of moral authority which rival groups choose to ignore or make an enemy of at their peril.

# Chapter 24

# POST-WAR REALITIES

BY the end of the 1930s the storm clouds of war were again gathering over Europe. As early as 1936 the Grand Master, Lt. Col. A D McInnes Shaw, was speaking out against appeasement when he warned his audience at an Orange rally: 'Surely nobody thought that this country could prevent war unless we had the strength to do so. What was the use of this or any other country talking in terms of peace unless we were prepared.'[1]

Old soldiers never die but the Grand Master was reading the runes correctly. When war came in 1939, the Orange view was that it represented a struggle for 'civil and religious liberty' against the forces of evil as represented in the Fascism of Germany and Italy. There is no reason to believe that the Order's response to the outbreak of hostilities was any less committed than it had been in 1914.[2] Given this, it is probable that some lodges would have had a struggle to survive during the war years and most certainly after it.

However, on the face of it, it appeared to be business as usual. In 1949, in the largest ever gathering in the town up till then, around 25,000 Orangemen arrived in Motherwell to celebrate the Boyne anniversary with the traditional procession and public meeting. Included in the procession were 28 lodges and 16 bands from Northern Ireland and amongst the guest speakers was a young Belfast clergyman who was just beginning to make a name for himself, the Rev. Ian K Paisley.[3] The usual resolutions were passed pledging loyalty to King and Constitution, support for Protestant Ulster and expressing pleasure in the continued prosperity of the Orange Order worldwide.[4]

The new Grand Master of the Loyal Orange Institution of Scotland was Francis D Dorrian, a coal contractor and ex-councillor from the Lanarkshire mining town of Bellshill. Dorrian had risen up through the ranks of the Order and had been Senior Deputy Grand Master to Shaw before the war. However, the movement he now led found itself in very different circumstances from the movement led by his predecessor. It would be obliged to meet new challenges not only to its internal cohesion and structure but also to its external relevance to post war Scottish society.

When Frank Dorrian joined the Orange Order, it still had some influence within the Unionist Party of Scotland. This influence became progressively weaker during the inter-war period despite the presence of a rump of Orange MPs in the party. By the outbreak of the war, it had declined to the point where the Order no longer had any real voice at all in the affairs of Scottish Unionism. Dorrian himself seemed to realise the new circumstances, for he resigned from the Unionist Party in 1939.[5]

Dorrian's resignation was indeed symbolic as it represented a portent of the future. The marriage of convenience so stealthily constructed by Lord Blythswood, Harry Long and others almost a century before was about to be finally dissolved. Of course, there had been a number of occasions in the past, most notably in the late 1890s and again in 1922, when this had looked on the cards, but other factors had always intervened to keep the reluctant partners together. It was the war and its aftermath which changed their relationship for good and in so doing signified the end of an era in the political history of Scotland.

Most Scots by this time were living in a secular society and party managers saw that there was no longer any lasting political advantage to be gained by pandering to religious loyalties. There was the added realisation that the 'Orange Vote' had always been of limited value. It promised much but delivered little, leading many Unionists to the conclusion that the party was jeopardising broader support by maintaining any links, however tenuous, with the Orange movement.

Other factors were also at work. Although the Unionists maintained a residue of Protestant working class support well into the mid 1960s, the party was by this time solidly middle class both in membership and in ethos. In outlook, it was becoming more national and less parochial.[6] It had also begun to attract increasing numbers of upwardly mobile and professional Roman Catholics, not only as voters but also as members and candidates.

These changes left the Orange Order in Scotland in a state of political impotence. Since it no longer had the ear of the Unionist Party, Orange leaders were effectively marooned in a political wilderness. Although they continued to support the Unionists, their attempts to convince the membership to follow suit met with only limited success. An increasing number of Orangemen were persuaded that their best interests lay in voting for the Labour Party and they remained unconvinced that such a vote was in any respect a betrayal of their principles.

In time, even the Grand Lodge came to accept this situation, however reluctantly. There was no longer any point in attempting to smear the Labour Party. Orange leaders were obliged to accept political reality for what it was and not for what they wanted it to be. Labour had participated in the wartime coalition government and had won a landslide election victory after the war. It had become an established and trusted part of the British political firmament.

An obvious by-product of the Order's estrangement from the Unionist political structure was the loss of any remaining vestige of the élite or upper class support it once enjoyed. At various times in the history of their relationship there had always been a small number of Tory grandees willing to lend their name to the Orange movement but since there were no longer any formal channels of communication existing between the two bodies, this practice came to an end. The death of Lt. Col. Sir Thomas C R Moore in 1971 not only signified the conclusion of this particular facet of Orange and Unionist relations but also broke the last remaining link with the past.[7]

Loss of political influence was not the only problem which beset the Order in the post-war years. It was also clear that clerical support for its activities was seriously waning. The Order's relationship with the mainstream churches, especially the Church of Scotland, had always been difficult. However, there had always been a small number of Kirk ministers willing to be associated publicly with the Orange movement, and they were supplemented, as it were, by an even smaller number of clerics from other denominations, usually independent evangelicals.

Although it is not possible to present exact figures, the level of clerical support for the Order appears to have progressively declined from the high point of the late nineteenth century onwards.[8] This decline partly reflected changing perceptions in the church and in society as an entity. The growing secularisation of Scottish society exacerbated the problems which the churches had always faced in appealing to working class Protestants as a whole. As the churches became increasingly middle class in ministry, membership and outlook, so they became even more of an irrelevance to many working class families.

The drift of most of the mainstream Protestant churches towards ecumenism has led them to reject the type of militant Protestantism espoused by the Orange Order and similar organisations. The search for what unites Christians rather than what divides them was and is in vogue. The Order, with its Reformation theology and its stockpile of grievances against the Church of Rome was considered to be an anachronism. Churchmen remain unimpressed by the Order's dire warnings that ecumenism will lead in only one direction: Rome.

Even those evangelical clergymen who might be expected to be at least sympathetic to some of the Order's views face difficulties in aligning themselves with the Orange movement. This is partly explained by the fact that the vast majority of Orangemen appear to have very little real commitment to any church, let alone evangelical theology.[9] The working class character and nature of Orangeism in Scotland does not lend itself easily to an evangelical lifestyle and committment.

The sympathetic view, sometimes expressed, that despite it all Orangemen tend to be Bible loving if not Bible reading has left most clergymen, whether liberal or conservative, quite unimpressed. The continuing difficulties which many District Lodges in Scotland have in obtaining the services of ministers willing to conduct their annual divine services or other events is another sign of the Church's continuing disapproval of the Order.

Disillusionment with the perceived 'Romeward' trend of the Kirk and other mainstream churches led Orangemen in Glasgow to establish their own independent church in 1979. The County Grand Orange Lodge of Glasgow purchased the disused Barony North Church in the city's prestigious Cathedral Square area. The building was refurbished and given a new name, the Glasgow Evangelical Church. The 'Orange Kirk' as it has become known, is strongly evangelical and reformed in theology and has retained a thriving congregation.

For most of the late 1940s and the 1950s, the Order languished in something of a political and religious vacuum. It was a quiet time compared to the previous two decades, punctuated only by the ritual of the annual processions and commemorations. A succession of Grand Masters came and went, all of whom had served a lengthy apprenticeship in the movement before assuming the top office. Although no doubt worthy individuals in their own right, they were largely unknown outside the ranks of the Order.[10] This placid state of affairs was disturbed briefly by the extraordinary rise of the Rev. Alan G Hasson.

Hasson had been raised by Free Church parents in Inverness and had joined the Orange Order in Partick whilst studying for the ministry at the University of Glasgow. On graduating, he became a Church of Scotland minister in Bonhill, near Dumbarton. It was there that his outspoken views and colourful sermons proved to be extremely popular with his largely working class parishioners, and his congregation grew from less than 300 to almost 1,000.[11]

Hasson's impact within the Orange Order was just as dramatic. In 1955, he founded and edited the *Vigilant*, which was to become the official journal of the movement and his own personal power base within it. He sought to revive the Order by raising the standards of membership. Hasson implored Orangemen to be on their best behaviour during processions and he waged a long and persistent campaign against the open abuse of alcohol by the membership at public demonstrations and rallies.

Hasson was determined to raise the religious commitment of the membership, which he regarded as crucial if the Order was to have any continuing relevance within Scottish society. He wanted nothing short of a full spiritual revival within the Orange movement. He attempted to have church attendance a condition of lodge membership and he introduced Sunday afternoon services in the Grand Lodge Halls in Glasgow. Outwith the Order, he was vociferous in various Kirk gatherings against ecumenism.

Hasson's oratorical and literary talents, popularity with the rank and file and his status as a minister, combined to see him elected as Grand Master of Scotland in 1958. He was the youngest person ever to hold this office and only the second minister. However, during his meteoric rise to the highest office, Hasson had stepped on a few toes and had made some enemies within the movement.

The Order had never liked its dirty linen being washed in public and Hasson's persistent criticism of the shortcomings of some of the membership had rankled with some senior Orange officials. As early as 1956, the Grand Lodge had reprimanded him for some of the views expressed in the *Vigilant*. Hasson offered to resign as editor and did so a year later following renewed displeasure. In 1959, he became embroiled in a platform argument at a Twelfth rally in Belfast, to the astonishment of Orangemen on both sides of the North Channel.

That same year at an Orange church service in Bathgate, Hasson launched into an attack on what he perceived to be the poor leadership qualities of many District Lodge officials. This proved too much for George Watson, the District Master of Armadale District No. 26 and a much respected figure in Grand Lodge circles. Watson charged Hasson with bringing the Order into disrepute and Hasson retaliated by suspending Watson and the warrant of the District Lodge.

This was a quite unprecedented situation in the history of the Loyal Orange Institution of Scotland. Armadale District No. 26 embraced the small mining towns of Armadale, Blackburn, Fauldhouse, Bathgate and Whitburn and was one of the numerically largest Orange districts in the country. The suspension of its warrant and of George Watson would not have been popular within the movement as a whole and would have caused untold damage to its cohesion and unity. Hasson had put his authority on the line, but other events were about to catch up with him.

In February 1960, the Grand Lodge convened a special meeting to attempt to sort out the impasse between Hasson and Watson. However, by that time, Hasson had become seriously ill and there was a suspicion that he may have been misappropriating Grand Lodge funds. Later that year, the Grand Lodge pressed charges in court against Hasson and he was obliged to resign as Grand Master. The ensuing court case and attendant publicity did nothing to enhance the reputation of the Order.

Hasson's fall within the Orange movement had been as meteoric as his rise. He was important as a Grand Master who was willing to face up to and tackle many of the criticisms which people outside the Order often make of it. Whatever else may be said or written about Alan Hasson, he at least had the courage to do this, which is more than can be said of many of the incumbents in that office before or since.

Loss of political influence and lack of clerical support were serious enough blows to the confidence and vitality of the Orange Order, but the most potentially damaging threat to its continuing survival were the changes which took place in the socio-economic structure of industrial Scotland during the 1950s and the 1960s. Entire communities were disrupted as massive urban regeneration and slum clearance programmes were enacted in a number of the country's largest towns and cities. This was occurring at the same time as the traditional heavy industries of coal mining, iron and steel and shipbuilding continued their steady decline, leaving the communities which depended on them increasingly fragmented as people moved elsewhere in search of new employment opportunities or else faced the prospect of unemployment or an uncertain future. Such upheavals within the urban working class communities of the Central Lowlands posed great difficulties to the stability and future prospects of the Orange movement, for it was in precisely these communities that it had developed and entrenched itself.

Perhaps the most serious disruption to the Order's membership occurred in Glasgow. It more than any other large urban settlement was subjected to large scale planning and re-development during this period. Many parts of the inner city were demolished, including almost all of Calton and Kinning Park and substantial parts of Bridgeton, Dalmarnock, Cowcaddens, Govan and Springburn, all districts where the Order had a significant presence. It is not possible to estimate exactly how many members were lost to the various local lodges during these moves in population and resettlement but it must have been a significant number. Certainly some District Lodges such as Anderston District No. 13 and Partick District No. 17 never fully recovered their former strength once the urban renewal programme was completed.[12]

It is interesting to contrast this situation with that of Liverpool at the same time. When similar inner city clearance programmes took place in that city, the Provincial Grand Orange Lodge of Liverpool opposed them. It regarded the break up of traditional Orange districts like Everton or Kirkdale as a 'Popish Plot', designed to weaken the influence of the Order in the city.[13] It is perhaps surprising that similar concerns did not emanate from Glasgow's Orangemen. This may have been due to the fact that the districts of Glasgow affected were not as ghettoised or as ethnically segregated as those in Liverpool.

The Order was clearly faced with a serious challenge but it was dynamic enough to adapt to the new circumstances in which it found itself. To begin with, it managed to compensate for some of the losses it sustained by simply spreading into the new housing schemes built by the city authorities to accommodate the people relocated from the old inner city districts. Huge housing estates were constructed on the periphery of Glasgow at Castlemilk, Drumchapel and Easterhouse and it was not long before Orange Lodges began to appear in each. Indeed, the establishment of lodges in Drumchapel led to it achieving District Lodge status and local Orangemen were numerous enough to fund the construction of an Orange Hall in the area.[14]

The spread of Orangeism into the new peripheral housing schemes or estates of the older towns and cities was not merely confined to Glasgow. In nearby Paisley, lodges were established in Foxbar and Glenburn. In Greenock, a lodge was established in Larkfield, and similarly in Airdrie, a lodge was established in Gartlea. This particular pattern of growth has continued to more recent times with a lodge established in the recently developed Pennyburn district of Kilwinning.[15]

Of equal significance has been the expansion of the Order into the new towns, some of which were created to accommodate the overspill from Glasgow. This was particularly true of Irvine and East Kilbride. Of course Irvine already had a long established Orange tradition but the relocation of numbers of Orangemen from Glasgow encouraged a revival of the movement's fortunes in the town and led to the establishment of a new District Lodge in the late 1970s. A new District Lodge was also established in East Kilbride but it has not been as successful.[16]

Even more recent developments have seen the Order spread into other areas of the country not accustomed to any previous Orange activity. This penetration into hitherto virgin territory has been very gradual and has certainly not been without controversy on occasion. Attempts to establish a lodge in Portree on the Isle of

Skye had to be abandoned due to the amount of local opposition it encountered, but similar opposition was successfully overcome in another part of the Highlands at Inverness, where a lodge was formed. Other lodges recently established include one at Forfar in the North East of Scotland and one in Hawick in the Scottish Borders.[17]

The major concern of people living in such areas is with what they consider to be the importation of sectarian strife into the life of their communities. Of course, this has been a persistent criticism made of the Order in Scotland and one which it has always struggled to refute. Lodges like those established in Inverness or Hawick are usually the result of the efforts of a few dedicated Orangemen who happen to live locally. It remains to be seen whether they will be able to sustain any momentum over a period of time. They do not have the advantage of being anchored to specific industrial communities which have always been the traditional breeding grounds of Orangeism in Scotland.

In fact, the migration of labour has remained a factor in the continued growth of the Orange movement. The revival of the Order in the ex-mining town of Linwood in 1957 was encouraged by the establishment of a major car factory in the locality at the same time. At its peak, 'Purple Heroes' LOL 144 had one of the largest memberships of any lodge in Scotland.[18] Although as yet less spectacular in growth, 'Bon Accord' LOL 701 owes its existence in Aberdeen to the development of the North Sea oil industry which attracted migrant workers from all over the country, some with Orange connections.[19]

An interesting variation on this particular theme was the migration of Orange steelworkers from Lanarkshire to the Northamptonshire town of Corby in the 1930s. On arrival in Corby in 1932, they established a lodge[20] which, needless to say, was a quite unknown phenomenon to the local inhabitants. By 1958, it seems six lodges were operating in and around the Midlands town.[21]

The Order was clearly a focus of ethnic solidarity for these migrant workers as it had been for the Ulstermen who arrived in Lanarkshire a century before. It may even be possible that some of Corby's migrant Orangemen were themselves the descendants of the Ulster migrants to Lanarkshire, thereby demonstrating the durability of Orangeism as a social cement spanning several generations, two centuries and three countries.

The lodges in Linwood and Aberdeen are contemporary examples of a long established pattern of development in the history of Orangeism in Scotland. The coal mining communities had long been used to labour migration and social upheaval. Many mining settlements often lasted only as long as local pits were worked, and when coal stocks became exhausted, able bodied miners and their families moved elsewhere for employment.

The transient nature of the mining industry was the main factor in the spread of Orangeism to other parts of the country.[22] The establishment of Orange Lodges in Fife and the Lothians in the early part of the twentieth century was the result of migrant Orange miners moving from exhausted pits in Ayrshire and Lanarkshire.[23]

More recently the East of Scotland has become the main area of growth for the Order in the post war period. A number of new District Lodges have been created:

| | |
|---|---|
| Alloa District No. 61 | established in 1968 |
| Bo'ness District No. 62 | established in 1968 |
| Grangemouth District No. 63 | established in 1972 |
| East Fife District No. 64 | established in 1979 |
| Highland District No. 65 | established in 1980[24] |

The upheavals of the 1950s and the 1960s were successfully overcome and in fact led to a major re-structuring of the Loyal Orange Institution of Scotland. The expansion of the movement into new areas of the country and the overall increase in membership then occurring provided the catalyst for a change in its organisation. That organisation was in need of an overhaul as it had changed little since the amalgamation of the 'Association' and the 'Institution' almost a century before in 1876.

The basic pyramid structure of organisation was left intact with the various primary lodges forming the base. At the next level up, these primary lodges would continue to be organised into District Lodges, based on geographical location. The new proposal was the establishment of permanent County Grand Lodges,[25] also grouped by geographical area, which would shoulder some of the routine and administrative workload previously undertaken by the Grand Lodge. This would result in a structure comprising a Grand Orange Lodge of Scotland at the top; a second tier of County Grand Lodges; a third tier of District Lodges and at the base, the primary lodges.

An important feature of this new structure was that it retained the mechanisms whereby members were able to pursue an Orange 'career' if they so wished. Representatives were elected from each tier to the next tier guaranteeing the essentially democratic nature of the Orange movement. Within each tier, elections were also held for office. It was thus possible for any member who was interested enough and who had the respect of his brethren to assume simultaneous office in his primary lodge, District Lodge, County Grand Lodge and the Grand Orange Lodge of Scotland.

The original proposal to establish County Grand Lodges was submitted to the Grand Lodge by Bellshill District No. 8 in 1964.[26] After two years of deliberation, the Grand Lodge finally agreed to create three County Grand Lodges:

The reason Grand Lodge accepted District No. 8's proposal for discussion was the continual increase in membership of the Institution. This was creating problems of administration and making Grand Lodge meetings extremely long and tedious as business of a very minor nature required to be discussed at that high level. It also meant that many Grand Lodge Officers had to travel extensively and spend considerable time in order to fulfil their duties. This prompted the members of Grand Lodge to consider the possibility of re-organisation.[27]

Another year elapsed before the following County Grand Lodges were established in November, 1967: the County Grand Orange Lodge of Ayrshire, Renfrewshire and Argyll; the County Grand Orange Lodge of Glasgow; and the County Grand Orange Lodge of Lanarkshire, Stirlingshire, Fife and the Lothians.[28]

Of course, the West of Scotland, the City of Glasgow and the mining areas of Central Scotland were the areas of the country where the Order had long established roots and the new structure succinctly reflected that fact. However, this was not the end of the reorganisation.

The continuing expansion of the Order in the East of Scotland led six District Lodges[29] in the newly created County Grand Orange Lodge of Lanarkshire, Stirlingshire, Fife and the Lothians, to petition Grand Lodge for the establishment of a separate County Grand Lodge for the region. This request was granted and the County Grand Orange Lodge of the East of Scotland was inaugurated in November, 1968.[30]

The creation of the four County Grand Lodges accomplished the main aim of easing the administrative burden of the Grand Lodge. A major task of the County Grand Lodges is the organisation of the annual Twelfth parades. Each of the four has the responsibility for holding its own separate procession at a different venue within its jurisdiction each year. The four different processions are usually spread out over a number of weekends in late June and early July so as to allow members the opportunity of participating in at least one of the other processions in Scotland. This arrangement also averts any potential problems the various primary lodges would have in hiring bands should the processions all be held on the same day.

It is quite clear that the Order has been able to compensate for the widespread demographic upheaval and social disruption it experienced by consolidating its foothold in its traditional areas of strength and by adapting to meet new challenges. Its expansion into the new peripheral housing schemes of the large urban conurbations, new towns and different parts of the country has underlined the determination of Orangemen to perpetuate their social relationships and traditions even when displaced from the communities which fostered and produced them.

The reason is not hard to find. The Orange Order matters to Orangemen and it is the importance which they attach to it which helps to explain its durability in Scottish society.

# Chapter 25

# 'THE TROUBLES'

HOWEVER regrettable, another factor which has kept Orangeism in the public mind in Scotland is the continuing 'troubles' in Northern Ireland. According to one historian:

> Working class Protestants in Scotland are both intimately involved in the Ulster paramilitaries and important as external allies. There has always been considerable traffic across the short stretch of sea between Ulster and Scotland. Many working class Scots feel equally at home on either side and have lived in both countries. The problems of Protestants in Belfast are thus also the problems of their friends and relations in Lowland Scotland. In addition, Ulster Loyalists have few other allies.[1]

The above view may be slightly overstated but there is undoubtedly a good deal of residual support for the Loyalist cause in Ulster amongst those working class Scots of Ulster Protestant ancestry and from certain other individuals and groups in Scottish society.

The Orange Order has been the traditional link uniting Loyalists on both sides of the North Channel. These ties are annually reinforced, and have been for well over a century now, at the Twelfth anniversary processions held in each country when friendships are renewed and new contacts established. Irish lodges and bands attend Scottish processions and Scottish lodges and bands reciprocate the custom.

The current politico-military campaign of the Irish Republican movement to end the partition of Ireland is, of course, utterly opposed by the Orange Order on both sides of the Irish Sea. For contemporary Orangemen, the struggle to maintain the Union, this time that of Northern Ireland with Great Britain, is the same struggle as that fought by their forefathers two generations before to preserve the Union between the whole of Ireland and Great Britain. Whilst Orangemen in Scotland fully support the Loyalist position in Ulster, there has been considerable debate and not insignificant friction generated within the movement as to how that support should be best exhibited.

From the outset of the current disturbances in the late 1960s, the Grand Orange Lodge of Scotland has been concerned that any support expressed by members should be within the confines of absolute legality. As a law abiding organisation craving respectability, the leadership was determined to ensure that any assistance given to the Loyalist population in Ulster was both legitimate and constructive in nature. One of its first actions was to establish an Ulster Relief Fund[2] for families in Northern Ireland who have suffered in any way as a result of the continuing violence.

In addition, the Order has organised various protest demonstrations and petitions of support through the years as events have unfolded in the Province. It has organised holidays in Scotland for the children of families caught up in the violence. The Order has continued to put the Unionist position to local politicians in Scotland and generally to keep the issue in the public eye. However, a number of rank and file Orangemen have believed that the Order was simply not doing enough and that its overall response to the crisis was much too moderate and ineffectual.

It is quite clear that an indeterminate number of Scottish Orangemen have supported and continue to support the various Loyalist paramilitary bodies in Ulster. Some members of the Order have joined the Scottish sections of these bodies or have engaged in criminal activities in Scotland, such as arms smuggling or armed robberies, to further their aims. The activities of Scottish Orangemen in the Ulster Defence Association or the Ulster Volunteer Force have, on occasion, led to convictions in the courts and long prison sentences for those involved.[3]

The publicity surrounding these cases has been a great embarrassment not only to the leadership of the Orange Order in Scotland but also to other ordinary Orangemen who prefer legitimate ways of assisting the cause. The Grand Lodge response has been an attempt to distance the Order as far as possible from the paramilitaries. Amongst the measures taken have been a ban on collections for the paramilitaries on Orange premises and a ban on the sale of their literature and any other merchandise at Orange meetings and rallies. At the same time, the Grand Lodge has been at pains to point out to the membership that solidarity with the Loyalists in Ulster is best served by the normal constitutional mechanisms which, Orangemen are reminded, they are pledged to uphold.

Matters came to a head on this issue in 1976 when the Orange leadership sought to expel from membership of the Order one Roddy MacDonald, the then leader of the Ulster Defence Association in Scotland. However, the motion to expel MacDonald was subsequently rejected by a meeting of the Grand Lodge. Faced with what was a clear challenge to their authority, a number of Grand Lodge Officers including the Grand Master, Thomas Orr, and the Grand Secretary, David Bryce, threatened to resign unless all paramilitary activity was unequivocally condemned by the Order.[4]

A special meeting of the Grand Lodge was re-convened for this purpose in

December, 1976. The meeting was asked to consider the resolution that the Order: 'utterly rejects all support, be it active or tacit, of terrorist organisations whose actions contravene the laws of the land.'[5] The gamble taken by Orr and his fellow officers paid off. The resolution was overwhelmingly adopted by those members present at the meeting. MacDonald eventually resigned from the Order in disgust.

Although some Orangemen continued to engage in paramilitary activity regardless, the leadership had made an important point both to the membership and to the outside world. The Grand Lodge had wanted the opportunity officially to reject all links with the paramilitaries and thus present the Order as a responsible organisation committed to a no less resolute but moderate approach to the Ulster question.

In truth, the Grand Lodge was yet again in a difficult position. It was obviously aware of the fair degree of grassroots support within the Order for at least a more bellicose stance in support of the Ulster Loyalists, yet this had to be balanced against the wishes of the majority of Scottish Orangemen for that support to remain within the boundaries of legitimate action. The leadership had demonstrated that it was firmly committed to pursuing its support for the Unionist population in Northern Ireland by wholly constitutional means and had not hesitated to criticise the paramilitaries:

> They have endangered the credibility of the Loyal Orange Institution of Scotland and have thus imperilled the constitutional policies being pursued by Grand Lodge. In plain language, who in Scotland will want to listen to anything the Orange Order has to say about Northern Ireland when misguided men claiming the name of Orange are constantly in our newspapers on arms charges or flaunting themselves on television boasting about shotguns and flamethrowers.[6]

The Grand Lodge reaction to those Orangemen with paramilitary connections was very much less ambiguous in nature than that which it displayed in 1912. However, the circumstances then were very different. In 1912, there was considerable public and political support for the Unionist cause in Ireland which created a climate within which the Order was able to turn a blind eye to the paramilitary activity of some of its members. For a variety of reasons such latitude is not possible today.

The vast majority of people in Scotland today, both Protestant and Roman Catholic, want absolutely nothing to do with 'the troubles' in Northern Ireland. There is a shared widespread revulsion at the catalogue of sectarian outrages which have been committed in the name of religion in the Province. Almost all sections of Scottish society are united in condemning these atrocities and there remains a generally held reluctance to take 'sides' in the Irish conflict. Most Scots are determined to ensure that nothing is said or done to promote sectarian discord in Scotland.

The leadership of the Orange Order in Scotland is acutely aware of these sentiments and is sensitive to them. However, despite its outright condemnation of all Protestant paramilitary activity, it is also aware that many people in Scotland still regard the Orange Order as a root cause of, or a net contributor to, the continuing troubles afflicting Northern Ireland.

Its position is not helped by those Orangemen who do want a harder line on Ulster. Some of them, mostly younger members, have gravitated into the ranks of more belligerent groups like the Scottish Loyalists. Formed in 1979, its activities are not dissimilar to those of the old Protestant Action Society in that the accent is on confrontation and direct action. This has led to some well publicised incidents involving the supporters of Irish Republicanism in Scotland, whose demonstrations have been the object of attack by militant Loyalists.[7]

In recent years there seems to have been a hardening of attitudes amongst some working class Roman Catholics in Scotland in their support for the Irish Republican movement. Whilst actual numbers remain very small, there is a definable commitment to the cause from those who are involved. The most visible sign of this is perhaps the growth of Republican Bands in the country which now number about six.[8] These bands take part in the annual commemoration of the Edinburgh born Socialist and Republican, James Connolly, and in other demonstrations and processions of various Irish and left wing groups.

A number of local authorities in Scotland have refused to give their permission to Irish Republican groups to hold processions for fear of encouraging public disorder.[9] This has led to accusations that they are giving in to intimidation from militant Loyalists. The Scottish Loyalists and like minded groups and individuals have certainly targeted Republican processions as a deliberate policy and the ensuing violence has led the police to take strong action when this has been required.

The Orange Order in Scotland continues to watch these events with a growing sense of unease. Whilst Orange processions are not subject to anything like the same scale of controversy or violence, there is a growing body of opinion in Scottish society which believes that these processions should also be prohibited or at least seriously curtailed. The view is put forward that if Republican processions are to be banned, then in the interests of even-handedness, Orange processions should be similarly banned. There is also the popular view that any processions or demonstrations with a perceived 'Ulster' connection should not be encouraged *per se*, as they only increase the climate of sectarianism in Scotland.

Orange leaders have argued that such people are not comparing like with like and that they are using the violence which often, though not always, accompanies Republican processions, as an excuse to have a go at the Orange Order. However, there is a growing awareness within the Orange movement that it needs to take more care in the image it projects to the Scottish public both in its public processions and in its responses to events in Ulster. Indeed, these twin problems have recently dovetailed together in a quite extraordinary way.

A damaging dispute has developed within Scottish Orangeism over the tendency of some Loyalist Bands to wear military style uniforms. This problem first surfaced at a Twelfth procession held in Broxburn in 1989. Orange leaders were furious that one band in the procession, the Young Cowdenbeath Volunteers Flute Band, were wearing replica uniforms of the Young Citizen Volunteers who were the youth wing of the original Ulster Volunteer Force.[10]

Orange leaders were concerned that this might be seen as support for the present day Ulster Volunteer Force, an illegal organisation. In response, they banned the Young Cowdenbeath Volunteers Flute Band from participating in any future Orange processions. When the lodge which hired the band for the Broxburn procession, 'Pride of Midlothian' LOL 160 protested, it promptly had its warrant suspended by the Grand Lodge.

Since 1991, a further two lodges, one in Airdrie and one in Grangemouth, have also had their warrants suspended by the Grand Lodge for hiring bands which have contravened its dress code in this way. This has led to the lodges involved forming a new organisation, the Independent Orange Order in Scotland, in retaliation to their suspension from the official body. The 'Independents' as they are known, now hold their own separate processions and hire the bands[11] which have been prohibited from participating in processions organised under the auspices of the Loyal Orange Institution of Scotland.

Whilst it remains too early to assess the impact of the split, it is important to keep a sense of proportion. The numbers involved in the breakaway group remains small, probably no more than about 500 in total. The overwhelming majority of the membership and bandsmen of the Orange Order in Scotland appear unmoved by the dispute. Its actual significance lies in the fact that it is the first serious division to occur within the Loyal Orange Institution of Scotland since its formation in 1876.

Of course in a real sense the dress code of the recalcitrant bands is only the tip of the iceberg. The dispute is really once again about the level and nature of the support which some Orangemen believe they should give to the Ulster Loyalists. The bans imposed by the Grand Lodge are in line with its declared policy that all such support should be within the absolute confines of legality. More militant Orangemen are obliged either to accept this situation or else leave the Orange Order and join other more bellicose organisations more in keeping with their thinking and propensities.

# Chapter 26

# SURVIVAL OF AN ORANGE CULTURE

T HE Orange Order has managed to retain a mass membership in Scotland.[1] The basis of this stability has been the Order's propensity to recruit and attract members from within family and kinship networks. Membership of an Orange Lodge had already become a family affair,[2] a tradition in many working class families by the First World War. This tradition has endured over succeeding generations to the present day. Whilst the Order, of course, continues to attract people from all walks of life and social circumstances, familial custom within the working class remains the most significant factor in its survival.

This phenomenon was tied to what may be termed the social relations of production. It has been emphasised that the growth and development of Orangeism in Scotland was primarily due to the rapid industrialisation of the country which occurred particularly in the mid to late nineteenth century. Economic circumstances change over periods of time and the story for most of the twentieth century has been one of gradual decline in those industries previously at the forefront of the Industrial Revolution. The coal mines, iron and steel mills, and the shipyards may now have closed but one legacy of their impact is the continued existence of Orange Lodges in a host of towns and villages across the old industrial belt of the Central Lowlands. It is a testimony to the vitality of the Orange Order that it has managed to survive the de-industrialisation of the economy and the resultant social disruption to the communities concerned, particularly in the post war decades.

One cannot really understand these processes unless the question is asked: what do Orangemen themselves think they are doing? What does the 'Orange' really mean to ordinary working class Orangemen today? Any explanations offered for the durability of Orangeism in Scottish life must surely begin from this starting point. Neglect of such a perspective leads to explanations of this subject which are too functional or theoretical in nature and as a result become divorced from what is actually occurring in reality.

What is quite clear from the history of the Orange movement in Scotland is that it truly is a survivor. Despite the dissolution of the movement in 1836; its fissures and schisms; its frequent involvement in disturbances and riots; the membership losses it sustained in two world wars; the challenges it has faced from rival groups and the widespread and continuing disapproval it faces from society at large, it soldiers on regardless, firm in the conviction that what it stands for is both timeless and relevant. In the past its ideology has been both a great strength and a great weakness. This ideology, still essentially rooted in the Victorian, imperialist era, continues to give the membership a set of beliefs to adhere to, however irrelevant these appear to contemporary society. Of course, the plain fact is that the Order is now completely impotent in the political and religious life of Scotland. In an age of blandness, conformity and moderation in matters of politics and religion, the uncompromising views promoted by the Orange Order seem not only archaic and extreme but also verging on the absurd to the movers and shakers, the opinion formers and the chattering classes of Scottish society.

Most ordinary Orangemen today remain unconcerned by such considerations. They remain aloof from middle class and liberal contempt. They could not care less what 'trendies' think of them.

For Orangemen, 'the Lodge' is a way of life. It is their life. It is perhaps difficult for people living comfortably in pleasant suburbs and enjoying some measure of financial security to comprehend fully this aspect of Orangeism. In those towns and villages ravaged by the worst effects of industrial decay and with little prospect of things improving, organisations like the Orange Order can and do offer a temporary escape from the often grim realities of everyday existence.

In times of economic uncertainty and hardship the communitarian values of mutual aid and brotherhood fostered in the lodge room and the social club offer a form of solace. In socially deprived areas of the country some lodges have either reduced their membership fees or entirely waived them for members who are unemployed or in financial difficulties. Crucially, membership of a lodge can give people a sense of 'belonging' to something which not only boosts self-confidence but also offers them a quite different perspective of their worth in a society from which many working class people are beginning to feel increasingly alienated and rejected.

In fact, the social role of the Orange Order has now come to assume a new importance as its political and religious role has progressively diminished. Whilst it would be inaccurate to imply that the Order has now become little more than a glorified social club, there is little doubt that the social side of its activities has perhaps been perceived as the major benefit to be derived from membership in the modern era.

The social aspect of Orangeism has been seriously neglected by historians and sociologists. Its most common manifestation is the annual 'Orange Walk'. It is unfortunate for the Order that it is often and solely judged on the basis of these ritual occasions.

The only time that Scottish Orangeism now really comes into the public gaze and grabs its attention is during these boisterous events, and for many impartial onlookers they present a not particularly edifying spectacle. However, the Order is quick to point out that it is not responsible for the activities of supporters lining the streets or accompanying the processions, many of whom are obviously in various stages of intoxication. Whilst this remains true, the Order's public image continues to be marred by the loutish and anti-social behaviour of such people.

Orangemen regard the 'Walk' as a traditional day out to be enjoyed to the full. It is 'their day'. They are uninterested in the generally held view that these processions represent a major contribution to sectarian division in Scotland. Orange leaders argue that there are people outside the ranks of the Order, not just 'lager louts', who enjoy these events and look forward to them every year. Whilst this is no doubt true, the Order is going to find it increasingly difficult to defend these occasions purely on the basis of them being a public affirmation of its loyalty to Queen and Country. For many Scots, probably the majority, the public celebration of a battle which took place in Ireland over three hundred years ago appears stupendously irrelevant and positively harmful to the life of the country.

The more private social aspect of Orangeism was reinforced in the 1960s when the Order in Scotland effectively abandoned any lingering adherence to temperance principles by sanctioning the licensing of Orange premises. In so doing, the Grand Lodge faced up to the realities of the public house oriented social life of many rank and file Orangemen. This situation was really forced upon them given the predilection of the membership towards the consumption of alcohol.

Orangemen tended to drink in certain public houses[3] but problems could arise in and outside such establishments if they came into contact with persons holding opposite views to their own. Trouble resulted and Orange officials, both local and national, became increasingly concerned that the reputation of the Order was being tarnished by such incidents.

Although Orangemen as individuals may have patronised certain public houses there was no official connection between them and the Order. All of the profits of their custom went straight to the publican. By opening their own social clubs, the Order could not only supervise the drinking of the membership but perhaps more importantly retain some of the revenue it generated.

The Order owns a considerable amount of property in the shape of the various Orange Halls scattered across the length and breadth of the Central Lowlands. Gradually, an increasing number of District Lodges began to open their own social clubs and were encouraged to do so by the breweries being willing to offer loans at low rates of interest for the expansion or refurbishment of Orange premises. As a result, most of the larger Orange Halls in Scotland are now licensed to sell alcohol. A Union of Orange Social Clubs[4] has been established which allows the member of one club access into any of the other clubs in the country.

Although a step regretted by some Orangemen, it has undoubtedly proved popular with the vast majority of the membership. As well as providing members with alcohol at a cheaper price than most public houses, the clubs offer them a wide and varied social scene. There are regular dances and cabarets. Snooker, darts and domino competitions are organised for male members and bingo and ladies nights are organised for female members. Parties are held for children and senior citizens.

This vibrant social scene is repeated on a daily basis in a host of such clubs across West Central Scotland throughout the year. The extent of this activity can be gauged by looking at a specific example. Local newspapers often carry news and reports of Orange social events. The following extracts are taken from the *Wishaw Press*:

> LOL—Entertainment in the Social Club this week begins on Thursday with the Thursday Club; Thursday evening, prize bingo; Friday evening, Ladies Committee dance, £1 entrance, all welcome; Saturday evening, Wishaw Purple Heroes Flute Band plus disco; Sunday Club, morning on Sunday, 25 April, there will be a domino tournament at 1.00pm.[5]

The above extract was taken from a page in the newspaper entirely devoted to the activities of various organisations in Wishaw including the Soroptimists; the Young Farmers' Club; the Boys Brigade; the Round Table; Rotary; the Motherwell Photographic Society; St Aidan's Operatic Society; and the Womens' Rural Institute. The page also carried a report on the annual installation of the office bearers and notice of the next meeting of the local Royal Black Preceptory.

The newspaper also has a number of pages devoted to district news. The format consists of a number of brief reports on current activities and items of interest from each community covered. Included in these reports were the following:

> Craigneuk—Orange Hall activities begin on Thursday with prize bingo at 8.00pm; Friday disco with Boyne Water Flute Band from 8.00pm; Sunday, Wishaw Flute Band practice; Tuesday, True Defenders Flute Band practice and Wednesday, LLOL 24 meeting.
>
> Harthill—On Saturday evening at the 30 Social Club, there will be dancing to Fanfare; Sunday evening, double bingo; Saturday, 1 May, dancing to the Miller Men; Sunday, 2 May, cabaret with Martini at 8.30pm and bingo at 9.45pm, all welcome.
>
> Newmains—LOL 56 and LLOL 126 hold their monthly prize bingo on Wednesday, 28 April at 7.30pm.[6]

There are some important points to be drawn from the above examples. To begin with, they underline the fact that in those localities where it has embedded itself, the Orange movement is regarded as being as much an integral part of normal community life as Rotary or the local church mens' club. This may be an unpalatable fact for some people to face but nevertheless it remains a fact. It is perhaps more difficult to grasp this concept because of the reluctance of the national press and media in Scotland to report on any Orange activities except in the most negative and sensational manner.

169

Brotherhood: 'Well done thou good and faithful servant'

More importantly, the extent of this social activity has contributed in no small measure to the retention of what may be termed an 'Orange Culture'.

The social clubs have reinforced the bonds of brotherhood fostered by the rituals and ceremonies performed in the Orange Lodges themselves by providing Orangemen with an even keener sense of their own identity within the wider community. The clubs also provide a focus of social interaction not only between and amongst Orangemen but with the outside world as well.

What has to be understood is that the 'Orange' is a way of life to thousands of ordinary Scots. The activities of any average Orangeman who also happens to be a member of a band will include perhaps two nights per week devoted to band practice. He will have a monthly lodge meeting to attend and other meetings if he is involved at District Lodge or County Grand Lodge level. In addition, he may also be in the 'Black' or in the Apprentice Boys of Derry or both. He will probably spend at least one night per week, perhaps two, at the social club, usually at the weekend.

This average Orangeman may have met his wife at an Orange function. They may have held their wedding and reception at the local Orange Hall. If they have children, their christening party may also be held there. The children will be entered on the cradle roll of the local lodge. This average Orangeman's father, almost certainly himself an Orangeman, if deceased, may have had an Orange funeral service.

Activity of this type is not merely confined to a dedicated minority of zealots. Rather, it is part and parcel of the everyday lives of thousands of ordinary working class Scots men and women across the length and breadth of the Central Lowlands. However much religious bigotry can be said to underpin much of this behaviour, there is something more going on here than mere anti-Catholicism. Whilst other 'No Popery' organisations have come and gone, the Orange Order has retained its mass membership and appeal because it has managed to prove its value socially to those who have become involved with it, generation after generation.

It is instructive to note that apart from a local sub-post office, often the only tangible reminder left of what were once busy and thriving industrial communities are the local Orange Lodges or Orange Bands. In localities such as, for example, Cairneyhill, Drumgelloch, Ferniegair, Shieldhill or West Benhar, the lodges and bands are almost the only vibrant symbols left of a once separate community existence. It would be going too far to say that they can be regarded as a focus of community identity, but their continued existence in such communities remains indicative of the complex social links binding Orange culture to community identity in many of the more economically depressed areas of Scotland.

In fact, even a cursory look at the Order's continued areas of strength in the country reads like a gazetteer of the nineteenth century Scottish coalfield. The 'Orange' retains a significance in the life of these communities because it has grown and developed in tandem with them and shared in their ups and downs. If a man's son can now no longer follow him into the local pit he can at least follow him into the local Orange Lodge. It is clear that many young men still choose to do this in a host of old pit villages and towns across the Central Lowlands.

It would be remiss not to mention another important element in the Order's social interaction with the wider community: its charitable work. Orangemen are instructed that charity is the highest moral virtue and a serious attempt has been made by the movement in Scotland to put this principle into action in recent times. Although its charitable work is limited, it has nevertheless become quite extensive in specific areas of activity.

Traditionally, Scottish Orangeism has been unable satisfactorily to fulfil its charitable obligations, not because of any lack of endeavour or enthusiasm but simply because of the modest means of its membership. It has compared unfavourably in the past with the Order in Canada, Ireland and even Australia where charitable work has always been to the forefront of the movement's activities. However, the revenue generated primarily by the social clubs has now allowed the movement in Scotland to engage earnestly in works for the charitable causes it has chosen to support.

These tend to be local hospitals, residential homes and churches. Donations vary in size but recent examples include £1,431 to Monklands General District Hospital from Airdrie District Social Club;[7] £5,000 to a local church building fund from Greengairs Social Club;[8] and £800 divided evenly between four Glasgow hospitals from Dennistoun District Social Club.[9] The Princess Louise Hospital for Disabled Ex-Servicemen in Erskine is a regular beneficiary of Orange fund-raising.[10] The Ladies Orange Association of Scotland is particularly active on this front but donations also arrive from a number of social clubs and District Lodges on a frequent basis. In addition, monies collected at the annual County Grand Orange Lodge of Glasgow Junior and Juvenile Rally are donated to the Royal Hospital for Sick Children in Glasgow.[11]

If it is a truism that charity begins at home, the Order has not been neglectful either of its own needs. Individual lodges still dispense benevolence to their members and their families as and when required and as circumstances allow. The Ladies Orange Association of Scotland has set aside a special fund for the benefit of the aged and infirm members. The Ulster Relief Fund is still running for the benefit of Loyalist families caught up in the violence of the Province.

Concern for the elderly has led the Order to embark on a more ambitious project with the setting up of the Scottish Orange Home Fund. The Order is attempting to establish its own retirement home for aged and infirm members similar to those established by Orange jurisdictions in Australia, Canada, Ireland and the United States of America. Such a project constitutes a major undertaking for the movement in Scotland given its financial resources and the social composition of the membership.

Largely ignored by wider society as a whole, Orange culture has nevertheless retained a curious fascination for the literati in Scotland and the public who support them. Orangeism has been the subject of a variety of books and successful stage and television plays in recent years.[12] The approach taken to the subject matter is universally patronising, where Orangemen are treated with the condescension that the sophisticated reserve for lesser breeds. Thus, for authors and playwrights alike, Orangemen are invariably characterised as irrational, drunken and often violent bigots without a saving grace.

Whilst stereotyping of this nature no doubt helps to sell books and theatre tickets, it has to be acknowledged that this is precisely how many people in society do see Orangemen. Until they do something positive to clean up their act at public processions and rallies, Orangemen are going to continue to be subjected to character assassination and criticism of this type.

Indeed, the Protestant working class in general and the values and institutions which many of them tend to support are often targets for similar abuse, which if it were directed against certain other groups in society would be met by outrage and condemnation from politicians, the press and the media. Orangemen, in particular, complain that they are not treated fairly in the press and media but the remedy is really in their own hands.

Despite its longevity, the Orange movement in Scotland remains an opaque society, still largely unknown but definitely unloved. Here indeed is a movement whose reputation has gone before it. It remains at the centre of a most curious paradox. It is an organisation which exemplifies so precisely the best and essential tenets of traditional working class society—mutual aid and communal solidarity—yet at the same time does so much to negate them. It really can be viewed as the black sheep of traditional working class culture.

Its future prospects appear undiminished. It is likely that its social and philanthropic role will expand as little more than lip service is paid to its political and religious obligations. For thousands of working class Scots, particularly those living in areas of economic recession, 'the Lodge' will continue to be a key element in their lives as it was for the generations who preceeded them. Orangeism will continue to be a family affair and be representative of the ties which bind.

It will be up to the reader to decide whether the Orange Order has been a positive or a negative force in the life of Scotland. Much will depend on one's own point of view and on one's actual experience of the movement in its various facets. History certainly suggests that Scotland's relationship with Orangeism has not been a happy experience.

Orangeism by its very nature represents a divisive element in society. It is not conducive to fostering harmonious community relations in the general sense. Of course, it is not the only divisive element in Scottish society nor is it the sole repository of sectarianism but it remains perhaps the most potent and certainly the most visible symbol of the religious divisions which have so afflicted life in West Central Scotland for so long.

Orangemen maintain that they have a 'humble and steadfast faith in Jesus Christ'. Who better, then, to have the last word: 'Ye shall know them by their fruits.'[13]

# Appendix 1

## The Royal Black Institution in Scotland

The origins of the Royal Black Institution remain a matter of conjecture even to Orange historians.[1] However, the impetus came from those Orangemen who wished to retain some of the more exotic degrees which had been developed in the wake of the formation of the Loyal Orange Institution of Ireland in 1795. The early history of the Orange movement in Ireland was marked by a long and often acrimonious controversy over which degrees should be formally recognised and worked in Orange Lodges. It was not until 1811 that some order was imposed when the Grand Lodge stipulated that only two degrees would be worked: the Orange and the Purple.

This did not satisfy those Orangemen who had formed an attachment to the degrees now officially proscribed by the Grand Lodge. In response, a number of so called 'Black' societies were established in order to preserve and work the old degrees and usages, some of which were derived or modified from the degrees worked in older societies such as the Orange Boys, irregular Masonic Lodges and the Knights of Malta. By the dissolution of 1836, a number of Black organisations were in existence including the Royal Black Association of Ireland, the Grand Black Order of Orangemen and the Loyal Black Association, none of which were on good terms with the Loyal Orange Institution.[2]

Curiously enough, the Loyal Black Association was an Irish offshoot of an older Scottish organisation known as the Grand Black Chapter of the Knights of Malta. This society seems to have existed in Scotland from the eighteenth century and quite possibly earlier.[3] It was exclusively Protestant in membership. It will be recalled that George Donaldson held senior office in this society in the 1830s.[4] Whether it once claimed ancestry from the staunchly Roman Catholic Sovereign Military and Hospitaller Order of St John of Jerusalem, Rhodes and Malta would be a moot point. Certainly, following the Reformation, a number of Knights converted to Protestantism and left the Order to set up Protestant equivalents in their respective countries.[5]

It was becoming increasingly clear to its proponents that the somewhat byzantine nature of the Black was in need of some uniform system of organisation. This eventually occurred on 16 September 1846, when members of the Loyal Black Association severed links with its parent body in Scotland and formed the Grand Black Chapter of Ireland or the Royal Black Institution as it is now known.[6] It absorbed the remaining rival Black societies in Ireland within a few years.

Although put on a more organised footing, relations between the newly established Grand Black Chapter and the Loyal Orange Institution remained strained. It was not until the early 1860s that their relationship settled down to one of mutual compatability. Within the Grand Black Chapter there was some debate as to whether its higher degrees should be restricted to selected members but this proposal was eventually rejected in favour of the view that all members should be entitled to receive all eleven degrees as by right.[7]

The Royal Black Institution began to increase its membership and received a major boost to its confidence and status with the recruitment of William Johnston of Ballykilbeg. He became its Sovereign Grand Master in 1855 and he was able through the strength of his personality and his organisational flair to raise dramatically the profile of the society.[8] It was soon chartering preceptories outside of Ireland.

The first preceptory formed in Scotland was 'Ancient Sons of William' RBP 118 which held its first meeting in Glasgow on 26 June 1856. Prior to this date, the preceptory members had met under a warrant as Royal Black Lodge No. 2 of the Grand Black Chapter of the Knights of Malta.[9] It would seem that the warrant simply transferred from this body to the Grand Black Chapter of Ireland.

Early extracts from the minute book of RBP 118 reveal that the monthly dues were three pence per member; fines were levied for non-attendance at meetings; the benevolent fund was known as 'the kist' and special fund raising was required for the purchase of 'black robes', presumably for its office bearers.[10] The preceptory is still working today.

Other early Scottish preceptories still in existence are 'Star of the North' RBP 171 Maryhill, formed in 1865, and 'Briton's Sons' RBP 187 Partick, formed in 1867.[11]

There are now approximately 60 preceptories in Scotland which are organised into 11 District Chapters. Of these preceptories, about 25 meet in the city of Glasgow and 13 in Lanarkshire.[12] Thus, the Institution is concentrated in West Central Scotland with only a handful of preceptories existing in the East of Scotland. Its growth has been static when compared with that of the Orange Institution, which has managed to expand gradually into other areas of the country.

It would be a misconception to regard the Royal Black Institution as in any way superior in status to the Loyal Orange Institution. In fact, they are quite distinct and separate societies within what constitutes the Orange Order. However, most Black Preceptories meet on Orange premises though on different evenings from Orange Lodges and one cannot join a Black Preceptory without first being a member in good standing of an Orange Lodge.

The Royal Black Institution is exclusively male and adult in membership. It does not permit women or children's sections. This obviously restricts its membership, which in Scotland is approximately 3,000.[13] Despite its existence in different countries, the Institution is controlled by its ruling body in Ireland, the Imperial Grand Black Chapter of the British Commonwealth. It issues all warrants and looks after the finances of the Institution.[14]

In Scotland, the Institution has an essentially two-tier structure of organisation. Local preceptories are grouped together geographically to form District Chapters. These in turn elect representatives to the Provincial Grand Black Chapter of Scotland, which is a purely administrative body. Its main functions are to ensure that the standard of degree work in the various preceptories is uniform and maintained satisfactorily and to organise the Institution's annual divine service and annual procession.

The annual procession of the Provincial Grand Black Chapter of Scotland is referred to by it as 'Black Saturday' or more colloquially as the 'Black Walk'. It is always held on the second Saturday in August. The purpose of the procession is to commemorate the Relief of Derry which occurred on 1 August 1689.

The Royal Black Institution is less 'political' and more religious in ethos than the Loyal Orange Institution. It offers its members moral and ethical instruction by means of a series of degrees comprising lectures and dramatic ceremonial. These degrees are symbolic interpretations of certain events in Old Testament history. In addition, a sense of human mortality is strongly inculcated in those going through some of these ceremonies.

The Institution regards itself as a bastion of reformed evangelical Protestantism. The Black Knight's Code:

- To be true and faithful to the Order at all times
- To spread the Gospel of his Christian Knighthood
- To uphold the honour and virtue of every Sir Knight
- To assist those who are less fortunate than himself
- To support his Preceptory and elected Officers
- To live up to the principles of the Order
- To be faithful to God, Church, Queen and Commonwealth[15]

# *Appendix 2*

## The Apprentice Boys of Derry Association in Scotland

The Apprentice Boys of Derry is an exclusively Protestant association formed to commemorate and keep alive the traditions surrounding the siege of Derry. The siege lasted 105 days from 7 December 1688 to 1 August 1689. The successful defence of the 'Maiden City', wooed but never won, secured Protestantism in the North of Ireland and paved the way for King William III's campaign in the rest of the country. This culminated in the victory won at the Battle of the Boyne on 1 July 1690.

The siege began to be commemorated by Irish Protestants as early as the 1700s. These celebrations were put on a more formal footing by Colonel John Mitchelburne, who had actually taken part in the defence of the city during the siege. He formed a club, the Apprentice Boys of Derry, to commemorate the event annually.[1] This idea proved popular, but it was not until the mid nineteenth century that other such clubs became firmly established.

The clubs tended to take their names from heroes of the siege and they are listed below with the dates of when they were founded:[2]

> Apprentice Boys of Derry Club (1714)
> Walker Club (1844)
> Murray Club (1847)
> Mitchelburne Club (1854)
> Browning Club (1863)
> No Surrender Club (1865)
> Campsie Club (1869)
> Baker Club (1927)

In 1859, the clubs then existing decided to form an association and the present day Apprentice Boys of Derry Association was born. A General Committee was appointed from the membership of the founder clubs to draw up the Association's rules and regulations.[3]

The key events of the siege, including the closing of the gates of the city by the 13 apprentices in December and the Relief of the city in August, were to be commemorated by formal annual processions and a divine service of thanksgiving. By the end of the nineteenth century these occasions were attracting people from all over Ireland and interest in the Association itself grew. It was soon obliged to consider chartering branches outside of Londonderry.

Interestingly enough, the first formal application submitted to set up a club outside Londonderry itself came from Glasgow in 1872.[4] This was then followed by applications from Omagh and later, Belfast. Whilst the Association decided against granting any charters outside of the city at this time, it had changed its position by the end of the century. It was then agreed that the existing clubs should become 'Parent Clubs' and be permitted to establish branch clubs in other parts of Ireland and beyond.

The first club established in Scotland was a branch of the Murray Club in Partick in 1903.[5] This was perhaps not too surprising given the large Ulster Protestant immigrant community living in the burgh at this time. One of the main traditions associated with the Apprentice Boys movement was already well established in Partick by the end of the nineteenth century. Thus Lundy was burnt in effigy at Whiteinch Cross every year.[6]

The Partick Murray Club received its charter on 26 January 1903.[7] A day later, a Glasgow branch of the No Surrender Club was established. It originally had 40 members and was the first club in Scotland to hold a procession in 1915. In those days it celebrated the Relief of Derry with a sail 'doon the watter' for members and their families.[8]

The Murray Club also established a branch club in Greenock in 1903. However, it did not survive the membership losses it sustained in the First World War.[9]

In fact, the initial progress of the Association in Scotland was slow. It was not until 1933 that another branch club was established. This was a branch of the

Mitchelburne Club in Govan.[10] Thus only three clubs existed in Scotland prior to the Second World War and these were all located in Glasgow.

Following the war the prospects of the Association dramatically improved. New branch clubs were established in the 1940s and 1950s at Irvine, Caldercruix, Bonnyrigg, Coatbridge, Cambuslang and Bellshill. This growth was reflected in the establishment of the Scottish Amalgamated Committee to administer and co-ordinate the Association's activities in Scotland.[11]

One of its first tasks was to organise an annual procession of all the clubs in Scotland. The first such procession took place in the old mining village of Caldercruix in 1959.[12] It was decided that the various branch clubs should take it in turn to host this event on the third Saturday in May each year.

The Scottish Amalgamated Committee has presided over a considerable expansion of the movement in the country, particularly in the last two decades. Branch clubs have been formed in places like Aberdeen, Perth and Methil. There are presently 42 branch clubs in Scotland organised by their parent clubs as follows:[13]

Apprentice Boys of Derry Club (1)
Browning Club (1)
Walker Club (7)
No Surrender Club (14)
Murray Club (3)
Campsie Club (11)
Mitchelburne Club (2)
Baker Club (3)

The Apprentice Boys of Derry Association is not a part of or officially connected with the Orange Order. It is a completely independent and separate society. However, there is a considerable overlap in membership between the two organisations. The vast majority of Apprentice Boys are also members of the Orange Order. Indeed, many branch clubs in Scotland stipulate membership of an Orange Lodge as a precondition of their own membership. Some clubs do admit people who are not members of the Orange Order.

There is significantly less ceremonial and degree work in clubs of Apprentice Boys compared to Orange Lodges and Black Preceptories. After what may be termed a probationary period, initiates must travel to Londonderry where their parent club will formally conclude their initiation within the actual walls of the city. Only then when a person becomes a 'Derry Made Man' does he become a full member of the Association.

The Apprentice Boys Association in Scotland has been less cautious and more militant than the Orange Order in its support for Loyalism in Northern Ireland. It has tended to take a slightly more belligerent stand on certain issues, including support for the Loyalist Prisoners Welfare Association.[14] It has also employed some of the bands proscribed by the Orange Order.[15]

# *Appendix 3*

## LOIGB Lodges in Scotland in 1830

| | | |
|---|---|---|
| 27 | Edinburgh | 142 Canongate |
| 29 | Girvan | McWinney's Inn |
| 43 | Edinburgh | 9 Greenside Place |
| 44 | Glasgow | |
| 83 | Glasgow | John Falconer's, Trongate |
| 97 | Dumfries | |
| 102 | Paisley | McLea's, Moss Street |
| 106 | Glasgow | Wilkie's, Gallowgate |
| 118 | Musselburgh | |
| 123 | Girvan | James Kennedy's |
| 126 | Stranraer | |
| 127 | Whithorn | |
| 129 | Crosshill | James McNeidger's |
| 130 | Dundee | Masonic Lodge, Morrowgate |
| 132 | Wigtown | |
| 137 | Kilmarnock | Black Bull, Portland Street |
| 156 | Creetown | |
| 167 | Glasgow | John Falconer's, Trongate |
| 173 | Dumfries | Black's, English Street |
| 176 | Glasgow | Christie's, Tavern, Argyle Street |
| 178 | Paisley | Donaldson's Tavern, Main Street |
| 183 | Wilsontown | Clarkson's Inn |
| 189 | Wilsontown | McCulloch's Inn |
| 193 | Dailly | |
| 197 | Newton | |
| 200 | Glasgow | Webster's Tavern, 62 Trongate |
| 201 | Pollockshaws | James Walker's, Main Street |
| 208 | Stranraer | Andrew McMaster's |
| 212 | Kirkcudbright | |
| 215 | Glenluce | |
| 216 | Newton Stewart | James Vernon's |
| 217 | Stoneykirk | |
| 218 | Larkhall | William Frame's, Main Street |
| 219 | Port Glasgow | James Erskine's |
| 220 | Dalkeith | |
| 228 | Maybole | James Edgar's |
| 230 | Glasgow | Nisbet's, Laigh Kirk Close |
| 245 | Gatehouse of Fleet | |
| 259 | Neilston | Mrs Anderson's |

*Source: Report from the Select Committee appointed to inquire into the origin, nature, extent and tendency of Orange Institutions in Great Britain and Colonies with minutes, appendices and index* (House of Commons, 1835) 605 XVII, *appendix 19, pp. 141-4*

# *Appendix 4*
## Membership of Royal Gordon Lodge in 1834

William Motherwell; Laurence W Craigie; William Leckie Ewing; Robert Adam; John J Bentley; Charles Stirling; Francis Adam; John K Jolly; William G Jolly; Peter Ferrie; Captain McArthur; Archibald McLellan; James R Dennistoun; John Thompson; James Young; Robert C Wilson; John Watkins; Alexander Dunlop; Robert Patterson; Thomas Stephenson Junior; David Connell; Gilbert K Boyle; Hector Grant; Alexander Buchanan; Alexander Galloway; John Campbell Douglas; A Gardner; John Bailey; Robert Crookes; John McFarlane; Thomas McGusty; James J Duncan

*Source:1835 Report, op. cit., p. 161*

# *Appendix 5*
## Army Regiments Holding LOIGB Warrants in 1830

| No. 30 | 13th Light Dragoons |
|--------|---------------------|
| No. 31 | Royal Sappers and Miners |
| No. 33 | 24th Regiment of Foot |
| No. 58 | 95th or Rifle Brigade |
| No. 64 | 35th Regiment |
| No. 65 | Royal Artillery Drivers |
| No. 66 | 43rd Regiment |
| No. 67 | Royal Artillery |
| No. 77 | Royal Horse Artillery |
| No. 84 | 42nd Foot (Highlanders) |
| No. 87 | 59th Foot |
| No. 94 | Rifle Brigade, 2nd Battalion |
| No. 104 | Rifle Brigade |
| No. 114 | 21st Foot |
| No. 125 | 7th Dragoons |
| No. 131 | 16th Light Dragoons |
| No. 165 | 51st Light Infantry |
| No. 181 | 6th Foot |
| No. 190 | 6th Dragoon Guards |
| No. 204 | 5th Dragoon Guards |
| No. 205 | Royal Artillery, 4th Battalion |
| No. 232 | Royal Artillery, 7th Battalion |
| No. 238 | 67th Foot |
| No. 241 | 29th Foot |
| No. 243 | Royal Sappers and Miners |
| No. 248 | Royal Artillery, 5th Battalion |
| No. 254 | Royal Artillery, 6th Battalion |
| No. 258 | 94th Foot |
| No. 260 | 17th Foot |
| No. 269 | 1st Royal Dragoons |

*Source: 1835 Report, op. cit., pp. 141-4*

# *Appendix 6*

## Grand Protestant Association of Loyal Orangemen of Scotland
## District and Primary Lodges in 1876

| | |
|---|---|
| No. 1 Airdrie | 6, 19 |
| No. 2 | |
| No. 3 Glasgow | 5, 24, 30, 162 |
| No. 4 Maybole | 85, 86, 87, 123, 231, 264 |
| No. 5 Edinburgh | 52 |
| No. 6 Paisley | 61, 74, 203, 1018, 1082 |
| No. 7 | |
| No. 8 Bellshill | 51, 55, 57, 121, 122, 192, 205, 244 |
| No. 9 Kilwinning | 95, 96, 129, 133 |
| No. 10 | |
| No. 11 Ayr | 3, 32, 46, 186, 250 |
| No. 12 Patna | 47, 83, 101, 220 |
| No. 13 Paisley | 4, 7, 15, 17, 22, 27, 50, 89, 102, 124 |
| No. 14 Dalry | 45, 48, 53, 63, 100, 150 |
| No. 15 Partick | 10, 25, 28, 43, 59, 64, 69, 98, 113, 116, 119, 139, 142, 153, 167, 209, 221, 225 |
| No. 16 Wishaw | 56, 66, 152, 211, 257, 68, 137 |
| No. 17 Glasgow | 60, 77, 156, 177, 183 |
| No. 18 Johnstone | 26, 42, 80, 103, 195 |
| No. 19 Port Glasgow | 16, 62, 79, 178, 219, 224, 226, 260 |
| No. 20 Rutherglen | 12, 25, 73, 191 |
| No. 21 Parkhead | 49, 115, 146, 163, 180, 296 |
| No. 22 Coatbridge | 1, 2, 8, 29, 31, 94, 109 |
| No. 23 Stevenston | 65, 82, 132, 147, 154, 166, 198 |
| No. 24 Glasgow | 106, 110, 172, 179, 1688 |
| No. 25 | |
| No. 26 Armadale | |
| No. 27 Dumbarton | 24, 140, 169 |
| No. 28 Pollockshaws | |
| No. 29 Kilmarnock | 67, 99, 141, 189 |
| No. 30 Renfrew | 23, 112, 196 |
| No. 31 Bridgeton | 108, 115, 210, 266 |
| No. 32 Slamannan | 20, 144, 227 |

# *Appendix 7*

## Loyal Orange Institution of Great Britain
## Scottish District and Primary Lodges in 1875

| | |
|---|---|
| No. 1 Glasgow | 54 (Helensburgh), 210 and 237 (Dumbarton), 175 (Yoker), 109 (Pollockshaws), 178 (Paisley), 288 (Johnstone), 197 (Coatbridge), |

|  | 201 (Dundee), 220 (Motherwell), 119, 125 and 202 (Govan), 89, 113, 117, 118, 124, 184, 200, 256, 395, 440, 644 (Glasgow) |
|---|---|
| No. 2 Glasgow | 145 (Busby), 244 (Coatbridge), 87, 91, 177, 231, 274 (Glasgow) |
| No. 1 Partick | 442 (Maryhill), 143, 144, 255, 438, 439, 441 (Partick) |
| No. 2 Ayrshire | 3, 5, 25, 37, 45, 47, 72, 75, 77, 138, 155, 208 |
| No. 3 Greenock | 82, 90, 108, 111, 112, 179, 182, 257, 258 |
| No. 4 Greenock | 80, 107, 115, 146, 173, 190 |
| No. 4 Edinburgh | 86, 437, 495 |

# Appendix 8

## Chronology of Orange Organisations in Scotland
## 1808-1876

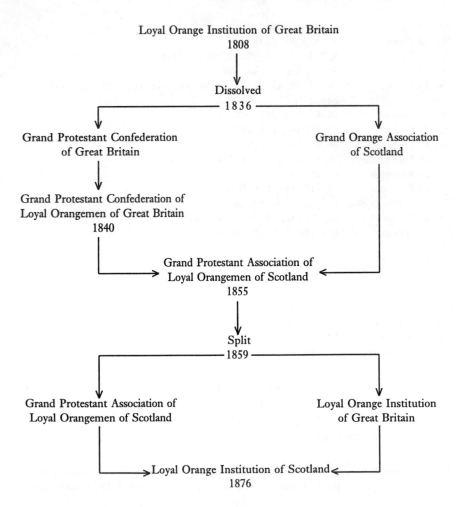

182

# Appendix 9
## Existing Temperance Lodges in Scotland

| | | |
|---|---|---|
| 33 | Dutch Blues | Bellshill |
| 103 | Thornie Tree | Kilwinning |
| 128 | Evangelical Christian Crusaders | Edinburgh |
| 130 | Joseph Baxter Memorial | Chryston |
| 210 | Sons of Joshua | Bridgeton |
| 213 | Thistle Temperance | Rutherglen |
| 217 | Harthill Temperance | Harthill |
| 269 | Churchman's Temperance | Calderbank |
| 340 | Old Boyne True Blues | Greenock |
| 669 | Star of Temperance | Motherwell |

# Appendix 10
## Clergymen with Orange Links

| | | | |
|---|---|---|---|
| 1860s: | *Rev. R H Dignum | Church of Scotland | Greenock |
| | *Rev. Robert Gault | Independent Evangelical | Partick |
| 1870s: | *Rev. Robert Thomson | Church of Scotland | Glasgow |
| | Rev. Campbell | | Kilbirnie |
| | Rev. Orr | | Kilbirnie |
| | Rev. Lorraine | | Dalry |
| | Rev. Robert MacGregor | | Holytown |
| | *Rev. Hugh MacKenzie | | Chapelhall |
| | Rev. John Thomson | Church of Scotland | Kilmarnock |
| | Rev. MacDougall | Church of Scotland | Stoneyburn |
| | Rev. James Muir | | Greengairs |
| | *Rev. James MacKay | Church of Scotland | Glasgow |
| | *Rev. P MacLachlan | Church of Scotland | Glasgow |
| | *Rev. Dr William Fraser | Free Church | Paisley |
| | *Rev. James Dodds | Church of Scotland | Glasgow |
| | *Rev. William F Mills | Episcopal Church | Paisley |
| | *Rev. William McDermott | | Johnstone |
| | *Rev. F R MacDonald | Church of Scotland | Paisley |
| | Rev. A M Lang | Church of Scotland | Paisley |
| 1880s: | *Rev. W Patrick | Congregational Church | Rutherglen |
| | *Rev. J Mitchell | Congregational Church | Glasgow |
| | *Rev. William Abernethy | | Elderslie |
| | *Rev. W Park | | Paisley |
| | *Rev. Thomas Fullerton | | Paisley |
| | Rev. Phelps | | Glasgow |
| | *Rev. John Campbell | | Edinburgh |
| | Rev. James Brandon | Church of Scotland | Clarkston |
| | Rev. D H Paterson | | Airdrie |

|       |                              |                         |             |
|-------|------------------------------|-------------------------|-------------|
|       | *Rev. Alexander Watt         |                         | Benhar      |
|       | *Rev. James Forrest          |                         | Harthill    |
| 1890s: | *Rev. J W Hodgkinson        |                         | Glasgow     |
|       | *Rev. James Collier          |                         |             |
|       | *Rev. William Davidson       |                         |             |
|       | *Rev. Robert McLelland       |                         |             |
|       | *Rev. Hugh Wilson            |                         | Bellshill   |
|       | *Rev. Joseph Druce           |                         | Armadale    |
|       | *Rev. William Winter         | Episcopal Church        | Coatbridge  |
|       | Rev. Duff MacDonald          |                         | Motherwell  |
|       | Rev. R S Bowie               |                         |             |
|       | Rev. Hood Wright             |                         | Craigneuk   |
|       | *Rev. A G Townsend           | Episcopal Church        | Partick     |
|       | *Rev. John Potter            |                         | Glasgow     |
| 1900s: | *Rev. R W Dobbie            |                         | Glasgow     |
|       | *Rev. George T Driver        |                         | Glasgow     |
|       | *Rev. David Ness             | Church of Scotland      | Whiteinch   |
|       | *Rev. John Weipers           | United Free Church      | Glasgow     |
|       | *Rev. James M Brisby         | Independent Evangelical | Glasgow     |
|       | Rev. W O Duncan              |                         | Clarkston   |
|       | Rev. R C Anderson            |                         | Greengairs  |
|       | *Rev. A L Bryan              |                         | Kirkintilloch |
|       | Rev. J Halliday              |                         | Glasgow     |
| 1910s: | *Rev. J G McGarvie          |                         |             |
|       | *Rev. Robert Dickson         |                         |             |
|       | *Rev. T M McKendrick         |                         | Clydebank   |
|       | Rev. George Goodfellow       |                         | Newarthill  |
|       | *Rev. J Victor Logan         | United Free Church      | Glasgow     |
|       | *Rev. William Whitehead      |                         |             |
|       | *Rev. William Edgar          |                         |             |
|       | *Rev. David Jack             |                         |             |
|       | Rev. A J Campbell            |                         |             |
|       | Rev. A MacLaren              |                         |             |
| 1920s: | *Rev. Andrew Duncanson      |                         |             |
|       | *Rev. A Boyd Thomson         |                         | Dalry       |
|       | *Rev. H C McColl             |                         | Kilbirnie   |
|       | Rev. James Muir              |                         | Kirkoswald  |
|       | Rev. David Swan              |                         | Maybole     |
|       | *Rev. Alexander Williamson   |                         | Maybole     |
|       | *Rev. George W Skilton       |                         | Saltcoats   |
|       | *Rev. James Anderson         |                         | Shotts      |
|       | Rev. Alexander Patterson     |                         | Fauldhouse  |
|       | Rev. D G Ross                |                         | Stirling    |
|       | *Rev. W Chalmers Smith       |                         |             |
|       | Rev. Frederick Watson        | Church of Scotland      | Bellshill   |
| 1930s: | Rev. Moffat Gillon          |                         | Edinburgh   |
|       | *Rev. William Sutherland     |                         | Wishaw      |
|       | Rev. R F Whiteley            |                         |             |

| | | |
|---|---|---|
| *Rev. John MacDougall | | Bridgeton |
| Rev. Russell Lewis | | Ardrossan |
| *Rev. Inglis M Black | | Leith |
| Rev. B P Verral | | Falkirk |
| *Rev. James Hamilton | | Blantyre |
| *Rev. John Ferguson | | Rutherglen |
| *Rev. James Francis | | Greenock |
| Rev. William Runciman | Church of Scotland | Johnstone |
| *Rev. Robert Daly | Church of Scotland | Glasgow |
| *Rev. Peter Cowan | Church of Scotland | Maryhill |
| *Rev. John Livingstone | Church of Scotland | Glasgow |
| *Rev. Robert Walker | | Springburn |
| *Rev. William B Lyons | | Dalmarnock |
| 1940s: N/A | | |
| 1950s: *Rev. James Hutchinson | | |
| *Rev. Alan G Hasson | Church of Scotland | Bonhill |
| 1960s: *Rev. Arnold Fletcher | Church of Scotland | Blackburn |
| 1970s: N/A | | |
| 1980s: *Rev. Gordon A McCracken | Church of Scotland | Whitburn |
| 1990s: *Rev. Ian Meredith | Church of Scotland | Blantyre |

*Denotes member of Orange Order.

# Appendix 11
## 'The Qualifications of an Orangeman'*

An Orangeman should have a sincere love and veneration for his Heavenly Father; a humble and steadfast faith in Jesus Christ, the Saviour of mankind, believing in Him as the only Mediator between God and man. He should cultivate truth and justice, brotherly kindness and charity, devotion and piety, concord and unity and obedience to the laws; his deportment should be gentle and compassionate, kind and courteous; he should seek the society of the virtuous and avoid that of the evil; he should honour and diligently study the Holy Scriptures and make them the rule of his faith and practice; he should love, uphold and defend the Protestant religion and sincerely desire and endeavour to propagate its doctrines and precepts; he should strenuously oppose the fatal errors and doctrines of the Church of Rome and scrupulously avoid countenancing (by his presence or otherwise) any act or ceremony of Popish worship; he should, by all lawful means, resist the ascendency of that Church, its encroachments and the extension of its power, ever abstaining from all uncharitable words, actions or sentiments towards his Roman Catholic brethren; he should remember to keep holy the Sabbath day and attend the public worship of God and diligently train up his offspring and all under his control in the fear of God and in the Protestant faith; he should never take the name of God in vain but abstain from all cursing and profane language and use every opportunity of discouraging these and all other sinful practices in others; his conduct should be guided by wisdom and prudence and marked by honesty, temperance and sobriety; the glory of God and the welfare of man, the honour of his Sovereign and the good of his country, should be the motive of his actions.

*Quoted in B Kennedy, *A Celebration: 1690-1990. The Orange Institution* (Belfast, 1990)

# NOTES

## Chapter 1

01 Steve Bruce, *No Pope of Rome* (Edinburgh, 1985), p. 25
02 *Ibid.*
03 Tom Gallagher, *Glasgow: the Uneasy Peace* (Manchester, 1987), p. 9
04 *Ibid.*
05 The 1798 Rebellion was not an exclusively Roman Catholic uprising. One of its leading figures, Wolfe Tone, was a Protestant, and the Society of United Irishmen had a significant number of Northern Presbyterians in its membership
06 James E Handley, *The Irish in Scotland 1798-1845* (Cork, 1945), pp. 89-90
07 *Ibid.*, p. 93
08 *Ibid.*, p. 95
09 *Ibid.*, p. 94
10 *Ibid.*, p. 95
11 Gallagher, *op. cit.*, p. 11
12 Alan Campbell, *Lanarkshire Miners: A Social History of their Trade Unions 1775-1874* (Edinburgh, 1979), p. 178
13 Handley, *op. cit.*, p. 287
14 *Ibid.*, p. 289
15 Gallagher, *op. cit.*, p. 9
16 The figure of 25 per cent seems to be generally accepted by most historians with an interest in the subject
17 Handley, *op. cit.*, p. 108
18 Campbell, *op. cit.*, p. 191
19 A T Q Stewart, *The Ulster Crisis* (London, 1967), p. 27
20 Rev. M W Dewar, Rev J Brown and Rev S E Long, *Orangeism: A New Historical Appreciation* (Belfast, 1967) p. 47
21 Ulster Protestants will hereafter be referred to in this work as 'Ulstermen'

## Chapter 2

1 Dewar, et al, *op. cit.*, p. 86
2 *Ibid.*, p. 97
3 *Ibid.*, pp. 98-99. Wilson was a member of Caledon Lodge No. 333 and both Sloan and Winter were members of Loughgall Lodge No. 603. Neither lodge is on the current roll of the Grand Lodge of Ireland

4   *Ibid.*, p. 98
5   R M Sibbett, *Orangeism in Ireland and Throughout the Empire*, vols. 1 and 2 (London, 1939), p. 357
6   Dewar et al, *op. cit.*, p. 112
7   *Ibid.*, p. 111
8   Rev Gordon McCracken, *Bygone Days of Yore: the Story of Orangeism in Glasgow* (Glasgow, 1990), p. 3
9   Billy Kennedy, *A Celebration: 1690-1990: The Orange Institution* (Belfast, 1990), p. 92
10  *Ibid.*
11  J R Weston, *Scottish Historical Review* vol. XXXIV
12  Sibbett, *op. cit.*, p. 481
13  A more detailed account of Colonel Fletcher's activities as a magistrate can be found in E P Thompson, *The Making of the English Working Class* (Harmondsworth, 1984), pp. 536, 557, 592, 621, 623, 633 and 743
14  Sibbett, *op. cit.*, p. 481
15  Kennedy, *op. cit.*, p. 92
16  McCracken, *op. cit.*, p. 3
17  *Report from the Select Committee appointed to inquire into the origin, nature, extent and tendency of Orange Institutions in Great Britain and Colonies with minutes, appendices and index* House of Commons (1835) 605 XVII. See Appendix 3 for a list of these lodges and their meeting places
18  Kennedy, *op. cit.*, p. 92
19  See p. 4
20  1835 Report, *op. cit.*, appendix 21, p. 186
21  Handley, *op. cit.*, p. 84
22  Campbell, *op. cit.*, p. 182
23  Handley, *op. cit.*, p. 307
24  1835 Report, *op. cit.*, appendix 2, p. 5
25  *Ibid.*, p. 45
26  *Ibid.*, appendix 22, p. 188
27  *Ibid.*, appendix 2, p. 5
28  *Ibid.*, appendix 2, p. 10
29  *Ibid.*, appendix 2, p. 60
30  *Ibid.*, appendix 21, p. 186
31  *Ibid.*, appendix 2, p. 72
32  *Ibid.*, appendix 18, p. 133
33  Nor was this perceived patronage confined to the licensed trade. A petition was presented to the Grand Lodge by some London Orangemen asking its officers to provide them with work on the docks. 1835 Report, *op. cit.*, appendix 2, p. 22
34  *Glasgow Chronicle*, 14 July 1821
35  McCracken, *op. cit.*, p. 5. The sum of £3, 4 shillings and eleven pence was raised
36  *Glasgow Herald*, 12 July 1822
37  McCracken, *op. cit.*, pp. 8-9
38  Handley, *op. cit.*, p. 306
39  *Ibid.*, p. 307

## *Chapter 3*

1   Sibbett, *op. cit.*, p. 483
2   Hereward Senior, *Orangeism in Ireland and Great Britain 1795-1836* (London, 1966), p. 166
3   Senior, *op. cit.*, pp. 165-7. Sibbett, *op. cit.*, p. 486, gives his date of initiation as 1819
4   Duke of York to William Woodbourne, Grand Secretary, 8 February 1821. 1835

Report, *op. cit.*, p. vi
5  Sibbett, *op. cit.*, p. 27 (vol. 2)
6  A summary of Cumberland's speech is given in Sibbett, *op. cit.*, pp. 41-4
7  *Ibid.*, p. 42
8  Sir James Balfour Paul, *Scots Peerage* (Edinburgh, 1907), pp. 557-9
9  Senior, *op. cit.*, pp. 165-7
10  1835 Report, *op. cit.*, appendix 2, p. 10
11  *Ibid.*, p. 44. The Duke certainly put his money where his principles were. In 1834, he paid £30 in dues to the Grand Lodge
12  *Ibid.*, appendix 2, p. 47
13  Craigie to Fairman, 6 April 1833. 1835 Report, *op. cit.*, appendix 22, p. 189
14  *Ibid.*, p. 162
15  *Ibid.*, p. 166
16  Joseph Irving, *The Book of Scotsmen* (Paisley, n.d.)
17  *Glasgow Courier*, 22 June 1833
18  Craigie to Fairman, 5 July 1833. 1835 Report, *op. cit.*, appendix 22, p. 193
19  See Appendix 4 for a list of members of Royal Gordon Lodge in 1835. 1835 Report, *op. cit.*, p. 161
20  1835 Report, *op. cit.*, appendix 21, p. 175

## Chapter 4

1  1835 Report, *op. cit.*, appendix 2, p. 27. The lodge in question was located in Ripponden. Some Orangemen in Rochdale were also expelled from the Order for supporting Reform
2  See Appendix 3
3  *Glasgow Herald*, 25 July 1831. It seems Orangemen were 'egged on' in their alcohol induced frenzy by large numbers of Ulstermen resident in the Newton district of the town who obligingly pointed out Irish Catholic victims
4  1835 Report, *op. cit.*, pp. 142-3
5  Ribbonmen were members of a secret Irish Catholic Society, which originated in Ulster. They are thought to have emerged in the wake of the suppression of the Defenders
6  *Glasgow Herald*, 24 July 1835
7  1835 Report, *op. cit.*, p. 143
8  *Glasgow Herald*, 14 September 1835
9  1835 Report, *op. cit.*, p. 143

## Chapter 5

1  Senior, *op. cit.*, p. 271
2  Sibbett, *op. cit.*, p. 145. Amongst the membership of the Select Committee was Daniel O'Connell
3  *Ibid.*, p. 147
4  *Ibid.*, pp. 164-6
5  Military Orangemen serving overseas were instrumental in introducing the Orange Order into Canada and New South Wales
6  Sibbett, *op. cit.*, p. 169
7  *Ibid.*, p. 171. Of this total, it was alleged there were 50,000 Orangemen in London!
8  *Ibid.*, p. 182
9  1835 Report, *op. cit.*, p. xxv
10  Fairman to the Duke of Gordon, 11 August 1832. 1835 Report, *op. cit.*, p. 183
11  Sibbett, *op. cit.*, p. 211
12  *Ibid.*, p. 226. The Irish Orangemen felt particularly aggrieved at the dissolution of their Institution. Whether or not British Orangemen were involved in conspiracies, they

argued, had nothing to do with them. However, the Select Committee made no distinction between them. It argued the Duke of Cumberland was Imperial Grand Master,
i.e., the leader of the Order in Ireland as well as Great Britain. The Grand Orange
Lodge of Ireland had also issued military warrants signed by the Duke; therefore Irish
Orangemen were also conspiring and should be suppressed as well

13 Apart from his strident political and religious views, the Duke's unpopularity arose
from an unfortunate incident involving his valet. Following a disagreement between
them, the valet was killed by Cumberland. The Duke claimed he acted in self defence
but many felt he had got away with murder due to his social position

## Chapter 6

1   Sibbett, *op. cit.*, p. 258
2   *Ibid.*, p. 270
3   *Ibid.*, pp. 270-1
4   *Ibid.*, pp. 271-2
4   Kennedy, *op. cit.*, p. 92
6   *Ibid.*
7   See p. 12. William Motherwell died, quite suddenly, of apoplexy in 1835 and is buried
    in Glasgow Necropolis
8   McCracken, *op. cit.*, p. 10
9   1835 Report, *op. cit.*, p. xxiii

## Chapter 7

1   *Glasgow Herald*, 15 July 1842
2   *Ibid.*, 16 July 1849
3   *Ibid.*, 19 July 1847
4   *Ibid.*
4   Campbell, *op. cit.*, p. 316
6   *Ibid.*
7   *Ibid.*, pp. 183-4
8   *Glasgow Sentinel*, 18 April 1857
9   Campbell, *op. cit.*, p. 238
10  *Glasgow Herald*, 17 July 1857
11  Campbell, *op. cit.*, p. 184
12  *Ibid.*
13  *Glasgow Herald*, 7 October 1857
14  Campbell, *op. cit.*, p. 184
15  *Glasgow Herald*, 13 July 1859
16  *Glasgow Sentinel*, 8 October 1859
17  Although there were a few Police Officers who were Orangemen, this does not by itself
    suggest there was any official collusion between the Paisley Constabulary and the local
    lodges in the town. It seems to imply that the police officers who took part in the
    procession as Orangemen were unwilling to give evidence against their brethern
18  *Glasgow Herald*, 18 July 1859
19  *North British Daily Mail*, 16 July 1859
20  See pp. 22 and 26

## Chapter 8

1   George Thomson, *The Third Statistical Account of Scotland: The County of Lanark*
    (Glasgow, 1960), pp. 40-52
2   Campbell, *op. cit.*, p. 101

3   *Ibid.*, p. 94
4   *Ibid.*
5   Francis II Groome, *Ordnance Gazeeter of Scotland* (Edinburgh, 1883)
6   *Ibid.*
7   Campbell, *op. cit.*, p. 94
8   See pp. 2-3
9   County Grand Orange Lodge of the East, 'Boyne Anniversary Programme', 1992
10  *Ibid.*
11  James Waugh, *Slamannan Parish Through the Changing Years* (?, 1977), pp. 126-127
12  County Grand Orange Lodge of the East, 'Boyne Anniversary Programme', 1990
13  Henry Patterson, *Class Conflict and Sectarianism: The Protestant Working Class and the Belfast Labour Movement* 1868-1920 (Belfast, 1980), p. xii
14  McCracken, *op. cit.*, p. 18
15  *North British Daily Mail*, 16 July 1873
16  McCracken, *op. cit.*, p. 23
17  County Grand Orange Lodge of Glasgow, 'Boyne Anniversary Programme', 1987
18  McCracken, *op. cit.*, p. 28. Thus, John A Baillie, a plater from Ireland, was first District Master of Glasgow District No. 24 and Joseph Moore, a weaver from Tyrone, was first District Master of Calton District No. 37
19  Thomson, *op. cit.*, p. 122
20  McCracken, *op. cit.*, p. 32
21  County Grand Orange Lodge of Glasgow, 'Boyne Anniversary Programme', 1987
22  McCracken, *op. cit.*, p. 21
23  *North British Daily Mail*, 16 July 1873
24  *Ibid.* The Orange Hall was located in Anderson Street
25  *Glasgow Herald*, 13 July 1886
26  *Greenock Post Office Guide*, 1885
27  *Glasgow Herald*, 14 July 1884
28  *Greenock Post Office Guide*, 1914. Victoria Orange Hall was located in Blackhall Street (District No. 34) and Britannia Orange Hall was located in Terrace Road (District No. 35)
29  *Dictionary of National Biography* (Oxford, 1975), vol. 1, p. 77
30  *Ibid.*
31  Campbell, *op. cit.*, p. 215
32  *Ibid.*, p. 222
33  *DNB, op. cit.*, p. 77
34  Campbell, *op. cit.*, p. 206
35  *Ibid.*, p. 223
36  *DNB, op. cit.*, p. 77
37  Campbell, *op. cit.*, p. 223
38  See p. 30. The lodge in question is LOL 8 which is still in existence today
39  *Glasgow Herald*, 17 July 1857
40  Campbell, *op. cit.*, p. 223
41  *North British Daily Mail*, 14 July 1873
42  *Ibid.*, 16 July 1873
43  Campbell, *op. cit.*, p. 224
44  See pp. 12-14 and 35-6
45  See pp. 88-9 for career of William Whitelaw
46  Harry McShane and Joan Smith, *No Mean Fighter* (London, 1978), p. 56
47  *Ibid.* See also T C Smout, *A Century of the Scottish People 1830-1950* (London, 1987), p. 99
48  Patterson, *op. cit.*, pp. xiv-xv
49  *Ibid.*, p. xv

## *Chapter 9*

1   Sibbett, *op. cit.*, p. 272. These figures seem grossly exaggerated
2   See p. 30
3   McCracken, *op. cit.*, p. 15
4   *Ibid.*, p. 16
5   *Ibid.*
6   *Ibid.*, p. 19
7   See pp. 39-40
8   McCracken, *op. cit.*, pp. 17-18
9   *Ibid.*, p. 18
10  *Ibid.*, p. 21
11  *Ibid.*
12  *Glasgow Herald*, 13 July 1876
13  County Grand Orange Lodge of the East, 'Boyne Anniversary Programme', 1992
14  Own research. See Appendix 6 for an incomplete list of Association lodges in 1876
15  This calculation is based on each lodge comprising 50 members. This figure is gener-
    ous, since a good number of lodges would have had considerably fewer than 50 mem-
    bers. There were always exceptions, of course, but these were unlikely to have been
    many
16  McCracken, *op. cit.*, p. 17
17  *Ibid.*, p. 22
18  Own research. See Appendix 7 for a probably incomplete list of Institution lodges in
    1875

## *Chapter 10*

1   *Glasgow Herald*, 14 July 1859
2   *Ibid.*, 13 July 1860
3   *Ibid.*, 15 July 1861
4   *Ibid.*, 14 July 1864
5   *Paisley Herald and Renfrewshire Advertiser*, 16 July 1859
6   *Glasgow Herald*, 14 July 1859
7   *Ibid.*
8   McCracken, *op. cit.*, p. 25
9   *North British Daily Mail*, 14 July 1868
10  *Ibid.*, 13 July 1870
11  *Glasgow Herald*, 17 July 1871
12  The driving force behind the repeal of the Party Processions Act was the MP for South
    Belfast and leading Orangeman, William Johnston of Ballykilbeg. Johnston became
    enshrined in Orange mythology when he led a then illegal Twelfth procession in 1867
    between Newtonards and Bangor, for which he was subsequently jailed for one month
13  *Glasgow Herald*, 13 July 1872. However, according to the *North British Daily Mail*'s
    account of this same event, the procession numbered 4,000, although it too reported a
    total of 31 lodges in attendance. This underlines perfectly the unreliability of newspa-
    per estimates of procession figures. Caution must be exercised in quoting from such
    sources
14  McCracken, *op. cit.*, pp. 26-7
15  *Glasgow Herald*, 14 July 1873
16  *Ibid.*
17  McCracken, *op. cit.*, p. 21
18  *Glasgow Herald*, 9 October 1889
19  County Grand Orange Lodge of the East, 'Boyne Anniversary Programme', 1992
20  *Ibid.*

21  *Ibid.*
22  See Appendix 8 for a chronology of Orange Societies operating in Scotland from c.1800 to the present day
23  Own research and McCracken, *op. cit.*, p. 23
24  *Ibid.*
25  Own research
26  County Grand Orange Lodge of the East, 'Boyne Anniversary Programme' 1992. Another lodge, LOL 505, existed in Dunfermline as early as 1875 but it does not appear to have survived very long
27  *Ibid.*
28  *Ibid.*
29  *Ibid.*, 1991
30  *Ibid.*
31  *Ibid.*
32  See p. 59 on establishment of female, junior and juvenile lodges
33  *Glasgow Herald*, 14 July 1902
34  *Ibid.*, 15 July 1903
35  *Ibid.*, 9 July 1906
36  *Ibid.*, 8 July 1907
37  I G C Hutchinson, 'Glasgow Working Class Politics' in R A Cage, ed, *The Working Class in Glasgow* (Beckenham, 1987) p. 128
38  See n. 15 to Chapter 9, p. 192
39  McCracken, *op. cit.*, p. 33
40  *Ibid.*
41  Stewart, *op. cit.*, p. 38
42  Gallagher, *op. cit.*, pp. 146-7
43  *Glasgow Herald*, 12 October 1922
44  McCracken, *op. cit.*, pp. 35-6

# *Chapter 11*

1  William S Marshall, 'Orangeism and the Scottish Working Class', *Scottish Labour History Review*, no. 4, Winter, 1990
2  See p. 11-12
3  Hutchinson, *op. cit.*, p. 127
4  Own research
5  *Ibid.*
6  County Grand Orange Lodge of Central Scotland, 'Boyne Anniversary Programme', 1988
7  County Grand Orange Lodge of the East, 'Boyne Anniversary Programme', 1990
8  In a recent edition of the *Orange Torch*, official journal of the Grand Orange Lodge of Scotland, the following article is indicative: 'Bro Donald Scott, "Sons of Gideon" LOL 420 writes to tell us about the remarkable family connections within the lodge's membership of 35 brethren. He has detected six father and son sets, one stepfather and son, six brothers, two grandfathers, two fathers-in-law and one pair of stepbrothers, not to mention sundry uncles and nephews.' June, 1991, p 5
9  Learned by the writer on the playground of Mossvale Primary School, Paisley, c.1960!
10  McCracken, *op. cit.*, p. 38
11  Scotland's National Bard was not a member of the Orange Order and even if he had lived long enough, it is doubtful if he would have entertained such a notion. Burns was a keen Freemason and Orangemen seem to have latched on to his celebration of the 'Brotherhood of Man', as an inspiration for their own movement. Such a view is inappropriate, since Burns can be regarded as a product of the 'Enlightenment' and as such saw in Freemasonry a metaphor for the essential unity of mankind, regardless of

religion, class or colour

12 Band fees are one of the largest expenses a primary lodge will incur in a single year and they account for a proportion of the dues each Orangeman pays to his lodge each month

13 *Greenock Post Office Directory*, 1912

14 *Glasgow Herald*, 18 March 1912

15 Sibbett, *op. cit.*, p. 640

## Chapter 12

1 *Glasgow Herald*, 12 July 1920

2 *Ibid.*, 14 July 1879

3 Norman Ritchie, *The Sentinel Centenniel 1875-1975* (Toronto, 1975)

4 The Order ignored the quite ruthless exploitation and cruelty which was inflicted upon various native peoples of these countries. It seems to have taken the view, widely shared in Victorian society, that such peoples were simply inferior and therefore Britain was performing a valuable civilising role for which they should be grateful

5 Ritchie, *op. cit.*

6 *Ibid.*

7 Gary Denniss, *The Spirit of the Twelfth* (Ontario, 1982), p. 115

8 Thomas Vertigan, *The Orange Order in Victoria* (Melbourne, 1979), p. 2

9 Oral Testimony, 16th Boys Brigade Company, Paisley

10 See p. 43

11 *Glasgow News*, 26 March 1880

12 *Glasgow Herald*, 13 July 1908

13 Gallagher, *op. cit.*, p. 27

14 Graham Walker, 'The Protestant Irish in Scotland', in T M Devine, *Irish Immigrants and Scottish Society* (Edinburgh, 1991), p. 60

15 As late as 1935 the Order was still passing resolutions at rallies in support of keeping the Sabbath sacred. *Glasgow Herald*, 8 July 1935

16 Temperance has never been popular with Orangemen in Scotland, despite the existence of a very small number of temperance lodges. These are listed in Appendix 9. Before World War One an attempt was made in Glasgow to establish a Temperance District Lodge. It only survived until 1921. See McCracken, *op. cit.*, p. 38. Most District Orange Halls in Scotland are now licensed to sell alcohol. The temperance lodges which have survived are 'temperance' in name only

## Chapter 13

1 *Glasgow Herald*, 11 July 1887

2 *Ibid.*, 13 July 1875

3 *Glasgow News*, 23 September 1875

4 Revelation 17

5 See pp. 1-2

6 Callum G Brown, 'Protestant Churches and the Working Class in Scotland', in Graham Walker and Tom Gallagher, eds, *Sermons and Battle Hymns* (Edinburgh, 1990), p. 76

7 *Ibid.*

8 Bruce, *op. cit.*, pp. 31-6

9 *Ibid.*, pp. 33-4

10 See p. 3

11 *Greenock Telegraph*, 13 July 1873

## Chapter 14

1 Hutchinson, *op. cit.*, p. 122

2  *Paisley and Renfrewshire Gazette*, May 1873
3  *Ibid.*, 27 September 1879; 4 October 1879 and 20 March 1880
4  *Glasgow Herald*, 28 March 1873
5  *Paisley and Renfrewshire Gazette*, 5 July 1879
6  *Glasgow Herald*, 13 July 1874
7  McCracken, *op. cit.*, p. 29
8  *Glasgow Post Office Guide*, 1882-83
9  *Paisley and Renfrewshire Gazette*, 8 November 1873
10  McCracken, *op. cit.*, p. 31
11  *Glasgow Post Office Guide*, 1873-74
12  *Ibid.*
13  McCracken, *op. cit.*, p. 31
14  *Glasgow Post Office Guide*, 1882-83
15  *Baillie*, no. 697
16  *Glasgow Post Office Guide*, 1882-83
17  *Baillie*, no. 1223
18  *Orange Torch*, February 1982
19  *Ibid.*
20  *Glasgow Herald*, 13 July 1874
21  *Paisley and Renfrewshire Gazette*, 3 October 1868
22  *Ibid.* and 14 November 1868
23  Hutchinson, *op. cit.*, p. 125
24  *Baillie*, nos 248 and 576
25  Peter F Anson, *Underground Catholicism in Scotland* (Montrose, 1970), p. 339
26  *Glasgow News*, 25 December 1877
27  Handley, *op. cit.*, p. 260
28  *Ibid.*
29  *Glasgow Herald*, 13 July 1878
30  *Ibid.*, 25 March 1882

# Chapter 15

1  Examples include Alexander Whitelaw, MP for Glasgow from 1874 until 1879; Charles Bine Renshaw, MP for Renfrewshire West from 1892 until 1906; and James Reid, MP for Greenock from 1900 until 1906
2  *Glasgow News*, 27 October 1881
3  *Paisley and Renfrewshire Gazette*, 30 March 1878
4  *Ibid.*
5  County Grand Orange Lodge of Glasgow, 'Boyne Anniversary Programme' 1987
6  *Greenock Post Office Directory*, 1885
7  Own research
8  *Glasgow News*, 22 October 1881
9  There were about 15 apologies in total. *Glasgow News*, 9 June 1881
10  *Ibid.*
11  *Ibid.*, 4 November 1881
12  *Ibid.*, 29 November 1881
13  *Orange Torch*, June 1990
14  *Glasgow News*, 8 November 1879
15  *Orange Torch*, June 1990
16  *Orange Torch*, September 1990 and *Who Was Who* supplied most of the biographical information on Campbell
17  *Paisley and Renfrewshire Gazette*, 10 October 1868 and 24 October 1868
18  *Ibid.*, 30 August 1873
19  *Ibid.*, 8 November 1873

20  *Glasgow News*, 10 November 1880
21  *Ibid.*
22  McCracken, *op. cit.*, p. 29
23  Hutchinson, *op. cit.*, p. 124
24  However, it is possible that Campbell may have joined LOL 258 in Pollockshaws. This lodge was located in his Parliamentary constituency and is now named after him as 'Lord Blythswood's True Blues'
25  Lord Blythswood was Provincial Grand Master of Renfrewshire East and was later Grand Master Masion of Scotland from 1885 until 1892
26  *Glasgow Herald*, 13 July 1908
27  For Belfast see Patterson, *op. cit.* For Liverpool See P J Waller, *Democracy and Sectarianism: A Political and Social History of Liverpool 1868-1939* (Liverpool, 1981)
28  Own research
29  *Glasgow Herald*, 13 July 1892
30  *Ibid.*, 13 July 1896
31  *Baillie*, no. 920
32  *Glasgow Herald*, 5 July 1892
33  *Ibid.*, 11 July 1892

## Chapter 16

1   Roy Douglas, *The History of Liberal Party 1895-1970* (London, 1971), p. 4
2   See pp. 16 and 80
3   *Glasgow Herald*, 13 July 1884
4   *North British Daily Mail*, 12 July 1886
5   The Bill was defeated on the second reading by 343 votes to 313 and was immediately followed by the dissolution of Parliament
6   Dewar et al, *op. cit.*, p. 151
7   *Glasgow Herald*, 14 July 1890
8   *Ibid.*, 13 July 1891
9   *Ibid.*, 10 July 1893
10  *North British Daily Mail*, 4 July 1892
11  Dewar et al, *op. cit.*, pp. 152-3
12  *Glasgow Herald*, 10 July 1893
13  *Ibid.*, 13 July 1876
14  *Ibid.*
15  See p. 77 for comments of George McLeod, Grand Master of Scotland and p. 81 for comments of Thomas Wetherall, Deputy Grand Master of Scotland
16  *Glasgow Herald*, 12 July 1897
17  Ritualism in the Church of England was the term given to certain church practices which were perceived as Roman Catholic or what Anglicans term 'High Church'. In 1897, a Church Discipline Bill was introduced in Parliament which banned Mass and the Confessional in the Church of England. However, the government's support for the Bill was, to say least, lukewarm, and when put to a free vote in the House of Commons it was unsuccessful
18  *Glasgow Herald*, 11 July 1898
19  *Ibid.*, 13 July 1900
20  *Ibid.*, 11 July 1904
21  *Paisley Daily Express*, 10 July 1905

## Chapter 17

1   Ruth 1:16
2   28 September 1912, now known as Ulster Day in Northern Ireland

3 *Glasgow Herald*, 13 June 1913. Following the merger of the Liberal Unionist Party with the Conservative Party in 1912, the generic term of Unionist was often used to denote the party. In effect, the Conservative Party absorbed the few remaining Liberal Unionists

4 Stewart, *op. cit.*, p. 65

5 Scottish Unionist MPs were: Charles Scott Dickson, MP for Glasgow Central; Sir George Younger, MP for Ayr Burghs; H J Mackinder, MP for Glasgow Camlachie; and Harry Hope, MP for Buteshire. The 2nd Lord Blythswood was also in attendance at the rally

6 *Glasgow Herald*, 13 June 1913

7 *Ibid.*, 14 July 1913

8 *Ibid.*, 30 March 1914

9 *Ibid.*

10 *Ibid.*

11 *Ibid.*

12 *Ibid.*, 14 July 1914

13 Dewar et al, *op. cit.*, p. 159. Poem written by Sir William Watson

14 See Gallagher, *op. cit.*, p. 72

15 Waller, *op. cit.*, p. 268

16 Stewart, *op. cit.*, pp. 88-104

17 *Ibid.*, p. 262. This figure almost certainly represents only a part of the financial contribution made by individual Orangemen and Orange Lodges in Scotland to the cause

18 *Glasgow Herald*, 14 June 1913

# Chapter 18

1 Sibbett, *op. cit.*, vol. 2, p. 644

2 McCracken, *op. cit.*, p. 38

3 County Grand Orange Lodge of Belfast, 'Boyne Anniversary Programme', 1992

4 *Ibid.*

5 Stewart, *op. cit.*, p. 241

6 County Grand Orange Lodge of Belfast, 'Boyne Anniversary Programme', 1992

7 A number of lodges in Scotland have commemorated these events on their banners or in their choice of name, including, 'Ulster Division Memorial' LOL 36 Govan; 'Ulster Defenders' LOL 76 Dalmarnock; and 'Falkirk Blues' LOL 120 Falkirk

8 Gordon Keyes, *Orangeism: Its Roots and Branches* (Toronto, 1980), p. 36

9 *Ibid.*, p. 38

10 *Ibid.*, p. 37

11 *Ibid.*

12 *Ibid.*

13 William Perkins Bull, 'From Brock to Currie', in Robert S Pennefather, *The Orange and the Black* (Toronto, 1984), p. 27

14 This occurred again during the Second World War. Amongst regiments then with an established Orange Lodge was Toronto Scottish. Pennefather, *op. cit.*, p. 28

15 *Ibid.*, p. 27

16 Vertigan, *op. cit.*, p. 89

17 *Ibid.*

18 County Grand Orange Lodge of Belfast, 'Boyne Anniversary Programme', 1992

19 These lodges include 'David Longwell Memorial' LOL 42 Maryhill; 'Thomas Barton Memorial' LOL 136 Maryhill; and 'James Carson Memorial' LOL 404 Wishaw

20 The author is obliged to Dr Graham Walker for permission to use this information

21 *Ibid.*

22 *Glasgow Herald*, 14 July 1919

23 Scottish immigrants were responsible for establishing the newest Orange Lodge in New South Wales when 'Star of Queanbeyan' LOL 82 was formed in 1982. *Sentinel*, May-June 1982
24 See Gallagher, *op. cit.*, p. 137 for remarks of Lord Scone, President of the Scottish Protestant League
25 County Grand Orange Lodge of the East, 'Boyne Anniversary Programme', 1993
26 The *Glasgow Herald* was consulted for this analysis
27 McCracken, *op. cit.*, p. 38
28 The author is again indebted to Dr Graham Walker
29 McCracken, *op. cit.*, p. 38
30 County Grand Orange Lodge of the East, 'Boyne Anniversary Programme', 1993
31 *Ibid.*
32 See n. 15 to Chapter 9, p. 192
33 Newspaper estimates of procession numbers include Bandsmen as well as Orangemen. However, not all Bandsmen are members of the Orange Order and therefore they should be deducted before calculating the number of 'Orangemen' on parade

## *Chapter 19*

1 It was not until 1928 that Glasgow schools were finally transferred into the state system
2 As one prominent Catholic social historian has pointed out: 'in no other predominantly Protestant country did Catholics enjoy such latitude in the educational sphere'. Gallagher, *op. cit.*, p. 103
3 See Gallagher, *op. cit.*, p. 104 and Bruce, *op. cit.*, p. 45
4 *Glasgow Herald*, 8 May 1935. Watson was not a member of the Orange Order but was in sympathy with most of its aims
5 It is worth bearing in mind that prior to 1918, Roman Catholic ratepayers could have been said to be subsidising 'non-denominational' schools as well as voluntarily funding their own schools
6 Gallagher, *op. cit.*, p. 106
7 *Glasgow Herald*, 7 April 1919
8 *Ibid.*, 28 March 1919
9 *Ibid.*
10 *Ibid.*, 30 March 1922
11 *Ibid.*, 23 March 1925
12 Bruce, *op. cit.*, p. 47
13 *Ibid.*, p. 42. The author is indebted to Bruce for much of the background information on Alexander Ratcliffe's early life
14 Alexander Ratcliffe, 'The Truth About Section 18 of the Education (Scotland) Act', p. 13
15 Bruce, *op. cit.*, p. 46
16 Much has been made of a report which was submitted to the General Assembly of Church of Scotland in 1923 entitled 'The Menace of the Irish Race to Our Scottish Nationality'. Although some remarks were made regarding the unfavourable prospects of successfully assimilating the Catholic Irish into Scottish society, it should be borne in mind that this was a minority report from a very small group of ministers, none of whom appeared to be members of the Orange Order. The report was completely out of step with mainstream Kirk thinking on this issue
17 *Protestant Advocate*, September/October 1923
18 This brief summary of Ratcliffe's views on the Orange Order was gleaned from a study of his second periodical, *Protestant Vanguard*, between the years 1933-39
19 *Protestant Advocate*, April/May 1927
20 F W S Craig, *British Parliamentary Election Results* (London, 1983)

# Chapter 20

1  See p. 97
2  For example, the activities of the 'Black and Tans' have been well documented
3  *Glasgow Herald*, 11 July 1921
4  *Ibid.*, 12 October 1922
5  *Ibid.*
6  *Ibid.*
7  *Ibid.*, 14 July 1924
8  For the relationship between the Labour Party and the Roman Catholic Church in Scotland at this time, see Gallagher, *op. cit.*, pp. 182-226
9  Gallagher, *op. cit.*, p. 108
10  Craig, *op. cit.*
11  *Ibid.*
12  *Glasgow Herald*, 27 November 1923
13  *Ibid.*, 26 November 1923
14  Craig, *op. cit.*
15  Ferguson was 'pro-government', relative to the two other candidates in the contest
16  See p. 125-7
17  Craig, *op. cit.*

# Chapter 21

1  At a Twelfth rally held at Dalry in 1926, a resolution was passed calling on Orangemen to continue supporting the OPPP
2  *Vanguard*, September 1937
3  *Glasgow Herald*, 11 July 1927
4  *Ibid.*, 9 July 1928
5  *Ibid.*, 9 July 1934
6  *Vanguard*, July 1935
7  Susan McGhee, 'Carfin and the Roman Catholic Relief Act of 1926', *Innes Review*, 16, 1, 1965
8  *Glasgow Herald*, 9 July 1924
9  *Ibid.*, 16 July 1924
10  *Ibid.*
11  *Ibid.*, 5 August 1924
12  *Ibid.*, 16 July 1924
13  *Ibid.*, 9 July 1924
14  McGhee, *op. cit.*
15  *Hansard*, 1926, vol. 200, p. 1585
16  *Ibid.*, p. 1587
17  *Ibid.*, p. 1595
18  *Ibid.*, p. 1590
19  *Glasgow Herald*, 16 December 1926
20  Apart from Lt. Col. T C R Moore (Ayr Burghs), four Scottish Unionist MPs who supported the amendment were Major G H M Broun-Lindsay (Partick); Sir S Chapman (Edinburgh South); Ian MacIntyre (Edinburgh West); and Sir R W Smith (Aberdeen and Kincardine). The sole Liberal was Sir Archibald Sinclair (Caithness and Sutherland)
21  See pp. 117-18
22  *Glasgow Herald*, 1 April 1940
23  McCracken, *op. cit.*, p. 39
24  Gallagher, *op. cit.*, p. 144
25  *Glasgow Herald*, 1 April 1940
26  *Ibid.*, 14 July 1924
27  McCracken, *op. cit.*, p. 39

28  *Glasgow Herald*, 1924-34
29  *Hansard*, 1932, vol. 272, pp. 260-330

## Chapter 22

1   See p. 44-5
2   There is a wide range of literature available on this subject. See McShane and Smith, *op. cit.*, for a sympathetic treatment of the concept. Iain McLean, *The Legend of Red Clydeside* (Edinburgh, 1983), offers something of a debunking exercise and J Hinton, *Labour and Socialism: a History of the British Labour Movement 1867-1974* (Brighton, 1983), a dispassionate but general view
3   Hinton, *op. cit.*, p. 106
4   J Melling, *Rent Strikes: The People's Struggle for Housing in West Scotland 1890-1916* (Edinburgh, 1983). See also the photographic display on the rent strikes in the People's Palace Museum in Glasgow
5   Melling, *op. cit.*, pp. 70-1
6   Harry McShane and Joan Smith, *Glasgow 1919: The Story of the the 40 Hours Strike* (Glasgow, n.d.)
7   For example, Alexander Stephen's of Linthouse and Barr and Stroud of Govan. *Glasgow Herald* 31 January 1919
8   *Ibid.*
9   *Glasgow Herald*, 2 February 1919
10  *The Times*, 1 February 1919
11  *Ibid.*, 3 February 1919
12  *Glasgow Herald*, 5 February 1919
13  *Ibid.*, 14 July 1919
14  *Ibid.*
15  James Buyers Black was born in Kirkcaldy, the son of a minister. He was a leading elder in the United Free Church and a member of its General Assembly for 20 years. Black was Ward Convenor (Blythswood) in the Central Unionist Association and was described as an insurance broker. *Glasgow Herald*, 23 November 1923; 24 November 1923; and 27 November 1923
16  The Labour Party won 29 seats in Scotland of which ten came from 15 Glasgow constituencies and nine from other constituencies in West Central Scotland. 42 per cent of electors in Glasgow voted Labour. In comparison with the 1918 General Election, Labour had only managed to win six seats and of these only one was in Glasgow (Govan)
17  Hinton, *op. cit.*, pp. 119-20
18  *Forward*, 3 February 1923
19  *Ibid.*
20  The irony here was that issuing dire warnings about the 'red menace' echoed the sentiments of the Roman Catholic Church at the same time
21  The Labour Party seems to have had particularly close relations with the Ancient Order of Hibernians in some of the inner city districts with strong Irish connections. *Glasgow Herald*, 27 October 1921
22  The *Glasgow Herald* was consulted for the period under review
23  Jonathan Harvey was a native of Armagh and was a successful Glasgow businessman. Royal Black Preceptory 752 in Kelvingrove is named after him
24  See p. 87-9
25  Craig, *op. cit.*
26  See p. 57

## Chapter 23

1   The focus of this section is the Orange Order's relationship to both the Scottish

Protestant League and the Protestant Action Society. It is not the intention to look in detail at militant Protestant movements. That particular ground has been well covered elsewhere, most notably by Bruce, *op. cit.*, pp. 42-107 and Gallagher, *op. cit.*, pp. 150-166

2 This is an aspect of the SPL's programme which has been perhaps underestimated as a partial explanation for its electoral success in Glasgow

3 Moderate was the term used by Conservatives and Unionists in local Council elections in Glasgow and elsewhere

4 *Glasgow Herald*, 6 November 1933

5 Bruce, *op. cit.*, p. 65

6 *Ibid.*, p. 55

7 *Protestant Vanguard*, 6 December 1933

8 *Ibid.*

9 John F Wilson and Robert McLellan

10 *Protestant Vanguard*, 8 November 1933

11 *Ibid.*, 27 June 1933

12 Bruce, *op. cit.*, p. 59

13 In 1934 Ratcliffe entered into an electoral pact with the Moderate Party whereby it would not oppose him in Dennistoun if Ratcliffe instructed his supporters to vote Moderate in all wards with no SPL candidates. This tactic probably sealed Ratcliffe's fate since it compromised his own independence in the eyes of the electorate. He now appeared to be in league with the very people he had spent a lifetime criticising

14 However, a particularly vicious incident occurred in 1925 when a procession was attacked at various points along its route in Glasgow. The disturbances carried on into the evening and a man was apparently shot in the Garngad district of the city. *Glasgow Herald*, 13 July 1925

15 For many unemployed working class Roman Catholics, Orange processions, particularly through districts where they tended to live in large numbers, were just another example of the same Protestant triumphalism displayed by Ratcliffe and the SPL and at least they presented an easier and more visible target upon which to vent their outrage

16 *Glasgow Herald*, 13 July 1931 and 11 July 1932

17 *Ibid.*, 10 July 1933

18 *Ibid.*

19 See p. 124

20 The police were again required to use batons to restore order and to defend themselves against attack. The main trouble spots were Gorbals, Gallowgate and Shettleston. Over 50 arrests were made

21 See Bruce, *op. cit.* and Gallagher, *op. cit.* The latter author has, in addition, devoted a separate book to the rise of the Protestant Action Society in Edinburgh: *Edinburgh Divided: John Cormack and No Popery in the 1930s* (Edinburgh, 1987). Whilst this work is very detailed, the present author does not believe it offers a satisfactory explanation for the rise and success of Cormack and his extraordinary movement

22 Gallagher, *op. cit.*, 158

23 The author is indebted to Bruce, *op. cit.* and Gallagher, *op. cit.*, for much of the biographical detail on John Cormack

24 Bruce, *op. cit.*, p. 84

25 Protestant Action Society membership form, c.1932

26 Bruce, *op. cit.*, pp. 94-5

27 *Ibid.*, p. 98

28 Gallagher, *op. cit.*, p. 160

29 Bruce, *op. cit.*, p. 89

30 Gallagher, *op. cit.*, p. 160

31 Gallagher, *Edinburgh Divided, op. cit.*, p. 98

32 Cormack rejoined the Order again in 1958. His old lodge, LOL 188, was renamed 'Cormack's Protestant Defenders' in his honour when he died
33 Gallagher, *Edinburgh Divided*, *op. cit.*, p. 118
34 County Grand Orange Lodge of the East, 'Boyne Anniversary Programme', 1993
35 Gallagher, *op. cit.*, p. 167

## *Chapter 24*

1 *Glasgow Herald*, 13 July 1936. ·
2 Unfortunately, not much information is available about Orange levels of recruitment but it is likely to have been substantial
3 Paisley was on better terms with the Orange Order at this time. He is not an Orangeman
4 *Glasgow Herald*, 11 July 1949
5 *Protestant Vanguard*, July 1939
6 In 1965, the party changed its name to the Conservative and Unionist Party. However, the accent was then very much on 'Conservative' and less on 'Unionist'
7 Moore was the last Orange MP to represent a Scottish constituency and the only one since 1945
8 See Appendix 10 for an incomplete list of clergymen associated with the Orange movement in Scotland
9 Of course, there are always exceptions to the rule. For example, LOL 128 in Edinburgh is composed entirely of evangelicals
10 These Grand Masters were Andrew Dalgliesh, Joseph Baxter and Thomas Corry
11 The author is again indebted to Bruce, *op. cit.*, for most of the material relating to Hasson
12 Anderston District No. 13 contained three lodges prior to the local urban renewal programme. These lodges were LOL 126; LOL 139; and LOL 141. It appears that only 'True Blues' LOL 139 has survived intact to the present day. Own research
13 Waller, *op. cit.*, p. 468
14 The relative strength of the Order in Drumchapel is probably the result of many of its inhabitants originating from Partick
15 These lodges are 'Truth Defenders' LOL 201 in Foxbar; 'Enniskillen True Blues' LOL 155 in Glenburn; 'True Blues' LOL 97 in Larkfield; 'Chosen Few' LOL 277 in Gartlea; and 'Lord Louis Mountbatten Memorial' LOL 411 in Pennyburn. Own research
16 Irvine District No. 56 and East Kilbride District No. 58 were both established in the late 1970s. One of the three lodges, LOL 300, which originally formed East Kilbride District No. 58, has been forced to close. Own research
17 These lodges are 'Star Of the North' LOL 700 in Inverness; 'Wishart Arch Defenders' LOL 444 in Forfar; and LOL 493 in Hawick. Own research
18 LOL 144 boasted 136 members in the early 1980s and it is still a numerically strong lodge. County Grand Orange Lodge of Ayrshire, Renfrewshire and Argyll, 'Boyne Anniversary Programme', 1994
19 LOL 701 was formed in 1978. Own research
20 This was probably LOL 58 working under the authority of the Loyal Orange Institution of England. An Orange Band was also formed in Corby. Own research
21 Christopher Harvie, *No Gods and Precious Few Heroes: Scotland 1914-1980* (London, 1981), p. 100. This figure needs to be treated with caution; even accepting that it may include adult, female and juvenile lodges it still seems somewhat high
22 And possibly England as well. It is possible that the existence of Orange Lodges in the Cumberland coalfield in the 1870s and 1880s may have been due to the migration of Scottish miners with Orange connections. It might also not be a coincidence that Bairds of Gartsherrie had extensive mining interests in the region at that time
23 See p. 54

24 Loyal Orange Institution of Scotland, *County Grand Lodges Silver Jubilee: An Historical Appreciation* (Glasgow, n.d.), unpaginated
25 In fact, this idea was not new. It had been briefly attempted between 1918 and 1925. *Ibid.*
26 *Ibid.*
27 *Ibid.*
28 *Ibid.*
29 The six District Lodges were Edinburgh District No. 5; Armadale District No. 26; Broxburn District No. 31; Falkirk District No. 36; East Lothian District No. 44; and Fife District No. 45. *Ibid.*
30 *Ibid.*

## Chapter 25

1 Bruce, *op. cit.*, p. 171
2 County Grand Lodges Silver Jubilee, *op. cit.*
3 For a detailed account of Loyalist paramilitary activity in Scotland see Bruce, *op. cit.*, pp. 170-90
4 *Glasgow Herald*, 13 December 1976
5 *Ibid.*
6 *Orange Torch*, February 1977
7 By 1982, the Scottish Loyalists claimed a membership of 1,500, but they had the ability to mobilise a lot more than this for street demonstrations. Gallagher, *op. cit.*, p. 297
8 The author witnessed a procession of these bands in Paisley in 1993
9 The trials and tribulations of, for example, the former Edinburgh District Council over granting permission to various Loyalist and Republican processions in the city has been well documented in the national press in recent years
10 Own research
11 Greengairs Thistle Flute Band have been similarly banned for wearing a replica uniform of the 36th (Ulster) Division

## Chapter 26

1 The membership is given as 80,000, organised into 900 lodges. This includes male adult; female adult; junior and juvenile lodges. Kennedy, *op. cit.*, p. 93. This figure seems too high. A more realistic figure may be some 50,000 based on the same calculations used before
2 See p. 58-9
3 In parts of Scotland there are still public houses whose clientele is predominantly one religion or the other
4 The Union of Orange Social Clubs has a roll of 27 clubs in Scotland and one club in Belfast
5 *Wishaw Press*, 23 April 1994
6 *Ibid.* LLOL refers to the Ladies' Loyal Orange Lodge
7 *Orange Torch*, February 1992
8 *Ibid.*
9 *Ibid.*, June 1991
10 For examples see reports and financial statements of Erskine Hospital for 1990 and 1991. In the former year, a total of £618 was donated by various Orange sources and a year later, sums donated amounted to £747
11 The sum of £500 was donated in 1991. County Grand Orange Lodge of Glasgow, 'Boyne Anniversary Programme', 1991
12 Plays include *Just Another Saturday* by Peter MacDougall which was broadcast on BBC 1 and *The Sash* by Hector MacMillan which enjoyed an extended run on the Glasgow stage.

Amongst novels dealing with Orangeism is *Its Colours They Are Fine* by Alan Spence. Orangeism is clearly a marketable 'genre'

13  Matthew 7:16

## *Appendix 1*

1  The most authoritative source on the origins of the Royal Black Institution is Aiken McClelland, *William Johnston of Ballykilbeg* (Lurgan, 1990), pp. 20-3
2  *Ibid.*
3  *Ibid.*
4  See p. 30
5  Joseph Attard, *Knights of Malta* (Marsa, 1992), p. 158
6  McClelland, *op. cit.*, p. 21
7  These degrees are Royal Black; Royal Scarlet; Royal Mark; Apron and Blue; Royal White; Royal Green; Royal Gold; Star and Garter; Crimson Arrow; Link and Chain; Red Cross
8  McClelland, *op. cit.*, p. 22
9  Provincial Grand Black Chapter of Scotland, 'Relief of Derry Anniversary Programme', 1983
10  *Ibid.*
11  Own research
12  *Ibid.*
13  This estimate is based on the same calculations used to determine Orange strength in this book
14  The Imperial Grand Black Chapter of the British Commonwealth has under its jurisdiction 970 preceptories as follows: Ireland (536); England (27); Scotland (62); Australia (20); Canada (203); New Zealand (20); Togo (1); and Ghana (1). In addition about 12 preceptories also exist in the United States of America. Kennedy, *op. cit.*, p. 71
15  Provincial Grand Black Chapter of Scotland, 'Relief of Derry Anniversary Programme', 1994

## *Appendix 2*

1  Apprentice Boys of Derry Association, 'Official Brochure of the Tercentenary Celebrations', 1988
2  *Ibid.*
3  *Ibid.*
4  *Ibid.*
5  Scottish Amalgamated Committee, 'Relief of Derry Anniversary Programme', 1990
6  Lundy was the Governor of Londonderry when the siege began. He wanted to surrender the city but was prevented from doing so by the actions of 13 apprentices who shut the gates of the city in the face of the Jacobite army. Lundy has become a demon figure in Ulster Protestant folklore. 'Relief of Derry', *op. cit.*
7  *Ibid.*
8  *Ibid.*
9  *Ibid.*
10  *Ibid.*
11  'Official Brochure', *op. cit.*
12  *Ibid.*
13  'Relief of Derry', *op. cit.*
14  *Ibid.*
15  Own research

# BIBLIOGRAPHY

The Bible (King James Authorised Version)

**Works of Reference**
Craig, F W S, *British Parliamentary Election Results* (Aldershot, 1989), (4 volumes)
*Dictionary of National Biography* (Oxford, 1975)
Groome, F H, *Ordnance Gazetteer of Scotland* (Edinburgh, 1883)
*Hansard*
Irving, J, *The Book of Scotsmen* (Paisley, n.d.)
Paul, Sir J B, *The Scots Peerage* (Edinburgh, 1907)
Stenton, M and Lees, S, *Who's Who of British Members of Parliament* (Hassocks, 1976), (4 volumes)
Thomson, G, *The Third Statistical Account of Scotland: The County of Lanark* (Glasgow, 1960)

**Primary Sources**
Apprentice Boys of Derry Association, *Official Brochure of the Tercentenary Celebrations*, 1988
Apprentice Boys of Derry Association: Scottish Amalgamated Committee, Relief of Derry Programmes
County Grand Orange Lodge of Ayrshire, Renfrewshire and Argyll, Boyne Anniversary Programmes
County Grand Orange Lodge of Central Scotland, Boyne Anniversary Programmes
County Grand Orange Lodge of the East, Boyne Anniversary Programmes
County Grand Orange Lodge of Glasgow, Boyne Anniversary Programmes
Dewar, M W, Brown, J, and Long, S E, *Orangeism: A New Historical Appreciation* (Belfast, 1967)
Kennedy, B, *A Celebration: 1690-1990. The Orange Institution* (Belfast, 1990)
Keyes, G, *Orangeism: Its Roots and Branches* (Toronto, 1980)
Loyal Orange Institution of Scotland, *The Orange Lodge: A Question and Answer Introduction to Scottish Orangeism* (Glasgow, n.d.)
Loyal Orange Institution of Scotland, *County Grand Orange Lodges Silver Jubilee: An Historical Appreciation* (Glasgow, n.d.)
Provincial Grand Black Chapter of Scotland, Relief of Derry Programmes

*Report from the Select Committee Appointed to Inquire into the Origin, Nature, Extent and Tendency of Orange Institutions in Great Britain and the Colonies with Minutes, Appendices and Index* (House of Commons, 1835) 605 XVII

Ritchie, N, *The Sentinel Centennial 1875-1975* (Toronto, 1975)

Vertigan, T, *The Orange Order in Victoria* (Melbourne, 1979)

### Secondary Sources: Books and Pamphlets

Anson, P F, *Underground Catholicism in Scotland* (Montrose, 1970)

Attard, J, *The Knights of Malta* (Marsa, Malta, 1992)

Bruce, S, *No Pope of Rome: Militant Protestantism in Modern Scotland* (Edinburgh, 1985)

Cage, R A, *The Working Class in Glasgow 1750-1914* (Beckenham, 1987)

Campbell, A B, *The Lanarkshire Miners: A Social History of their Trade Unions 1775-1874* (Edinburgh, 1979)

Checkland, O and S, *Industry and Ethos: Scotland 1832-1914* (Edinburgh, 1989)

Cooney, J, *Scotland and the Papacy* (Edinburgh, 1982)

Denniss, G, *The Spirit of the Twelfth* (Gravenhurst, Canada, 1982)

Devine, T M, *Irish Immigrants and Scottish Society* (Edinburgh, 1991)

Dickson, T, *Capital and Class in Scotland* (Edinburgh, 1982)

Douglas, R, *History of the Liberal Party 1895-1970* (London, 1971)

Foster, J, *Class Struggle and the Industrial Revolution* (London, 1974)

Foster, J and Woolfson, C, *The Politics of the UCS Work-In* (London, 1986)

Gallagher, T, *Edinburgh Divided: John Cormack and No Popery in the 1930s* (Edinburgh, 1987)

Gallagher, T, *Glasgow: The Uneasy Peace* (Manchester, 1987)

Gibbon, P, *The Origins of Ulster Unionism* (Manchester, 1975)

Gray, R, *The Aristocracy of Labour in Nineteenth Century Britain 1850-1914* (Oxford, 1973)

Handley, J E, *The Irish in Scotland 1798-1845* (Cork, 1945)

Harvie, C, *No Gods and Precious Few Heroes: Scotland 1914-1980* (London, 1981)

Hinton, J, *Labour and Socialism: A History of the British Labour Movement 1867-1974* (Brighton, 1983)

MacKenzie, P, *Letters of the Tory Orange Conspirators in Glasgow to Colonel Fairman* (Glasgow, 1835)

McClelland, A, *William Johnston of Ballykilbeg* (Lurgan, 1990)

McCracken, G A, *Bygone Days of Yore: The Story of Orangeism in Glasgow* (?, 1990)

McLean, I, *The Legend of Red Clydeside* (Edinburgh, 1983)

McShane, H and Smith, J, *Glasgow 1919: The Story of the 40 Hours Strike* (Glasgow, n.d.)

McShane, H and Smith, J, *No Mean Fighter* (London, 1978)

Melling, J, *Rent Strikes: The People's Struggle for Housing in West Scotland 1890-1916* (Edinburgh, 1983)

Mills, C W, *The Sociological Imagination* (Harmondsworth, 1980)

O'Farrell, P, *The Irish in Australia* (Sydney, 1986)

Patterson, H, *Class Conflict and Sectarianism: The Protestant Working Class and the Belfast Labour Movement 1868-1920* (Belfast, 1980)

Pennefather, R S *The Orange and the Black: Documents in the History of the Orange Order in Ontario and the West 1890-1940* (Canada, 1984)

Ratcliffe, A, *The Truth About Section 18 of the Education (Scotland) Act* (?, n.d.)

Report and Financial Statements of Erskine Hospital: years ending 1990 and 1991

Senior, H, *Orangeism in Ireland and Great Britain 1795-1836* (London, 1966)

Sibbett, R M *Orangeism in Ireland and Throughout the Empire* (London, 1939)

Smout, T C, *A Century of the Scottish People 1830-1950* (London, 1987)

Stewart, A T Q, *The Ulster Crisis* (London, 1967)

Strawthorn, R, *Ayrshire: The Story of a County* (Ayr, 1975)

Thompson, E P, *The Making of the English Working Class* (Harmondsworth, 1984)

Walker, G, and Gallagher, T, *Sermons and Battle Hymns: Protestant Popular Culture in Modern Scotland* (Edinburgh, 1990)

Waller, P J, *Democracy and Sectarianism: A Political and Social History of Liverpool 1868-1939* (Liverpool, 1981)

Waugh, J, *Slamannan Parish Through the Changing Years* (?, 1977)

Weber, M, *The Protestant Ethic and the Spirit of Capitalism* (London, 1976)

Wood, I S, *Scotland and Ulster* (Edinburgh, 1994)

## Secondary Sources: Articles

Gallagher, T, 'Protestant Extremism in Urban Scotland 1930-1939: its Growth and Contraction', *Scottish Historical Review*, 178, 1985

McCaffrey, J F, 'The Origins of Liberal Unionism in the West of Scotland', *Scottish Historical Review*, 50, 1971

McGhee, S, 'Carfin and the Roman Catholic Relief Act of 1926', *Innes Review*, 16, 1, 1965

Marshall, W S, 'Orangeism and the Scottish Working Class', *Scottish Labour History Review*, no. 4, Winter, 1990

Smith, J, 'Labour Tradition in Glasgow and Liverpool', *History Workshop*, 17, Spring, 1984

## Secondary Sources: Journals, Newspapers and Periodicals

*Baillie; Forward; Glasgow Chronicle; Glasgow Courier; Glasgow Herald; Glasgow News; Glasgow Sentinel; Greenock Telegraph; History Workshop; Innes Review; North British Mail; Orange Torch; Paisley Daily Express; Paisley Herald and Renfrewshire Advertiser; Paisley and Renfrewshire Gazette; Protestant Advocate; Scottish Historical Review; Scottish Labour History Review; Sentinel (Australia); Sentinel (Canada); The Times; Vanguard; Vigilant; Wishaw Press*

# INDEX

*No entries have been given for 'Conservative and Unionist Party', 'Glasgow' or 'Ulster', as these recur so frequently throughout the text and references to them can easily be located by a brief inspection of the book's contents.*